A Handbook on Computer Science

A Handbook on Computer Science

Editors

Izaan Ahmed & Hasad Demirci

scitus academics

A Handbook on Computer Science
Edited by **Izaan Ahmed & Hasad Demirci**

Printed in 2017

ISBN: 978-1-68117-194-4
Library of Congress Control Number: 2015952017

SCITUS Academics LLC,616,
Corporate Way, Suite 2, 4766,
Valley Cottage, NY 10989

www.scitusacademics.com

Preface

Computer science is a discipline that extents theory and practice. It needs thinking both in abstract terms and in concrete terms. The practical side of computing can be seen everywhere. Computer science also has strong connections to other disciplines. Many problems in science, engineering, health care, business, and other areas can be solved efficiently with computers, but finding a solution requires both computer science expertise and knowledge of the particular application domain. Computer science has a wide range of spheres. These embrace computer architecture, software systems, graphics, artificial intelligence, computational science, and software engineering. Drawing from a common core of computer science knowledge, each specialty area emphases on particular challenges.

A Handbook on Computer Science encompasses all the formulae and important theoretical aspects of computer science, with appropriate diagrams, whenever it is appropriate. An extensive coverage of key points for additional information is also given.This handbook covers all the essential concepts and terms in computer science.

Table of Contents

A Handbook on Computer Science

1

Engineering Mathematics

CONTENTS

1 Mathematical Logic

Mathematicallogicisasubfieldofmathematicsexploringtheapplications offormallogictomathematics. Topically, mathematicallogicbearsclose connections to metmathematics, the foundations of mathematics, and theoretical computer science.

Propositional Logic

A proposition or statement is a sentence which is either true or false. If a proposition is true, then we say its truth value is true, and if a proposition is false, we say its truth value is false.

- Logical constants: true, false
- Propositional symbols: P, Q, S, (atomic sentences)
- Wrapping parentheses: (…)
- Sentences are combined by connectives:

$\wedge$ ...and	[conjunction]
...or	[disjunction]
...implies	[implication / conditional]
..is equivalent	[biconditional]
...not	[negation]

Examples of PL Sentences

- P means "It is hot."
- Q means "It is humid."

- R means "It is raining."
- $(P \wedge Q) \rightarrow R$

  "If it is hot and humid, then it is raining"
- $Q \rightarrow P$

  "If it is humid, then it is hot"
- A better way:

  Hot = "It is hot"

  Humid = "It is humid"

  Raining = "It is raining"

First Order Logic

First-order logic is a formal system used in mathematics, philosophy, linguistics, and computer science. It is also known as first-order predicate calculus, the lower predicate calculus, quantification theory, and predicate logic. First-order logic uses quantified variables over (non-logical) objects.

- propositional logic assumes the world contains facts,
- first-order logic (like natural language) assumes the world contains
  a. **Objects:** people, houses, numbers, colors, baseball games, wars ...
  b. **Relations:** red, round, prime, brother of, bigger than, part of, comes between ...
  c. **Functions:** father of, best friend, one more than, plus ...

First-order logic is symbolized reasoning in which each sentence, or statement, is broken down into a subject and a predicate. The predicate modifies or defines the properties of the subject. In first-order logic, a predicate can only refer to a single subject. First-order logic is also known as first-order predicate calculus or first-order functional calculus.

A sentence in first-order logic is written in the form Px or P(x), where P is the predicate and x is the subject, represented as a variable. Complete sentences are logically combined and manipulated according to the same rules as those used in Boolean algebra.

In first-order logic, a sentence can be structured using the universal quantifier (symbolized $\forall$) or the existential quantifier ($\exists$). Consider a subject that is a variable represented by x. Let A be a predicate "is an apple," F be a predicate "is a fruit," S be a predicate "is sour"', and M be a predicate "is mushy." Then we can say

$\forall x : Ax \Rightarrow Fx$

which translates to "For all x, if x is an apple, then x is a fruit." We can also say such things as

$\exists x : Fx \Rightarrow Ax$

$\exists x : Ax \Rightarrow Sx$

$\exists x : Ax \Rightarrow Mx$

Where the existential quantifier translates as "For some."

First-order logic can be useful in the creation of computer programs. It is also of interest to researchers in artificial intelligence (AI). There are more powerful forms of logic, but first-order logic is adequate for most everyday reasoning.

Syntax of FOL: Basic Elements

- Constants KingJohn, 2, NUS,...
- Predicates Brother, >,...
- Functions Sqrt, LeftLegOf,...
- Variables x, y, a, b,...
- Connectives $\neg$, $\Rightarrow$, $\wedge$, $\vee$, $\Leftrightarrow$
- Equality =
- Quantifiers $\forall$, $\exists$.

2 Combinatorics

Combinatory is a branch of mathematics concerning the study of finite or countable discrete structures.

Permutations

Permutation relates to the act of **rearranging**, or **permuting**, all the members of a set into some sequence or order (unlike combinations, which are selections of some members of the set where order is disregarded). For example, written as tuples, there are six permutations of the set $\{1,2,3\}$, namely: (1,2,3), (1,3,2), (2,1,3), (2,3,1), (3,1,2), and (3,2,1). As another example, an anagram of a word, all of whose letters are different, is a permutation of its letters.

The number of ways of obtaining an *ordered* subset of k elements from a set of n elements is given by

$$ {}_nP_k \equiv \frac{n!}{(n-k)!} $$

Combinations

Combination is a way of selecting items from a collection, such that (unlike permutations) the order of selection does not matter. In smaller cases it is possible to count the number of combinations. For example given three fruits, say an apple, an orange and a pear, there are three combinations of two that can be drawn from this set: an apple and a pear; an apple and an orange; or a pear and an orange. More formally, a *k*-**combination** of a set S is a subset of k distinct elements of S. If the set has n elements, the number of k-combinations is equal to the binomial coefficient

$$\binom{n}{k} = \frac{n(n-1)\ldots(n-k+1)}{k(k-1)\ldots1},$$

Counting

Combinatorics,alsoreferredtoasCombinatorialMathematics,isthefield ofmathematicsconcernedwithproblemsofselection,arrangement,and operationwithinafiniteordiscretesystem.Itsobjectiveis:Howtocount withoutcounting.Therefore,oneofthebasicproblemsofcombinatoryis to determine the number of possible configurations of objects of a given type.

The be a positive integer. A composition of n is a way of writing n as an ordered sum of one or more positive integers (called parts). For example, the compositions of 3 are 1+1+1, 1+2, 2+1, and 3. Let f (n):= the number of compositions of n in which all parts belong to the set {1, 2}

n r = n × · · · × n (r factors)

Listsoflengthrand(n)r:= n × (n – 1) × ··· × (n – r + 1) Permutations of length r may be formed.

Summation

The **rule of sum** or **addition principle** is a basic counting principle. Stated simply, it is the idea that if *a* ways of doing something and *b* ways of doing another thing and It is not do both at the same time, then there are *a* + *b* ways to choose one of the actions.

The summation formula for

$$|S_1| + |S_2| + \ldots + |S_n| = |S_1 \cup S_2 \cup \ldots \cup S_n|$$

$$\sum_{i=1}^{N} C(k+i-1, i) = ?$$

Generating functions and Recurrence relations

The Method of Generating Functions to get a closed form expression for f (n) from (*) we use the so- called method of generating functions F(x)

$$F(x) = f(0) + f(1)x + f(2)x^2 + f(3)x^3 + ...$$

A few general principles for using generating functions to construct counting arguments (e.g. counting the number of subsets or number of total orderings) that can be remixed to count different quantities

If fn is a function defined on the positive integers, then a relation that expresses fn + k as a linear combination of function values of integer index less than n + k, in which a fixed constant in the linear combination is written ai, is called a recurrence relation

$$f_{n+k} = a_1 f_{n+k-1} + a_2 f_{n+k-2} + ... + a_k f_n$$

Asymptotes

In statistics, asymptotic theory, or large sample theory, is a generic framework for assessment of properties of estimators and statistical tests. Within this framework it is typically assumed that the sample size n grows indefinitely, and the properties of statistical procedures are evaluated in the limit as n→ ∞. Asymptotic theory is applied by treating the asymptotic results as approximately valid for finite sample sizes. The importance of the asymptotic theory is that it often makes possible to carry out the analysis and state many results which cannot be obtained within the standard finite-sample theory.

3 Set Theory

Set theory, branch of mathematics that deals with the properties of well-defined collections of objects, which may or may not be of a mathematical nature, such as numbers or functions. The theory is less valuable in direct application to ordinary experience than as a basis for precise and adaptable terminology for the definition of complex and sophisticated mathematical concepts.

Sets

A Set is any well-defined collection of "**objects**."

A **set** is a collection of objects that have something in common or follow a rule. The objects in the set are called its elements. Set notation uses curly braces, with elements separated by commas. So the set of outwear for Kyesha would be listed as follows:

$A = \{\text{coat, hat, scarf, gloves, boots}\}$, where A is the name of the set, and the braces indicate that the objects written between them belong to the set.

Ways of Describing Sets

- List the elements

  $A=\{1,2,3,4,5,6\}$

- Give a verbal description

  "A is the set of all integers from 1 to 6, inclusive"

- Give a mathematical inclusion rule

$A=\{\text{Integers } x \mid 1 \leq x \leq 6\}$

Relations

A relation is a set of ordered.

Any subset of a Cartesian product of sets is called a relation.

(I.e., a relation is a set of ordered pairs.)

If X and Y are sets and $\rho \subset X \times Y$, we say that ρ is a relation from X to Y.

(We can also say that ρ is a relation between the elements of X and Y.)

If $\rho \subset X \times X$, we say that ρ is a relation in X. If $(x, y) \in \rho$, we often write $x \rho y$.

Examples.

- The relation of equality in a nonempty set X.
  $\rho 1 := \{(x, x): x \in X\}$,
  thus $(x, y) \in \rho 1 \subset X \times X$ iff $x=y$.
- The relation of divisibility in N^+.
  $\rho 2 := \{(m, n) \in N^+ \times N^+ : \exists k \in N^+ \; n = k \cdot m\}$,
  thus $(m, n) \in \rho 2 \subset N^+ \times N^+$ iff $m \mid n$,
  that is n can be divided by m without remainder (n is divisible by m).

Functions

A **function** is a relation between a set of inputs and a set of permissible outputs with the property that each input is related to exactly one output. An example is the function that relates each real number x to its square x^2. The output of a function f corresponding to an input x is denoted by $f(x)$ (read "f of x"). In this example, if the input is -3, then the output is 9, and we may write $f(-3) = 9$. Likewise, if the input is 3, then the output is also 9, and we may write $f(3) = 9$. (The same output may be produced by more than one input, but each input gives only one output.) The input variable(s) are sometimes referred to as the argument(s) of the function.

Let X and Y be sets.

A relation $f \subset X \times Y$ is called a function from X to Y if

- D(f) = X ,
- ∀x ∈ X the set {y ∈ Y: (x, y) ∈ f} has exactly one element.

Groups

A group G is a finite or infinite set of elements together with a binary operation (called the group operation) that together satisfy the four fundamental properties of closure, associativity, the identity property, and the inverse property. The operation with respect to which a group is defined is often called the "group operation," and a set is said to be a group "under" this operation. Elements A, B, C, ... with binary operation between A and B denoted AB form a group if

- Closure: If A and B are two elements in G, then the product AB is also in G.

Associativity: The defined multiplication is associative, i.e., for all A,B,C,∈ G, .(AB)C = A(BC)

Identity: There is an identity element I (a.k.a. 1, E, or e) such that IA = AI = A for every element .A ∈ G

Inverse: There must be an inverse (a.k.a. reciprocal) of each element. Therefore, for each element A of G, the set contains an element B = A^{-1} such that A A^{-1} = A^{-1} A = I.

Partial Orders

A **partially ordered set** (or **poset**) formalizes and generalizes the intuitive concept of an ordering, sequencing, or arrangement of the elements of a set. A poset consists of a set together with a binary relation that indicates that, for certain pairs of elements in the set, one of the elements precedes the other.

A relation "≤" is a partial order on a set S if it has:

Reflexivity: $a \geq a$ for all $a \in S$.

Antisymmetry: $a \geq b$ and $b \leq a$ implies a = b.

Transitivity: $a \geq b$ and $b \leq c$ implies $a \leq c$.

Lattice

A **lattice** is a partially ordered set in which every two elements have a unique supremum (also called a least upper bound or join) and a unique infimum (also called a greatest lower bound or meet).

A lattice-ordered set is a poset $(L, \leq)$ in which each two-element subset $\{a,b\}$ has an infimum, denoted $\inf\{a,b\}$, and a supremum, denoted $\sup\{a,b\}$. There is a natural relationship between lattice-ordered sets and lattices. In fact, a lattice $(L, \wedge, \vee)$ is obtained from a lattice-ordered poset $(L, \leq)$ by defining $a \wedge b = \inf\{a,b\}$ and $a \vee b = \sup\{a,b\}$ for any $a,b \in L$. Also, from a lattice $(L, \wedge, \vee)$, one may obtain a lattice-ordered set $(L, \leq)$ by setting $a \leq b$ in L if and only if $a = a \wedge b$. One obtains the same lattice-ordered set $(L, \leq)$ from the given lattice by setting $a \vee b = b$ in L if and only if $a \vee b = b$. (In other words, one may prove that for any lattice, $(L, \wedge, \vee)$, and for any two members a and b of L, $a \wedge b = b$ if and only if $a = a \vee b$.

Boolean algebra

A Boolean algebra (BA) is a set A together with binary operations $+$ and $\cdot$ and a unary operation $-$, and elements 0, 1 of A such that the following laws hold: commutative and associative laws for addition and multiplication, distributive laws both for multiplication over addition and for addition over multiplication, and the following special laws:

- $x + (x \cdot y) = x$
- $x\,(x + y) = x$
- $x + (-x) = 1$
- $x\,(-x) = 0$

Graph theory is the study of graphs which are mathematical structures used to model pair wise relations between objects. To analyze the graph theory application two problem areas are considered.

- Classical problem
- Problems from applications

A graph may be undirected, meaning that there is no distinction between the two vertices associated with each edge, or its edges may be directed from one vertex to another. No attention is paid to the position of points and the length of the lines. Thus, the two graphs are the same graph.

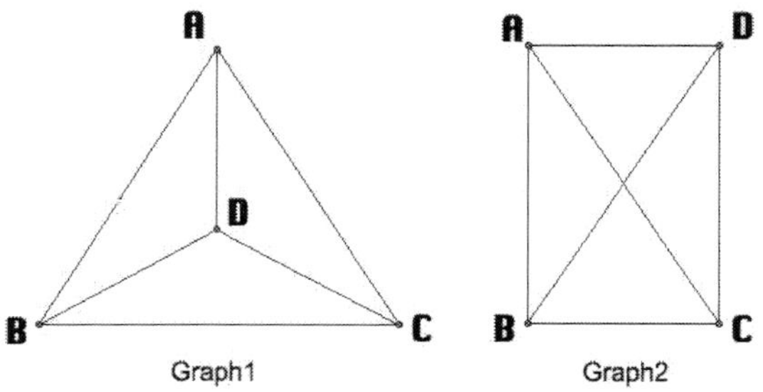

Connectivity

Connectivity is one of the basic concepts of graph theory: it asks for the minimum number of elements (nodes or edges) that need to be removed to disconnect the remaining nodes from each other. It is closely related to the theory of network flow problems. The connectivity of a graph is an important measure of its robustness as a network.

- A connected graph is an undirected graph that has a path between every pair of vertices
- A connected graph with at least 3 vertices is 1-connected if the removal of 1 vertex disconnects the graph

4 Graph Theory

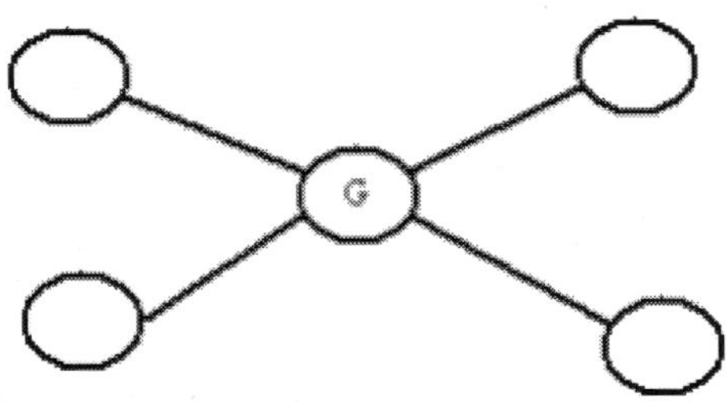

Similarly, a graph is one edge connected if the removal of one edge disconnects the graph.

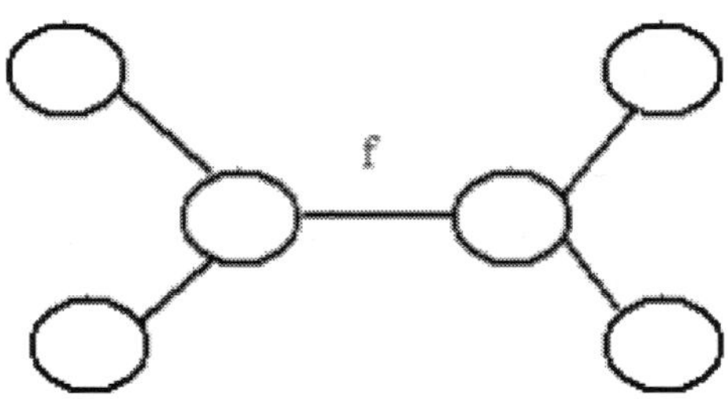

Vertex Connectivity vs. edge Connectivity: Connectivity based on edges gives a more stable form of a graph than a vertex based one. This happens because each vertex of a connected graph can be attached to one or more edges.

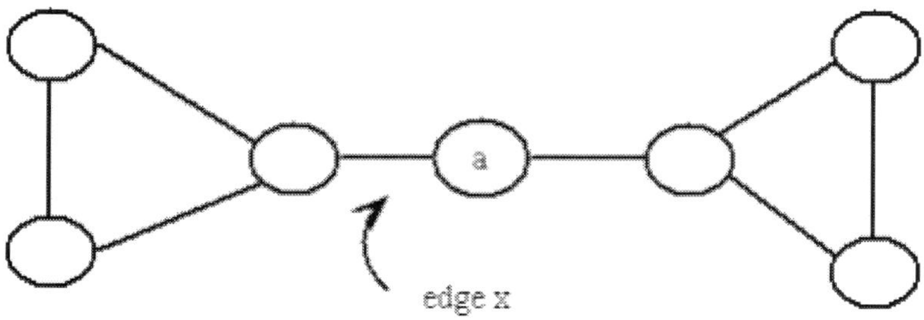

As shown in figure graph g is one edge and one vertex connected. The removal of vertex x has the same effect with a possible removal of vertex a. The same definitions apply to k-connected graphs:

- A connected graph is k-connected if the removal of k vertices disconnects the graph.
- A k-edges connected graph is disconnected by removing k edges

Spanning Trees

A spanning subgraph is a subgraph which has the same vertex set as the original graph. A spanning tree is a tree that is spanning.

A spanning tree of a network is a subgraph that

- Connects all the vertices together; and
- Contains no circuits.

For example:

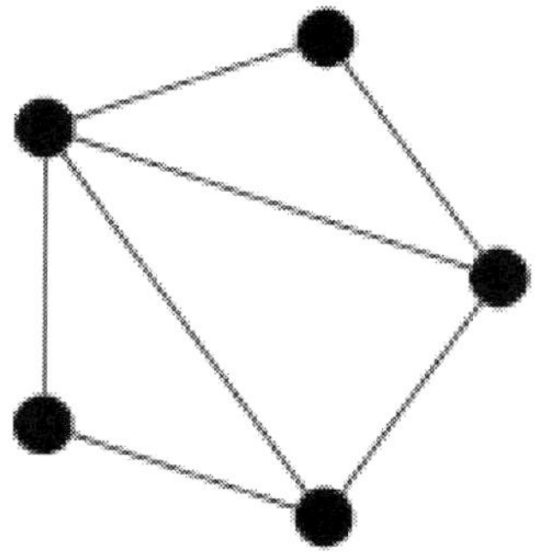

The spanning tree

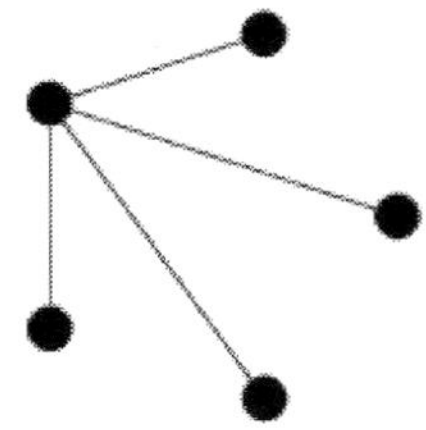

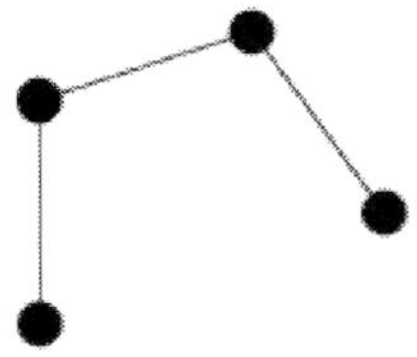

Whereas the subgraph is not a spanning tree (it is a tree, but it is not spanning).

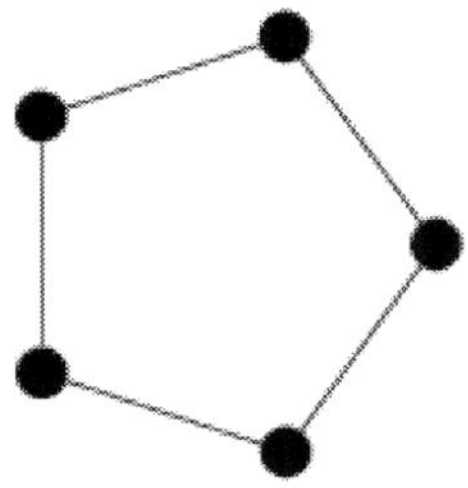

The subgraph is also not a spanning tree (it is spanning, but it is not a tree).

Cut Vertices

A cut vertex is a vertex that when removed (with its boundary edges) from a graph creates more components than previously in the graph. It is important to note that the above definition breaks down if G is a complete graph, since we cannot then disconnect G by removing vertices.

Vertex-Cut set

A vertex-cut set of a connected graph G is a set S of vertices with the following properties.

- The removal of all the vertices in S disconnects G.
- The removal of some (but not all) of vertices in S does not disconnects G.

Consider the following graph

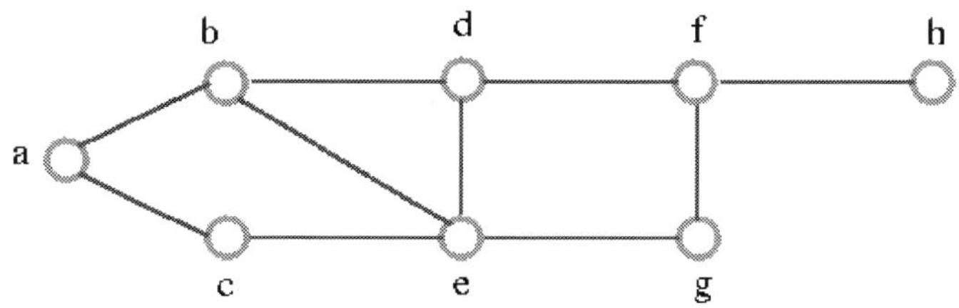

We can disconnect the graph by removing the two vertices b and e, but we cannot disconnect it by removing just one of these vertices. The vertex-cut set of G is {b, e}.

Cut Edge

A cut edge is an edge that when removed (the vertices stay in place) from a graph creates more components than previously in the graph.

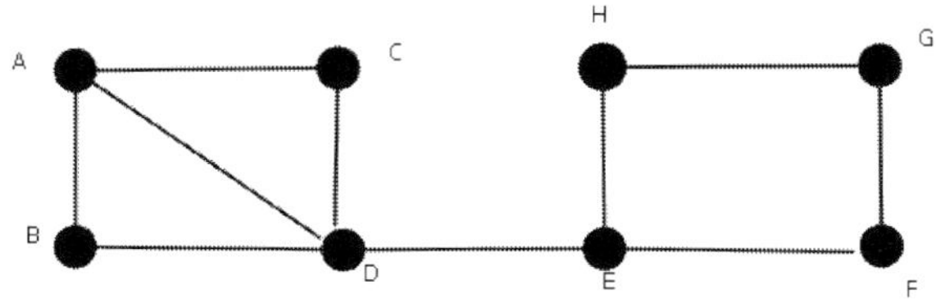

Covering Graph

A graph C is a covering graph of another graph G if there is a covering map from the vertex set of C to the vertex set of G. A covering map f is a surjection and a local isomorphism: the neighborhood of a v vertex in C is mapped bijectively onto the neighborhood of f(v) in G.

Let G = (V, E) and C = (V_2, E_2) be two graphs, and let f: V_2 □ V be a surjection. Then f is a covering map from C to G if for each v ∈ V_2, the restriction of f to the neighborhood of v is a bijection onto the neighborhood of f(v) ∈ V in G. Put otherwise, f maps edges incident to v one-to-one onto edges incident to f(v).

Example:

In the following figure, the graph C is a covering graph of the graph H.

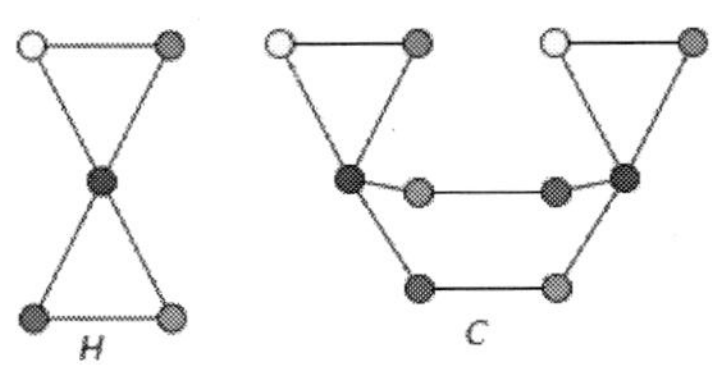

Matchings: A matching or independent edge set in a graph is a set of edges without common vertices. It may also be an entire graph consisting of edges without common vertices. Bipartite matching is a special case of a network flow problem.

- A matching is a subset of edges in a graph which have no common vertices.
- A matching M is maximum if as many vertices are matched as possible.
- An M-alternating path in a graph is one in which the edges are alternately in M and G\M.

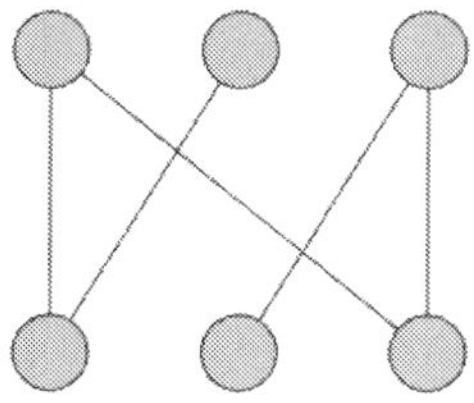

Matching M ⊆ E shown as dashed lines:

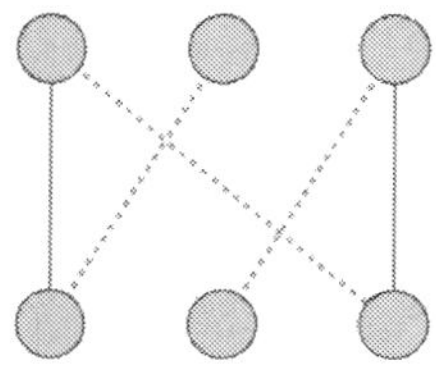

Independent Set

Two sets A and B are said to be independent if their intersection A intersection B = empty set, where empty set is the empty set. *For example*, {A, B, C} and {D,E} are independent, but {A,B,C} and {C,D,E} are not. Independent sets are also called disjoint or mutually exclusive.

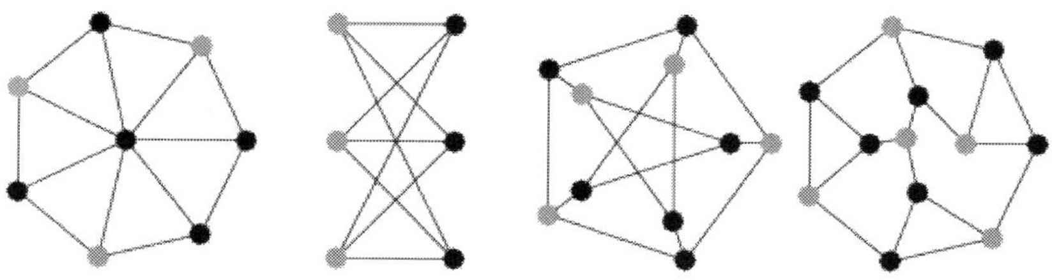

An independent vertex set of a graph G is a subset of the vertices such that no two vertices in the subset represent an edge of G. The figure above shows independent vertex sets consisting of two subsets for a number of graphs (the wheel graph W_8, utility graph $K_{3,3}$, Petersen graph, and Frucht graph).

Planarity

A graph G is planar if it can be drawn in the plane in such a way that no two edges meet each other except at a vertex to which they are incident. Any such drawing is called a plane drawing of G.

For example, the graph K_4 is planar, since it can be drawn in the plane without edges crossing.

K_4

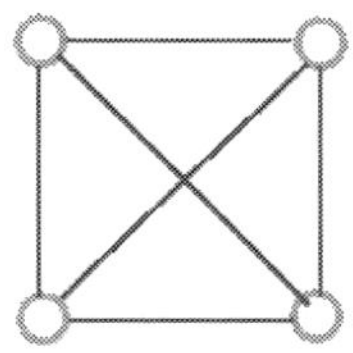

The three plane drawings of K4 are:

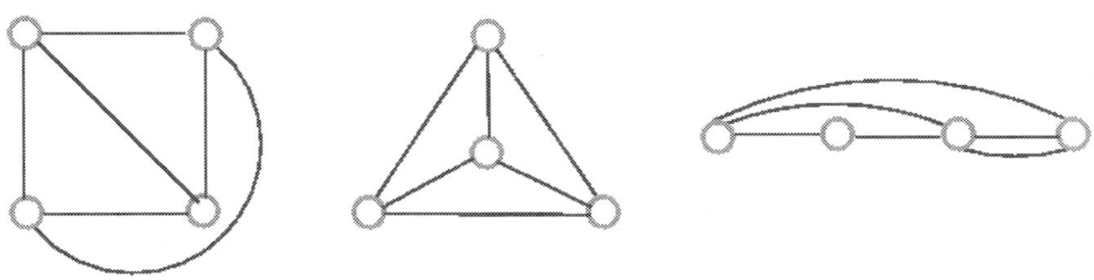

The five Platonic graphs are all planar.

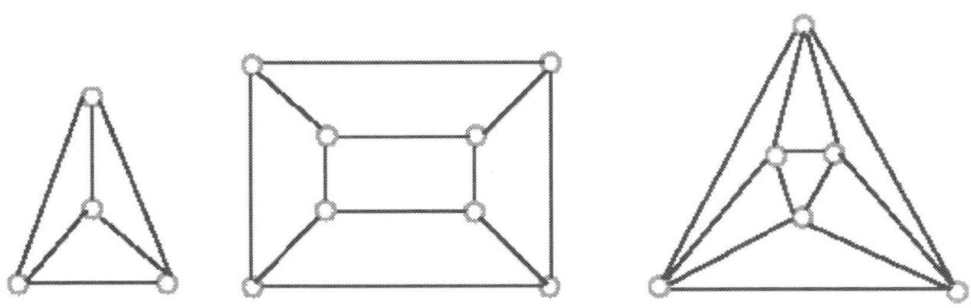

Graph Coloring

The proper coloring of a graph is the coloring of the vertices and edges with minimal number of colors such that no two vertices should have the same color. The minimum number of colors is called as the chromatic number and the graph is called properly colored graph

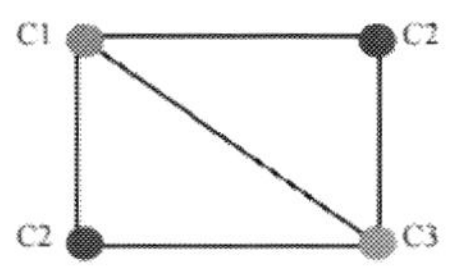

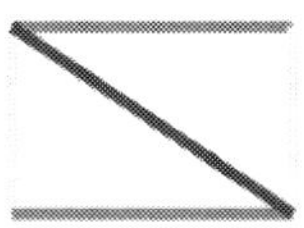

Isomorphism of Graphs

An isomorphism of G to H is a bijection f: V (G) →V (H) such that uv ∈ E(G) iff f(u)f(v) ∈ E(H).

If there is an isomorphism from G to H, then we say G is isomorphic to H, denoted by G ≅ H.

Claim: The isomorphism relation is an equivalence relation on the set of all graphs.

An isomorphism class of graphs is an equivalence class of graphs under the isomorphism relation.

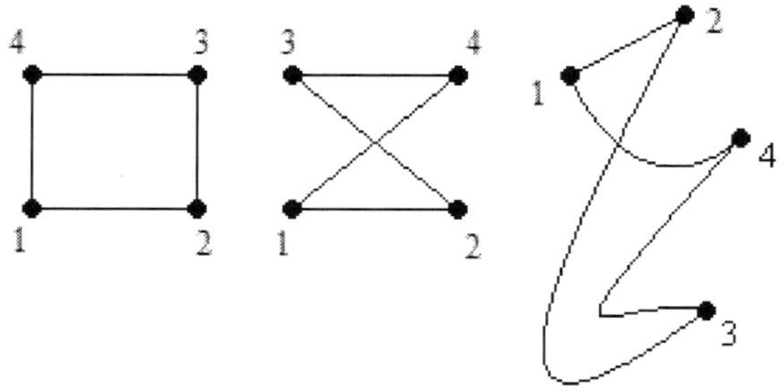

5 Probability

Probability is the measure of the likeliness that an event will occur.

Mean, Median, and Mode

The mean, median and mode are types of average.

The range gives a measure of the spread of a set of data.

$$P(Z)=\frac{1}{\sqrt{2\pi}}e^{-\frac{Z^2}{2}};\ -\infty \leq Z \leq \infty$$

$$\text{and } Z=\frac{x-\mu}{\sigma}$$

$$Z=\frac{x-np}{\sqrt{npq}}$$

$$\text{Median}=\frac{x_{n/2}+(x_{n/2}+1)}{2};\text{n is even}$$

$$=x_{n+1/2};\text{n is odd}$$

$$=L_{med}+(\frac{N/2-F}{F})xw$$

Where L_{med} = lower level of median class

$N = \Sigma f_i$

F = Cumulativefrequencyuptothemedianclass(Cumulativefrequency of the preceding class)

f = Frequency of the median class

Mode: Value of 'x' corresponding to maximum frequency.

$$L_{mode} + \frac{f_m - f_1}{(2f_m - f_1 - f_2)} \times h$$

Where L_{mode} = lower limit of modal class

f_m, = frequency of modal class

f_1 = preceding frequency of modal class

f_2 = Following frequency of modal class

Note: Mode = 3 Median - 2 Mean [for Asymmetric distribution]

Mean = Mode = Median [for Symmetric distribution]

Axioms of Probability

1. Let A and B be two events.

   $$P(A^c) = 1 - P(A)$$

2. P(□) = 0; RA) where □ is the empty set
3. If A and B are events and $A \subseteq B$ then

   $P(A) \leq P(B)$.4. If A is an event then $P(A) \leq 1$.
5. If $A = \{a_1, a_2, \ldots, a_n\}$ is a finite event then

   $$P(A^c) = \sum_{i=1}^{n} P(a_i)$$

6. If $A = \{a_1, a_2, a_3, \ldots\}$ is a countable infinite event then

   $$P(A) = \sum_{i=1}^{\infty} P(a_i)$$

7. For any two events A and B we have

   P(A ∪ B) = P(A) + P(B) – P(A □ B)
8. For any three events A, B and C we have

   P(A∪B ∪C) = P(A)+P(B)+P(C)−P(A□B)−P(A□C)−P(B

□C) + P(A□B □C).9. P(S) = 1; S is sample space.

10. max(0, P(A) + P(B) - 1) 5 P(A n min(P(A). P(B))

$11. \max(0, P(A) + P(B) - 1) \leq P(A \cap B) \leq \min(P(A), P(B))$

$12. \max(P(A), P(B)) \leq P(A \cup B) \leq \min(1, P(A) + P(B))$

$13. \max(0, P(A_1) + P(A_2) .... + P(A_n) - (n-1)) \leq P(A_1 \cap A_2)... \cap A \leq \min(P(A_1), P(A_2) .... P(A_n))$

$14. \max(P(A_1), P(A_2)....., P(A_n)) \leq P(A_1 \cup A_2 .... \cup A_n) \leq \min(1, P(A_1) + P(A_2)... + P(A_n))$

$$15. P(A / B) = \frac{P(A \cap B)}{P(B)}$$

$16. P(A / B) = P(A)$; independent events

$17. p(E_1 \cap E_2 \cap ..... \cap E_n) = P(E_1).P(E_2)....P(E_n)$; independent events

$$18. \text{Rule of total probability}: P(X) = \sum_{i=1}^{n} P(E_i) P(X \setminus E_i)$$

19.Baye's Theorem

$$P(E_1 \setminus X = \frac{P(E_1).P(X \setminus E_1)}{P(E_1).P(X \setminus E_1) + P(E_2).P(X \setminus E_2) + P(E_3).P(X \setminus E_3)}$$

Ingeneral,

$$P(X \setminus E_1) = \frac{P(E_1).P(X \setminus E_1)}{\sum_{i=1}^{n} PP = (E_i).P(X \setminus E_i)}$$

Random Variable (Stochastic Variable)

Randomvariableassignsarealnumbertoeach Let X be a discrete random variable_ then P(X) = P(X < x)v) is caned distribution function

1. $\sum_{i=0}^{n} P(i) \text{ of } X$

2. Mean or Expectation of $X = \mu = E(X)\sum_{i=1}^{n} x_i P(x_i)$

3. Variance of $X = \sigma^2 = E(X^2) - [E(X)]^2 = \sum_{i=1}^{n} (x_i - \mu)^2 P(x_i)$

4. Standard deviation of $X = \sigma = \sqrt{\text{Variance}}$

5. $\sum_{i=1}^{n} P(x_i) = 1$

Types of Random Variables

1. Discrete Random Variable: "Finite set of values" or "Countably infinite".
2. Continuous Random Variable (Non-discrete): "Infinite number of uncountable values".

Discrete Distributions

1. *Binomial Distribution*: The probability that the event will happen exactly r times in n trials i.e. r successes and n- r failures will occur.

   $P(X = r) = P(r) = \sum {}^{n}C_{r} P^{r} q^{n-r}$

   $\text{Mean} = E(x) = np$

   $\text{Variance}(\sigma^2) = V(x) = npq = np(1-p)$

   $S.D(\sigma) = \sqrt{npq} = \sqrt{np(1-p)}$

Where r = 0, 1, ...n

q = 1-p

n = fixed number of trials

p = probability of success

Poisson Distributions

$$P(X = x) = \sum \frac{e^{-\lambda}.\lambda^{x}}{x!}; x = 0, 1, 2,.., \infty$$

Where X = Discrete random variable

λ = Parameter of distribution (positive constant)

Mean (μ) = variance ($\sigma 2$) = λ

S.D. = Square root of λ

Poisson distribution

Continuous Distribution

Let X be continuous random variable, then

(i) Density functions:

$$P(X \leq a) = \int_{-\infty}^{a} f(x).dx$$

$$P(a \leq X \leq b) = \int_{a}^{b} f(x).dx$$

(ii) Mean = $E(x) = \int_{-\infty}^{\infty} f(x).dx$

(iii) Variance of X = $V(x) = \int_{-\infty}^{\infty} [x - E(x)]^2 .f(x)dx = E(x^2) - (E(x))^2$

$$= \int_{-\infty}^{\infty} x^2 f(x)dx - \left[\int_{-\infty}^{\infty} xf(x)dx \right]^2$$

$$= \int_{-\infty}^{\infty} f(x)dx = 1$$

(iv)

1. Uniform Distribution (Rectangular Distribution)

(i) Density Function:

$$f(x) = \frac{1}{b-a}; \quad a \le x \le b$$
$$= 0; \qquad \text{otherwise}$$

(ii) Cumulative function:

$$P(X \le x) = \int_{-\infty}^{x} f(x).dx = \begin{cases} 0 & ;\text{if } x \le a \\ \dfrac{x-a}{b-a} & ;\text{if } a \le x \le b \\ 1 & ;\text{if } x > b \end{cases}$$

(iii) Mean (μ) = (a + b)/2 = E(X)

(iv) Variance (σ^2) = $(b-a)^2/12$

2. Normal Distribution

The Normal Distribution has:

mean = median = mode

Symmetry about the center 50% of values less than the mean and 50% greater than the mean

(i) Density Function

$$f(x) = \frac{1}{\sigma\sqrt{2\pi}}.e^{-\frac{1}{2}\left(\frac{x-\mu}{\sigma}\right)}; -\infty \le x \le \infty, \sigma > 0, -\infty < \mu < \infty$$

(ii) Normal distribution is symmetrical

(iii) Mean = μ; Variance = σ2

(iv) $f(x) \ge 0$ for all x

(v) $\int_{-\infty}^{\infty} f(x).dx = 1$

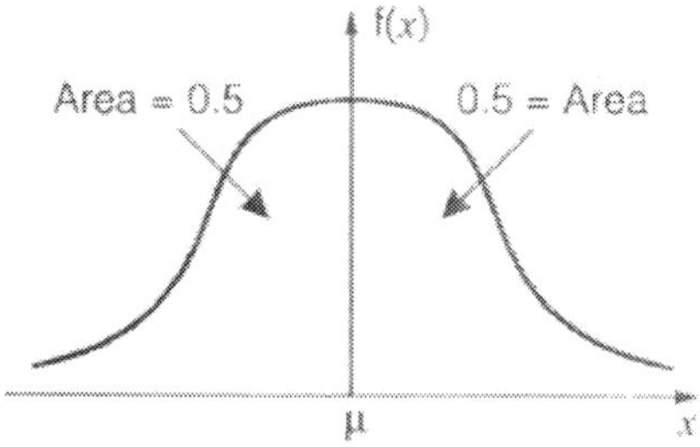

(vi).

$$P(Z) = \frac{1}{\sqrt{2\pi}} e^{-\frac{Z^2}{2}}; \ -\infty \le Z \le \infty$$

$$\text{and } Z = \frac{x-\mu}{\sigma}$$

$$Z = \frac{x-np}{\sqrt{npq}}$$

(When approximating binomial by normal)

Z = Standard normal variate

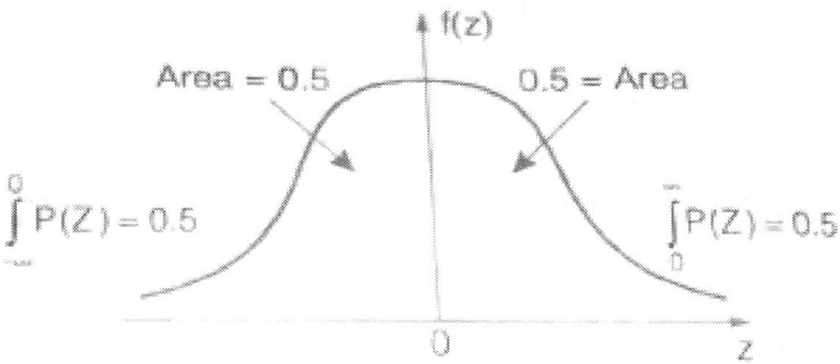

3. Exponential Distribution

(i) Density function:

$$f(x) = \lambda . e^{-\lambda x} \quad ; x > 0$$
$$= 0 \quad ; \text{Otherwise}$$

(ii) Mean (μ) = 1/□ = S.D (σ)

(iii) Variance (σ^2) = 1/□^{2}

6 Linear Algebra

Linear algebra is the branch of mathematics concerning vector spaces and linear mappings between such spaces. It includes the study of lines, planes, and subspaces, but is also concerned with properties common to all vector spaces.

Algebra of matrices

A matrix is an m × n array of scalars from a given field F. The individual values in the matrix are called entries.

Example:

$$A = \begin{bmatrix} 2 & 1 & 3 \\ -1 & 2 & 4 \end{bmatrix} \qquad B = \begin{bmatrix} 1 & 2 \\ 3 & 4 \end{bmatrix}$$

The size of the array is–written as m × n, where m is number of rows, and n is number of columns

Notation:

$$A = \begin{bmatrix} a_{11} & a_{12} & \dots & a_{1n} \\ a_{21} & a_{22} & \dots & a_{2n} \\ a_{n1} & a_{n2} & \dots & a_{mn} \end{bmatrix} \leftarrow \textit{Rows}$$

Columns

A: = uppercase denotes a matrix

a: = lower case denotes an entry of a matrix a ∈ F.

Special matrices

(1) If m = n, the matrix is called square. In this case we have

(1a) A matrix A is said to be diagonal if

$aij = o \quad i \neq j$

(1b) A diagonal matrix A may be denoted by diag (d_1, d_2,... ,d_n)

Where:

$aii = d_i \;\; aij = 0 \quad j \neq i.$

The diagonal matrix diag(1, 1,..., 1) is called the identity matrix and is usually denoted by

$$I_n = \begin{bmatrix} 1 & 0 & \cdots & 0 \\ 0 & 1 & & \\ \vdots & & \ddots & \\ 0 & & & 1 \end{bmatrix}$$

Or simply I, when n is assumed to be known. 0 = diag(0,..., 0) is called the zero matrix.

(1c) A square matrix L is said to be lower triangular if

$lij = 0 \quad i < j$

(1d) A square matrix U is said to be upper triangular if

$uij = 0 \quad i > j.$

(1e) A square matrix A is called symmetric if

aij = aji.

(1f) A square matrix A is called Hermit Ian if

$aij = \overline{a}ij\,(\overline{Z} := Complex\,Conjugate\,of\;Z$

(1g) Eij has a 1 in the (i, j) position and zeros in all other positions.

(2) A rectangular matrix A is called nonnegative if

$aij \geq 0 \; all \;\; i, j.$

It is called positive if

$aij > 0 \; all \;\; i, j.$

Each of these matrices has some special properties, which we will study during this course.

Determinant

The determinant of a matrix is a special number that can be calculated from a square matrix.

Calculating the Determinant

First of all the matrix must be **square** (i.e. have the same number of rows as columns). Then it is just basic arithmetic. Here is how:

For a 2×2 Matrix

For a 2×2 matrix (2 rows and 2 columns):

$$A = \begin{bmatrix} a & b \\ c & d \end{bmatrix}$$

The determinant is:

|A| = ad – bc

"The determinant of a equals a times d minus b times c"

It is easy to remember when you think of a cross:

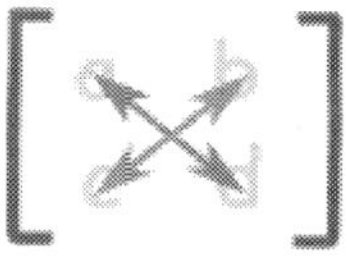

- Blue means positive (+ad),
- Red means negative (-bc)

A Matrix is an array of numbers:

$$\begin{bmatrix} 3 & 8 \\ 4 & 6 \end{bmatrix}$$

A Matrix: (This one has 2 Rows and 2 Columns)

The determinant of that matrix is (calculations are explained later): $3\times 6 - 8\times 4 = 18 - 32 = -14$

System of leaner Equation

These are all linear equations:

$y = 2x + 1 \qquad 5x = 6 + 3y \qquad y/2 = 3 - x$

Example: $\mathbf{y = 2x + 1}$ is a linear equation:

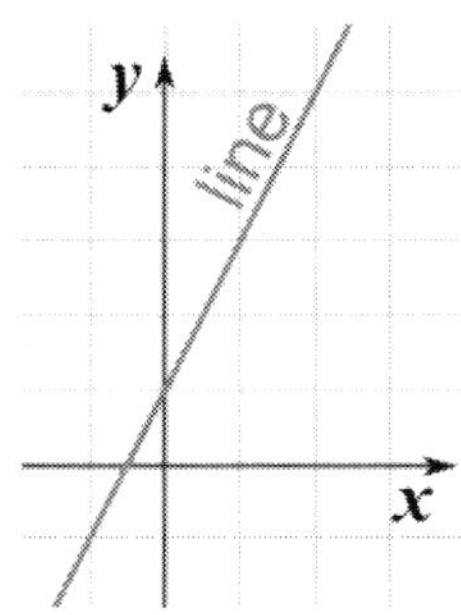

The graph of $\mathbf{y = 2x + 1}$ is a straight line

- When x increases, y increases **twice as fast**, hence 2x
- When x is 0, y is already 1. Hence +1 is also needed
- So: y = 2x + 1

Here are some example values:

x	$y = 2x + 1$
-1	$y = 2x(-1) + 1 = -1$
0	$y = 2x0 + 1 = 1$
1	$y = 2x1 + 1 = 3$
2	$y = 2x2 + 1 = 5$

Eigen Values

Consider an n × n matrix a and a scalar □. By definition □ is an eigenvalue of A if there is a nonzero vector $\vec{u}$ in R^n such that.

$AC = \lambda C.$

Using the matrix multiplication properties, we obtain

$(A - \lambda I_n)C = 0.$

This is a linear system for which the matrix coefficient is $A - \lambda I_n$. We also know that this system has one solution if and only if the matrix coefficient is invertible, i.e. $\det(A - \lambda I_n) \neq 0$. Since the zero-vector is a solution and C is not the zero vector, then we must have

$\det(A - \lambda I_n) = 0$

Example: Consider the matrix

$$A = \begin{pmatrix} 1 & -2 \\ -2 & 0 \end{pmatrix}$$

The equation $\det(A - \lambda I_n) \neq 0$ translates into

$$\begin{vmatrix} 1-\lambda & -2 \\ -2 & 0-\lambda \end{vmatrix} = (1-\lambda) - 4 = 0$$

Which is equivalent to the quadratic equation

$\lambda^2 - \lambda - 4 = 0$

Solving this equation leads to

$$\lambda = \frac{1+\sqrt{17}}{2}, and\ \lambda = \frac{1-\sqrt{17}}{2}$$

In other words, the matrix A has only two eigenvalues.

Eigen vectors

Let A be a square matrix of order n and λ one of its eigenvalues. Let X be an eigenvector of A associated to λ. We must have

$$AX = \lambda X\ or\ (A - \lambda I_n)X = 0.$$

This is a linear system for which the matrix coefficient is $A - \lambda I_n$. Since the zero-vector is a solution, the system is consistent. In fact, we will in a different page that the structure of the solution set of this system is very rich. In this page, we will basically discuss how to find the solutions. It is quite easy to notice that if X is a vector which satisfies $AX = \lambda X$, then the vector $Y = cX$ (for any arbitrary number c) satisfies the same equation, i.e. $AY = \lambda Y$. In other words, if we know that X is an eigenvector, then cX is also an eigenvector associated to the same eigenvalue.

Example: Consider the matrix

$$A = \begin{pmatrix} 1 & 2 & 1 \\ 6 & -1 & 0 \\ -1 & -2 & -1 \end{pmatrix}$$

First we look for the eigenvalues of A. These are given by the characteristic equation det $(A - \lambda I_3)$, i.e.

$$\begin{vmatrix} 1-\lambda & 2 & 1 \\ 6 & -1-\lambda & 0 \\ -1 & -2 & -1-\lambda \end{vmatrix} = 0.$$

If we develop this determinant using the third column, we obtain

$$\begin{vmatrix} 6 & -1-\lambda \\ -1 & -2 \end{vmatrix} + (-1-\lambda)\begin{vmatrix} 1-\lambda & 2 \\ 6 & -1-\lambda \end{vmatrix} = 0.$$

Using easy algebraic manipulations, we get

$$-\lambda(\lambda+4)(\lambda-3) = 0.$$

7 Numerical Methods

Numerical methods for ordinary differential equations are methods used to find numerical approximations to the solutions of ordinary differential equations (ODEs). Their use is also known as "numerical integration", although this term is sometimes taken to mean the computation of integrals.

LINEAR ALGEBRAIC EQUATIONS

A linear equation is an algebraic equation in which each term is either a constant or the product of a constant and (the first power of) a single variable. Linear equations can have one or more variables.

A linear algebraic equation (or as well a linear equation) is an algebraic equation of the first degree in all unknowns, that is, an equation of the form

$$a_1x_1 + \cdots + a_nx_n = b.$$

Every system of linear algebraic equations can be written in the form

$$a_{11}x_1 + a_{12}x_2 + a_{13}x_3 = b_1$$
$$a_{21}x_1 + a_{22}x_2 + a_{23}x_3 = b_2$$
$$a_{31}x_1 + a_{32}x_2 + a_{33}x_3 = b_3$$

$$A = \begin{bmatrix} a_{11} & a_{12} & a_{13} \\ a_{21} & a_{22} & a_{23} \\ a_{31} & a_{32} & a_{33} \end{bmatrix}_{3\times3}, X = \begin{bmatrix} x_1 \\ x_2 \\ x_3 \end{bmatrix}_{3\times1}, B = \begin{bmatrix} b_1 \\ b_2 \\ b_3 \end{bmatrix}_{3\times1}$$

where m and n are natural numbers; the a_{ij} (i=1,...,m; j=1,...,n) are called the coefficients at the unknowns and are given; the b_i (i=1,...,m) are called the free terms and are also given; the x_i (i=1,...,n) are called the unknowns and need to be found. A solution of the system of linear algebraic equations (1) is a set of values $c_1,...,c_n$ such that each equation of the system becomes an identity when the ci are substituted for the corresponding unknowns. For applications the most important case is that in which the coefficients at the unknowns, the free terms and the values of the unknowns are numbers (complex, real or integers), but one can also consider the case when they belong to an arbitrary field P.

LU Decomposition

LU decomposition (decomposition into a lower and upper triangular matrix) is recommended when dealing with equation systems where the matrix A does not alter but the right hand side (the vector z) does. Both the Gaussian elimination and the Gauss-Jordan method involve both the right hand side and the matrix in their algorithm. Consecutive solutions of an equation system with an altering right hand side can be computed faster with LU decomposition.

The LU decomposition splits a matrix A into a product of a lower triangular matrix L with an upper triangular matrix U.

$$A = LU \quad \text{with} \quad L = \begin{bmatrix} l_{11} & 0 & \cdots & 0 \\ l_{21} & l_{22} & \ddots & \vdots \\ \vdots & & \ddots & 0 \\ l_{n1} & \cdots & \cdots & l_{nn} \end{bmatrix} \quad \text{and}$$

$$U = \begin{bmatrix} u_{11} & u_{12} & \cdots & u_{1n} \\ 0 & u_{22} & & \vdots \\ \vdots & \ddots & \ddots & \vdots \\ 0 & \cdots & 0 & u_{nn} \end{bmatrix}$$

Principal minors of A are non-singular.

$$AX = B \Rightarrow LUX = B \left[\text{Since } A = LU\right]$$

$$A = \begin{bmatrix} a_{11} & a_{12} & a_{13} \\ a_{21} & a_{22} & a_{23} \\ a_{31} & a_{32} & a_{33} \end{bmatrix} = \begin{bmatrix} 1 & 0 & 0 \\ l_{21} & 1 & 0 \\ l_{31} & l_{32} & 1 \end{bmatrix} \begin{bmatrix} u_{11} & u_{12} & u_{13} \\ 0 & u_{22} & u_{23} \\ 0 & 0 & u_{33} \end{bmatrix} \text{(Doolittle's method)}$$

$$A = \begin{bmatrix} a_{11} & a_{12} & a_{13} \\ a_{21} & a_{22} & a_{23} \\ a_{31} & a_{32} & a_{33} \end{bmatrix} = \begin{bmatrix} l_{11} & 0 & 0 \\ l_{21} & l_{22} & 0 \\ l_{31} & l_{32} & l_{33} \end{bmatrix} \begin{bmatrix} 1 & u_{12} & u_{13} \\ 0 & 1 & u_{23} \\ 0 & 0 & 1 \end{bmatrix} \text{(Crout's method)}$$

Order of computation in Doolittle's method such as:

In Doolittle's method the equations are set-up row-wise for A's elements.

- First row of

  $A \Rightarrow u_{11} = a_{11}$

  $u_{12} = a_{12}$

  $u_{13} = a_{13}$

- Second row of

  $A \Rightarrow l_{21} = \frac{a_{21}}{a_{11}}; u_{22} = a_{22} - \frac{a_{21}}{a_{11}}.a_{12}$

  $u_{23} = a_{23} - l_{21}u_{13}$

- Third row of

  $A \Rightarrow l_{31} = \frac{a_{31}}{a_{11}}; l_{32} = \frac{1}{u_{22}}\left[a_{32} - \frac{a_{31}}{a_{11}}.a_{12}\right]$

  $u_{33} = a_{33} - l_{31}.u_{13} - l_{33}u_{23}$

ROOT FINDING METHOD

There are some types of root finding method such as:

Regular-falsi Method

The Regula falsi method is also called as regula Falsi Method. This is oldest method for computing the real roots of an algebric equation. With the use of this method wecan find two numbers a and b such that equations f(a) and f(b) are of different sign. Hence the root lies between the point a and b for the graph of y = f(x) and must cross the x axis for the point x = a and x = b.

The Regula–Falsi Method is a numerical method for estimating the roots of a polynomial f(x). A value x replaces the midpoint in the Bisection Methodand serves as the new approximation of a root of f(x). The objective is to make convergence faster. Assume that f(x) is continuous.

Algorithm for the Regula–Falsi Method: Given a continuous function f(x)

- Find points a and b such that a < b and f(a) * f(b) < 0.
- Take the interval [a, b] and determine the next value of x_1.
- If $f(x_1) = 0$ then x_1 is an exact root, else if $f(x_1) * f(b) < 0$ then let a = x_1, else if $f(a) * f(x_1) < 0$ then let b = x_1.
- Repeat steps 2 and 3 until $f(x_i) = 0$ or $|f(x_i)| \leq$ DOA, where DOA stands for degree of accuracy.

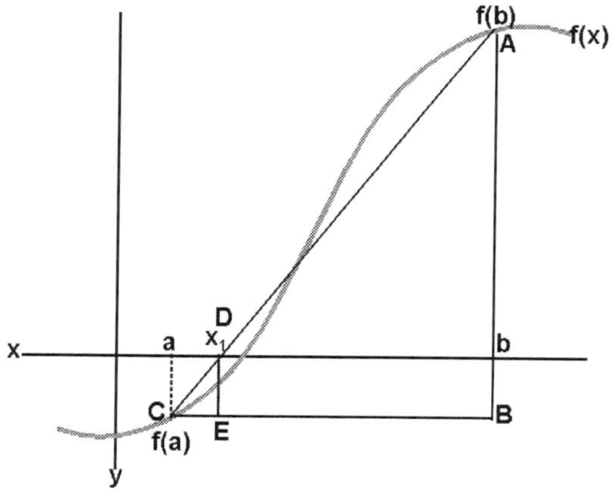

EC / BC = E / AB

$[x - a] / [b - a] = [f(x) - f(a)] / [f(b) - f(a)]$

$x - a = [b - a][0 - f(a)] / [f(b) - f(a)]$

$x = a + [b - a][-f(a)] / [f(b) - f(a)]$

$x = a - [b - a] f(a) / [f(b) - f(a)]$

Secant method

In numerical analysis, the secant method is a root-finding algorithm that uses a succession of roots of secant lines to better approximate a root of a function f. The secant method can be thought of as a finite difference approximation of Newton's method.

Variation of Newton's Method:

- Approximates derivative
- Requires two starting x values

Let x_k denote approximation to root of f(x) at step k.

Using Newton's Method, next approx. is

$$x_{k+1} = x_k - f(x_k)/f'(x_k)$$

Since the derivative

$$f'(x) = \lim_{\Delta x \to 0} \frac{f(x) - f(x - \Delta x)}{\Delta x}$$

Can be approximated as

$$f'(x_k) \approx \frac{f(x_k) - f(x_{k-1})}{x_k - x_{k-1}} = \frac{y_k - y_{k-1}}{x_k - x_{k-1}}$$

the expression for x_{k+1} can be approximated as

$$x_{k-1} = \frac{x_{k-1}y_k - x_k y_{k-1}}{y_k - y_{k-1}}$$

- It can find complex roots
- Faster convergence, no guarantee of convergence
- Order of convergence = 1.62

Bisection Method

Bisection method is the simplest among all the numerical schemes to solve the transcendental equations. This scheme is based on the intermediate value theorem for continuous functions.

Consider a transcendental equation f (x) = 0 which has a zero in the interval [a, b] and f (a) * f (b) < 0. Bisection scheme computes the zero, say c, by repeatedly halving the interval [a, b]. That is, starting with

c = (a+b) / 2

the interval [a,b] is replaced either with [c,b] or with [a,c] depending on the sign of f (a) * f (c) . This process is continued until the zero is obtained. Since the zero is obtained numerically the value of c may not exactly match with all the decimal places of the analytical solution of f (x) = 0 in the interval [a,b]. Hence any one of the following mechanisms can be used to stop the bisection iterations:

- C1. Fixing a priori the total number of bisection iterations N i.e., the length of the interval or the maximum error after N iterations in this case is less than | b-a | / 2N.
- C2. By testing the condition $|c_i - c_{i-1}|$ (where i are the iteration number) less than some tolerance limit, say epsilon, fixed a priori.
- C3. By testing the condition $|f(c_i)|$ less than some tolerance limit alpha again fixed a priori.

Algorithm - Bisection Scheme

Given a function f (x) continuous on an interval [a, b] and f (a) * f (b) < 0

Do

c = (a+b)/2

if f (a) * f (c) < 0 then b = c

else a = c

While (none of the convergence criteria C1, C2 or C3 is satisfied)

Example

Find a root of f (x) = 3x + sin(x) - exp(x) = 0.

The graph of this equation is given in the figure.

It's clear from the graph that there are two roots, one lies between 0 and 0.5 and the other lies between 1.5 and 2.0.

Consider the function f (x) in the interval [0, 0.5] since f (0) * f (0.5) is less than zero.

Then the bisection iterations are given by

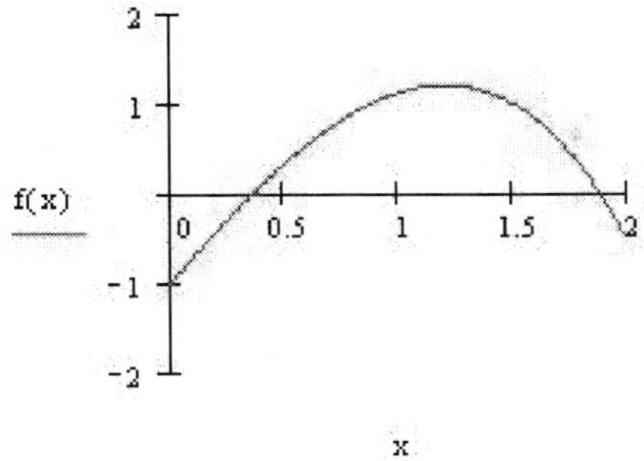

Iteration No.	a	b	c	f(a) * f(c)
1	0	0.5	0.25	0.287 (+ve)
2	0.25	0.5	0.393	-0.015 (-ve)
3	0.65	0.393	0.34	9.69 E-3 (+ve)
4	0.34	0.393	0.367	-7.81 E-4 (-ve)
5	0.34	0.367	0.354	8.9 E-4 (+ve)
6	0.354	0.367	0.3605	-3.1 E-6 (-ve)

So one of the roots of $3x + \sin(x) - \exp(x) = 0$ is approximately 0.3605.

Newton-Raphson Method

If you have ever tried to find a root of a complicated function algebraically, you may have had some difficulty. Using some basic concepts of calculus, we have ways of numerically evaluating roots of complicated functions. Commonly, we use the Newton-Raphson method. This iterative process follows a set guideline to approximate one root, considering the function, its derivative, and an initial x-value.

You may remember from algebra that a root of a function is a zero of the function. This means that at the "root" the function equals zero. We can find these roots of a simple function such as: $f(x) = x^2 - 4$ simply by setting the function to zero, and solving:

$$f(X) = X^2 - 4 = 0$$
$$(X+2)(X-2) = 0$$
$$X = 2 \ or \ X = -2$$

The Newton-Raphson method uses an iterative process to approach one root of a function. The specific root that the process locates depends on the initial, arbitrarily chosen x-value.

$$x_{n+1} = x_n - \frac{f(x_n)}{f(x_n)}$$

Here, xn is the current known x-value, f(xn) represents the value of the function at xn, and f'(xn) is the derivative (slope) at xn. xn + 1 represents the next x-value that you are trying to find. Essentially, f'(x), the derivative represents f(x)/dx (dx = delta-x). Therefore, the term f(x)/f'(x) represents a value of dx.

$$\frac{f(x)}{f(x)} = \frac{f(x)}{f(x)/\Delta x} = \Delta x$$

The more iteration that are run, the closer dx will be to zero (0). To see how this works, we will perform the Newton-Raphson method on the function that we investigated earlier, f(x) = x^2-4. Below are listed the values that we need to know in order to complete the process.

$$f(x) = x^2 - 4$$
$$f(x) = 2x$$
$$x_0 = 6$$

n	x_n	$f(x_n)$	$f'(x_n)$	x_{n+1}	dx
0	**$x_0 = 6$**	$f(x_0 = 32)$	$f'(x_0 = 12)$	**$x_1 = 3.33$**	
1	**$x_1 = 3.33$**	$f(x_1) = 7.09$	$f'(x_1) = 6.66$	**$x_2 = 2.27$**	dx = 1.06
2	**$x_2 = 2.27$**	$f(x_2) = 1.15$	$f'(x_2) = 4.54$	**$x_3 = 2.01$**	dx = .26
3	**$x_3 = 2.01$**	$f(x_3) = 0.04$	$f'(x_3) = 4.02$	**$x_4 = 2.00$**	dx = 0.01

Thus, using an initial x-value of six (6) we find one root of the equation $f(x) = x^2-4$ is $x=2$. If we were to pick a different inital x-value, we may find the same root, or we may find the other one, $x=-2$.

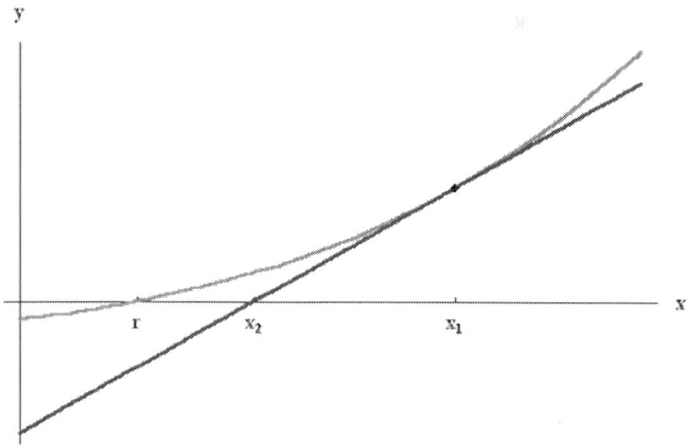

NUMERICAL INTEGRATION

Numerical integration is the approximate computation of integral using numerical techniques. The numerical computation of an integral is sometimes called quadrature.

It is the process of finding or evaluating a definite integral $I = \int_a^b f(x)dx$ from a set of a numerical values of of the integrand f(x).

There are two types of numerical integration rules such as:

- Trapezoidal rules
- Simpson's rules

Trapezoidal Rules

The trapezoidal rule is a method for approximating a definite integral by evaluating the integrand at two points.

The formal rule is given by

$$\int_a^b f(x)dx \approx \frac{h}{2}[f(2)+f(b)]$$

Where $h = b - a$.

This rule comes from determining the area of a right trapezoid with bases of lengths f(a) and f(b) respectively and a height of length h. When using a graph to illustrate the trapezoidal rule, the height of the right trapezoid is actually horizontal and the bases are vertical. This may be confusing to someone who is seeing the trapezoidal rule for the first time.

Simpson's Rules

There are some steps such as:

(i) It gives exact result when polynomial of degree ≤ 3.

(ii) If we are evaluating $I = \int_a^b f(x)dx$ by Simpson's rules then

$$\text{Error} = -\frac{h^5}{90}.f^{iv}(\xi)\times n_i \; (a \leq \xi \leq b)$$

(iii) Simpson's rule is more accurate as compare to trapezoidal rule, since it is a fourth order method as compared to trapezoidal rule which is second order.

(iv) Simpson's $1/3^{rd}$ rule

$$\int_{x_0}^{x_0} ydx = \frac{h}{3}[(y_0+y_n)+2(y_2+y_4+\ldots+y_{n-2})+4(y_1+y_3+\ldots+y_{n-1})$$

(v) Simpson's 3/8 rule

$$\int_{x_0}^{x_0} ydx = \frac{3h}{8}[(y_0+y_n)+2(y_3+y_6+\ldots+y_{n-3})+3(y_1+y_2+\ldots+y_{n-1})$$

(vi) If tabulation (step size) is halved, the error in Simpson's rule evaluation of the integral is reduced by a factor of '16'.

8 Calculus

Limit: A limit is the value that a function or sequence "approaches" as the input or index approaches some value.

In formulas, a limit is usually written as

$$\lim_{x \to c} f(n) = L$$

and is read as "the limit of *f* of *n* as *n* approaches *c* equals *L*". Here "lim" indicates *limit*, and the fact that function *f*(*n*) approaches the limit *L* as *n* approaches *c* is represented by the right arrow (), as in

$$f(n) \to L$$

Continuity of a Function in Calculus

A function f(x) is said to be continuous at x = a if

$$\lim_{x \to a} f(x) = f(a)$$

A function is said to be continuous on the interval [*a*, *b*] if it is continuous at each point in the interval.

If f(x) is continuous at x = a then,

$$\lim_{x \to a} f(x) = f(a) \qquad \lim_{x \to a^-} f(x) = f(a) \qquad \lim_{x \to a^+} f(x) = f(a)$$

Differentiability

A function f is differentiable at a point c if $\lim_{h \to 0} \frac{f(c+h)-f(c)}{h}$ exists.

Similarly, f is differentiable on an open interval (a, b) if $\lim_{h \to 0} \frac{f(c+h)-f(c)}{h}$ exists for every c in (a, b).

Basically, f is differentiable at c if f'(c) is defined, by the above definition. Another point of note is that if f is differentiable at c, then f is continuous at c.

Mean Value Theorem

In mathematics, the mean value theorem states, roughly: that given a planar arc between two endpoints, there is at least one point at which the tangent to the arc is parallel to the secant through its endpoints.

The theorem is used to prove global statements about a function on an interval starting from local hypotheses about derivatives at points of the interval.

More precisely, if a function *f* is continuous on the closed interval [*a*, *b*], where $a < b$, and differentiable on the open interval (*a*, *b*), then there exists a point *c* in (*a*, *b*) such that

$$f'(c) = \frac{f(b)-f(a)}{b-a}$$

Theorem of Integral Calculus

Suppose F is a real-valued function that is differentiable on an interval [a, b] of the real line, and suppose F' is continuous on [a, b]. Then

$$\int_a^b F'(t)\,dt = F(b) - F(a).$$

For example, if you want to integrate x^2 over [0, 1], the Fundamental Theoremsaysthatit'sonlynecessarytofindafunctionFon[0,1]withderivative x^2; say $F(x) = x^3/3$; then $\int_a^b x^2 dx = \int_0^1 F'(x)\,dx = F(1) - F(0) = 1/3$.

Improper Integral and Definite Integral

This is the definite integral where either one or both of the limits of integration are infinite, or the integrand is infinite.

Improper Integrals with Infinite Limits:

$$\int_{-\infty}^{b} f(x)\,dx = \lim_{a \to -\infty} \int_a^b f(x)\,dx$$

$$\int_a^{\infty} f(x)\,dx = \lim_{b \to \infty} \int_a^b f(x)\,dx$$

If the limit exists and have finite values, we say that the improper integral converges. Otherwise, we say that the integral diverges.

Partial Derivative

In mathematics, a partial derivative of a function of several variables is its derivative with respect to one of those variables, with the others held constant (as opposed to the total derivative, in which all variables are allowed to vary). Partial derivatives are used in vector calculus and differential geometry.

Thepartialderivativeofafunctionf(x,y,...)withrespecttothevariable x is variously denoted by

$$f_x', f_x, \partial_x f, \frac{\partial}{\partial x} f, \text{ or } \frac{\partial f}{\partial x}$$

Sinceingeneralapartialderivativeisafunctionofthesamearguments as was the original function, this functional dependence is sometimes explicitly included in the notation, as in

$$f_x(x, y, \ldots), \frac{\partial f}{\partial x}(x, y, \ldots)$$

Example:

Let f(x, y) = y^3x^2. Calculate $\frac{\partial f}{\partial x}(x, y)$

Solution:

To calculate $\frac{\partial f}{\partial x}(x, y)$, we simply view y as being a fixed number and calculate the ordinary derivative with respect to x. The first time you do this, it might be easiest to set y = b, where b is a constant, to remind you that you should treat y as though it were number rather than a variable. Then, the partial derivative $\frac{\partial f}{\partial x}(x, y)$ is the same as the ordinary derivative of the function g(x) = b3x2. Using the rules for ordinary differentiation, we know that

$$\frac{dg}{dx}(x) = 2b^3x$$

Now, we remember that b = y and substitute y back in to conclude that

$$\frac{\partial f}{\partial x}(x, y) = 2y^3x$$

Total Derivative

The total derivative is the derivative with respect to t of the function y = *f*(t, u_1, ..., u_m) that depends on the variable t not only directly but also via the intermediate variables $u_1 = u_1(t, u_1, \ldots, u_m), \ldots, u_m = u_m(t, u_1, \ldots, u_m)$. It can be calculated using the formula

$$\frac{\partial y}{\partial t} = \frac{\partial f}{\partial t} + \frac{\partial f}{\partial u_1}\frac{\partial u_1}{\partial t} + \ldots + \frac{\partial f}{\partial u_m}\frac{\partial u_m}{\partial t}$$

The total derivative of a function f(t, x, y, ...) with respect to t is implemented in the Wolfram Language as dt[f[t, x, y, ...], t].

Example:

Elevation of land above sea level, H, depends on two map coordinates x, y in the following way:

$$H(x, y) = e^{-0.01(x^2+y^2)}.$$

A car travels thorough this terrain, so its coordinates depend on time in the following way:

$x(t) = -7 + 10\cos(10t)$, $y(t) = 4 + 10\sin(10t)$.

Find the speed with which the altitude of the car increases or decreases at $t = 0$.

Solution

$$\frac{dH}{dt} = \frac{\partial H}{\partial x}\frac{dx}{dt} + \frac{\partial H}{\partial y}\frac{dy}{dt}$$

$$= -0.02xe^{-0.01(x^2+y^2)} \cdot (-100\sin(10t))$$

$$-0.02ye^{-0.01(x^2+y^2)} \cdot (100\cos(10t))$$

At $t = 0$, $x = 3$, $y = 4$, this becomes

$$\frac{dH}{dt} = (2{\cdot}3{\cdot}0 - 2{\cdot}4{\cdot}1)e^{-0.01\cdot 25} \boxed{= -8e^{-0.25} \approx -6.230}$$

Maximum and Minimum

In mathematics, the maximum and minimum (plural: maximums or maxima and minimums or minima) of a function, known collectively as extrema (singular: extremum), are the largest and smallest value that the function takes at a point either within a given neighborhood (local or relative extremum) or on the function domain in its entirety (global or absolute extremum).

Suppose a surface given by f(x, y) has a local maximum at (x_0, y_0, z_0); geometrically, this point on the surface looks like the top of a hill. If we look at the cross-section in the plane $y = y_0$, we will see a local maximum on the curve at (x_0, z_0), and we know from single-variable calculus that $\frac{\partial z}{\partial x} = 0$ at this point. Likewise, in the plane $x = x_0$, $\frac{\partial z}{\partial y} = 0$. So if there is a local maximum at (x_0, y_0, z_0), both partial derivatives at the point must be zero, and likewise for a local minimum. Thus, to find local maximum and minimum points, we need only consider those points at which both partial derivatives are 0. As in the single-variable case, it is possible for the derivatives to be 0 at a point that is neither a maximum nor a minimum, so we need to test these points further.

Example: Verify that $f(x, y) = x^2 + y^2$ has a minimum at (0, 0).

First, we compute all the needed derivatives:

$$f_x = 2x \quad f_y = 2y \quad f_{xx} = 2 \quad f_{yy} = 2 \quad f_{xy} = 0$$

The derivatives fx and fy are zero only at (0,0). Applying the second derivative test there:

$D(0,0) = f_{xx}(0,0) f_{yy}(0,0) - f_{xy}(0,0)^2 = 2 \cdot -2 - 0 = -4 < 0$, so there is a local minimum at (0,0), and there are no other possibilities. So there are no local maxima or minima. The surface is shown in figure.

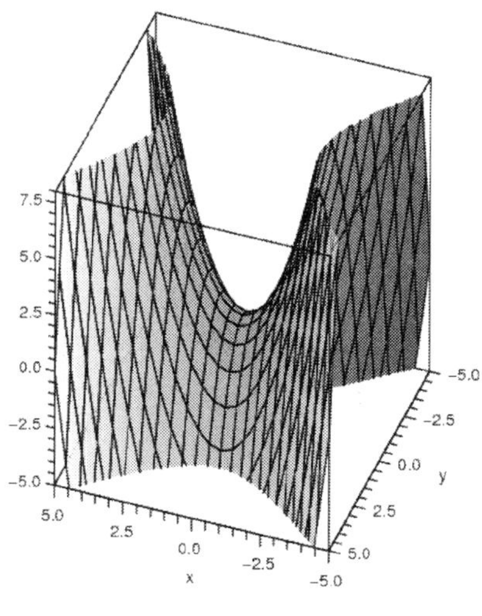

A Handbook on Computer Science

2

Digital Logic

CONTENTS

1 Logic Function

LOGIC GATES

A logic gate is an idealized or physical device implementing a Boolean function; that is, it performs a logical operation on one or more logical inputs, and produces a single logical output.

- Basic Gates – OR, AND, NOT
- Universal Gates –
- Arithmetic Gates – EX-OR, EX-NOR

NOT Gate

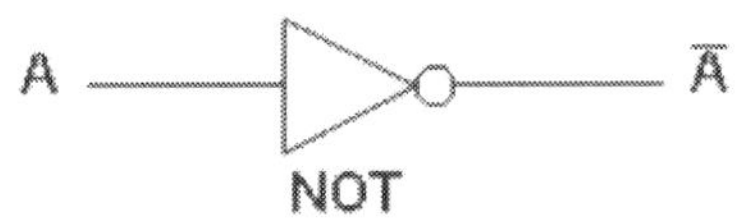

Input A	Output Y = $\bar{A}$
0	1
1	0

OR Gate

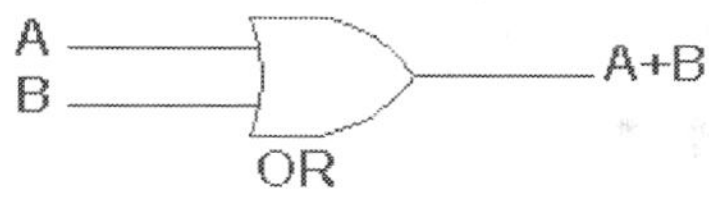

Inputs		Output
A	B	Y = A+B
0	0	0
0	1	1
1	0	1
1	1	1

AND Gate

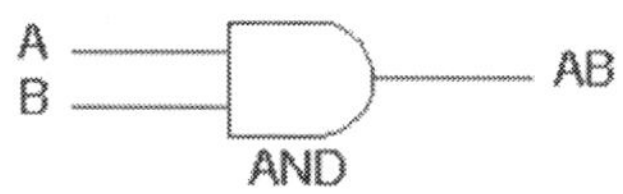

Inputs		Output
A	B	Y = AB
0	0	0
0	1	0
1	0	0
1	1	1

NOR Gate

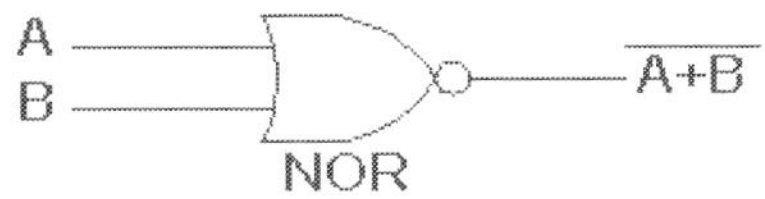

Inputs		Output
A	B	$Y = \overline{A+B}$
0	0	1
0	1	0
1	0	0
1	1	0

NAND Gate

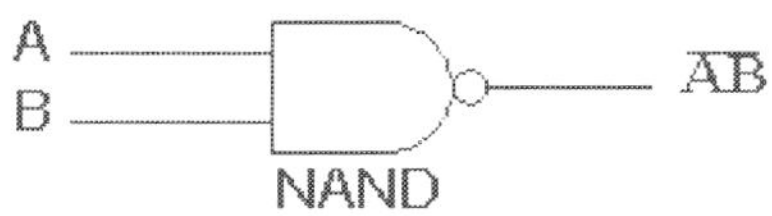

Inputs		Output
A	B	$Y = \overline{AB}$
0	0	1
0	1	1
1	0	1
1	1	0

EXOR Gate

Inputs		Output
A	B	$Y = A \oplus B$
0	0	0
0	1	1
1	0	1
1	1	0

EXNOR Gate

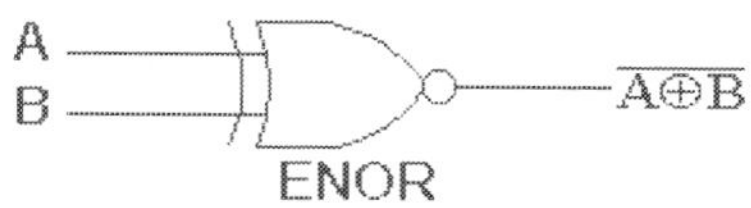

Inputs		Output
A	B	$Y = \overline{A \oplus B}$
0	0	1
0	1	0
1	0	0
1	1	1

Number of NAND or NOR Gates

Logic Gate	No. of NAND Gates	No. of NOR Gates
AND	2	3
OR	3	2
NOT	1	1
EXOR	4	5
EXNOR	5	4

Implementation of Gates using NAND

- AND gate :

- OR gate :

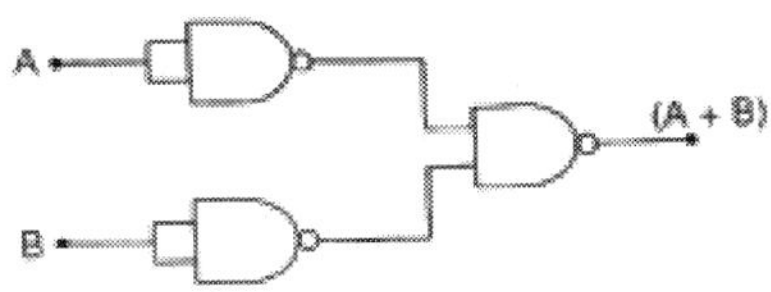

- NOT gate :

- EXOR gate :

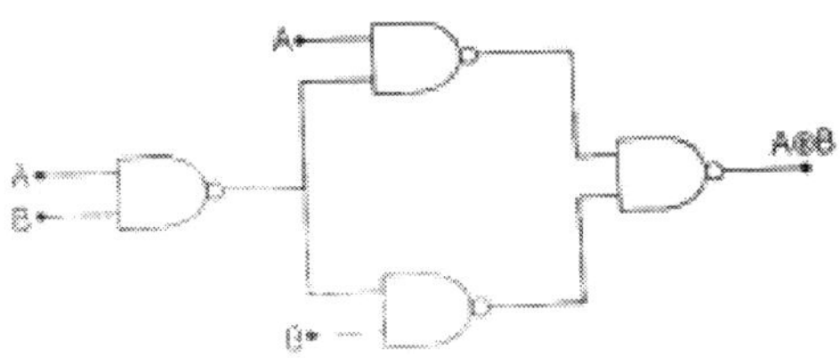

- EXNOR Gate :

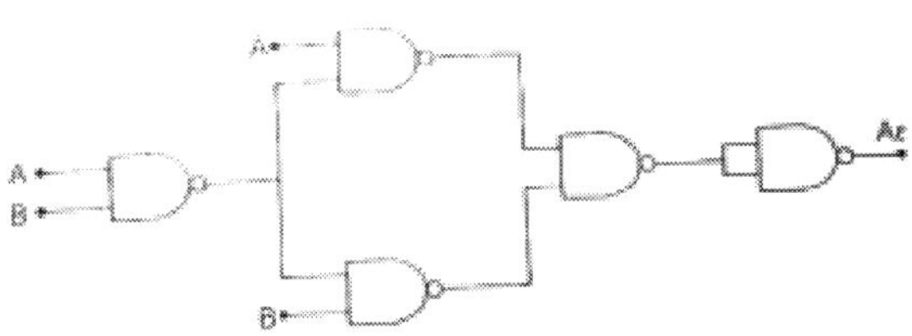

Implementation of Gates using NOR

- AND gate :

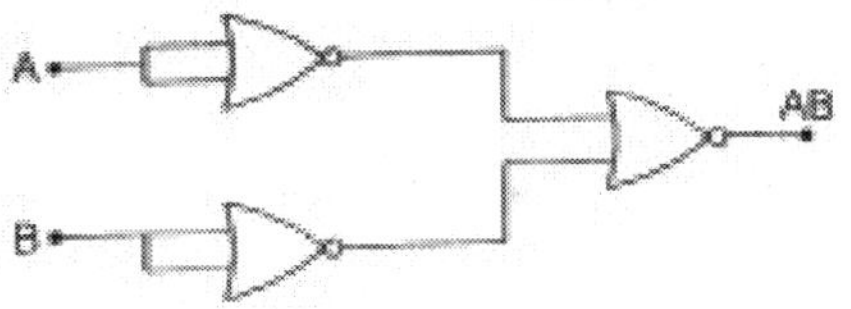

- OR gate :

- NOT gate :

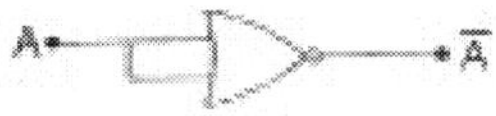

- EXOR gate :

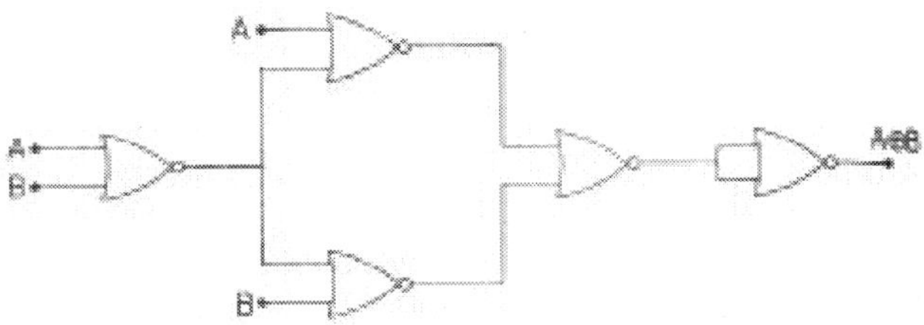

- EXNOR gate :

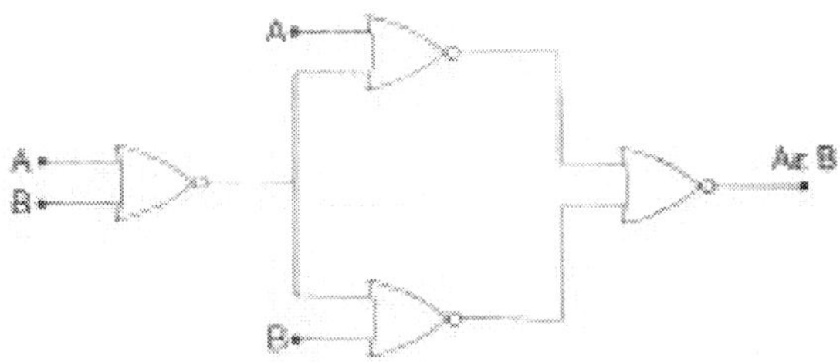

2 Minimization

Boolean Algebra Laws

Identity Law:

- A+A = A
- A•A = A

Communicative Law:

- A+B = B+A
- A • B = B • A

Associative Law:

- (A + B) + C = A + (B + C)
- (A B) C = A (B C)

Distributive Law:

- A (B + C) = A B + A C
- A + (B C) = (A + B) (A + C)

Negation Law

- (A') = A'
- (A)'' = A

Redundance Law

- A + A B = A
- A (A + B) = A

De Morgan's Theorem

- (A + B)' = A' • B'

- (A • B)' = A' + B'

NOTE:

Break the Line Change the Sign

Some Other Formula:

- A' + A = 1
- A' • A = 0
- A + A' B = A + B
- A(A' + B) = A • B
- 0 + A = A
- 1 + A = 1
- 1 • A = A
- 0 • A = 0
- A+AB = A
- A(A+B) = A

NOTE:

- **NAND and NOR gates do not follow associative law.**
- **NAND and NOR gates follow communicative law.**
- **OR, AND, EXOR, EXNOR follow communicative and associative law both.**

Duality Theorem

In digital electronics, there are two basic types of topologies, AND-OR and OR-AND.

OR-AND topology is also known as Product of Sums. AND-OR topology is also known as Sum of Products.

"*Usingdualitytheorem,SumofProductsisconvertedtoProductofSumsandvice versa. Each OR gate is changed to AND gate and vice versa*".

OR-AND Topology (Product of Sums)

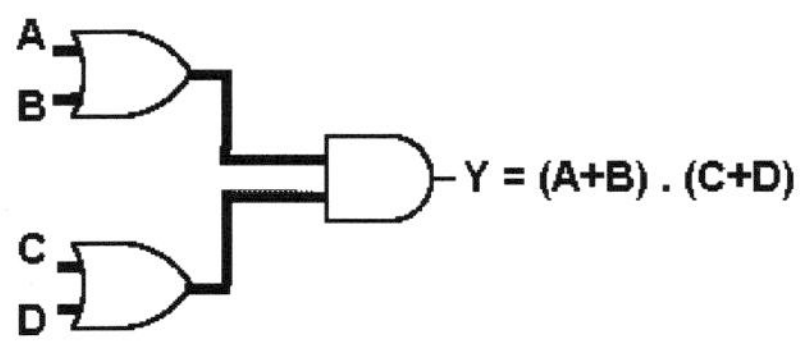

AND-OR Topology (Sum of Product)

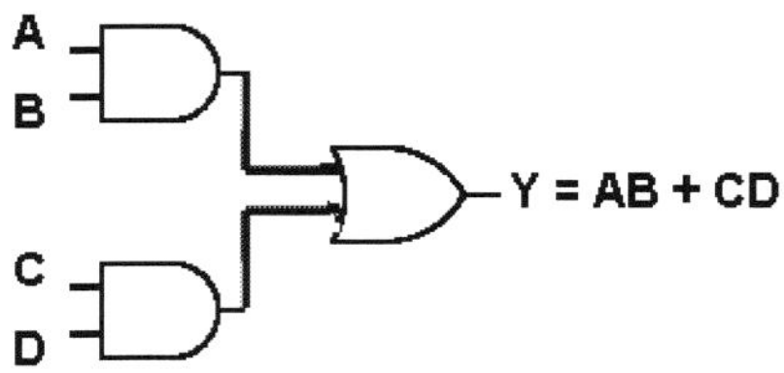

3 Combinational Circuit

Combinational circuit is circuit in which we combine the different gates in the circuit for example encoder, decoder, multiplexer and de-multiplexer. Some of the characteristics of combinational circuits are following.

- The output of combinational circuit at any instant of time depends only on the levels present at input terminals.
- The combinational circuit do not use any memory. The previous state of input does not have any effect on the present state of the circuit.
- A combinational circuit can have an n number of inputs and m number of outputs.

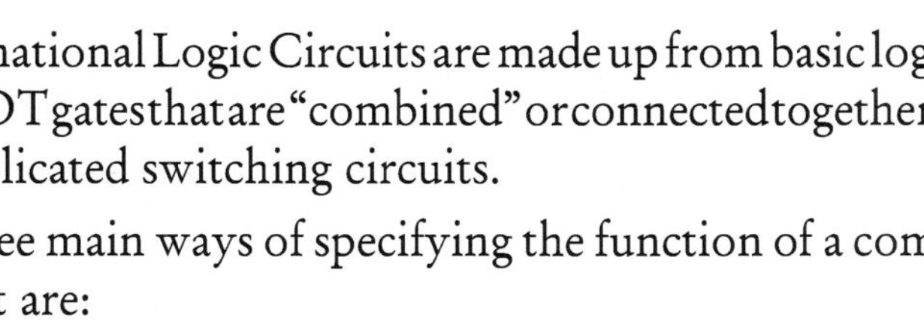

Combinational Logic Circuits are made up from basic logic NAND, NOR or NOT gates that are "combined" or connected together to produce more complicated switching circuits.

The three main ways of specifying the function of a combinational logic circuit are:

- Boolean algebra – This forms the algebraic expression showing the operation of the logic circuit for each input variable either True or False that results in a logic "1" output.

- Truth Table – A truth table defines the function of a logic gate by providing a concise list that shows all the output states in tabular form for each possible combination of input variable that the gate could encounter.
- Logic Diagram – This is a graphical representation of a logic circuit that shows the wiring and connections of each individual logic gate, represented by a specific graphical symbol that implements the logic circuit.

Half Adder

Half adder is a combinational logic circuit with two inputs and two output. The half adder circuit is designed to add two single bit binary numbers A and B. It is the basic building block for addition of two single bit numbers. This circuit has two outputs carry and sum.

Block Diagram

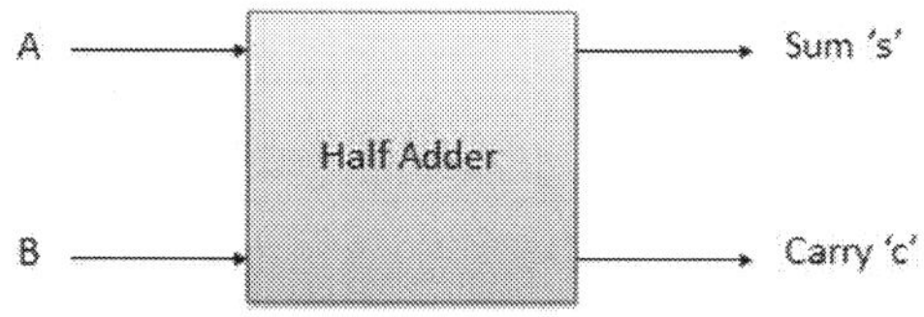

Truth Table

Input	Output	
A	B	S C
0	0	0 0
0	1	1 0
1	0	1 0
1	1	0 1

Circuit Diagram

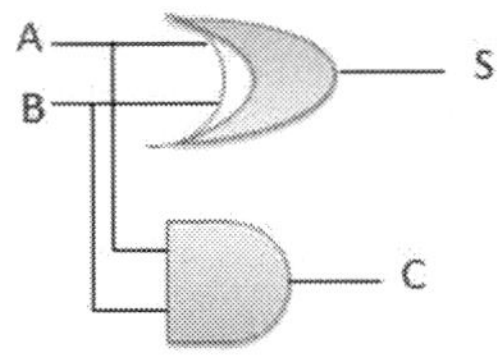

Full Adder

Full adder is developed to overcome the drawback of Half Adder circuit. It can add two one-bit numbers A and B, and carry c. The full adder is a three input and two output combinational circuit.

Block Diagram

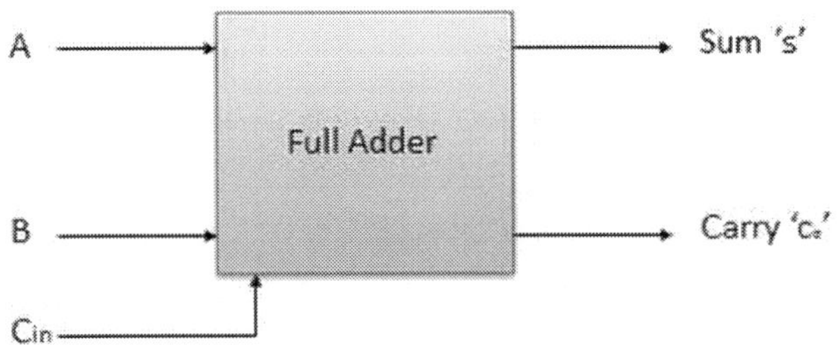

Truth Table

Input			Output
A	B	C_{in}	S C_o
0	0	0	0 0
0	0	1	1 0
0	1	0	1 0

0	1	1	0 1
1	0	0	1 0
1	0	1	0 1
1	1	0	0 1
1	1	1	1 1

Circuit Diagram

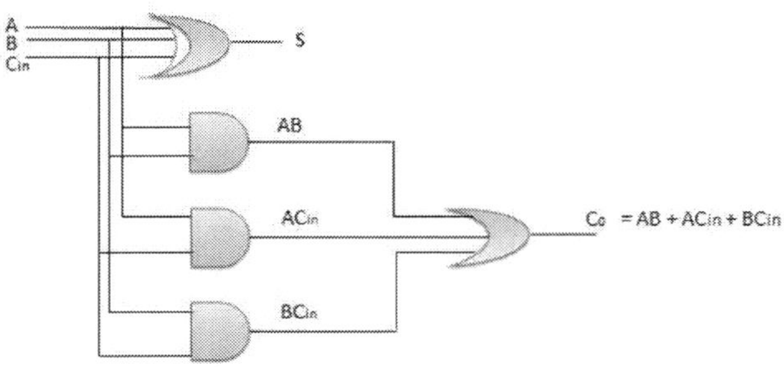

Half Subtractors

Half subtractor is a combination circuit with two inputs and two outputs (difference and borrow). It produces the difference between the two binary bits at the input and also produces a output (Borrow) to indicate if a 1 has been borrowed. In the subtraction (A-B), A is called as Minuend bit and B is called as Subtrahend bit.

Truth Table

Inputs		Output	
A	B	(A-B)	Borrow
0	0	0	0
0	1	1	1

1	0	1 0
1	1	0 0

Circuit Diagram

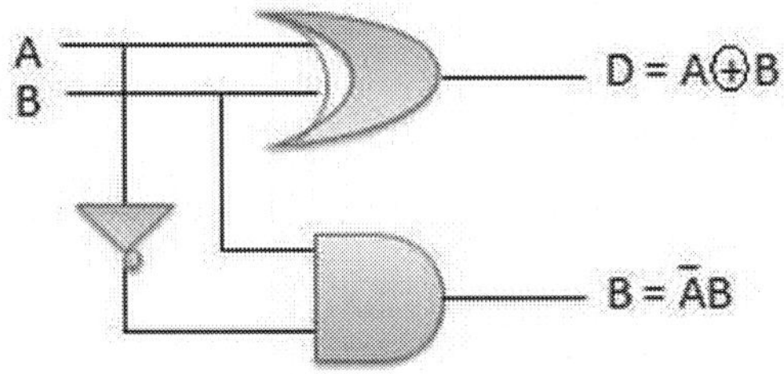

Full Subtractors

The disadvantage of a half subtractor is overcome by full subtractor. The full subtractor is a combinational circuit with three inputs A,B,C and two output D and C'. A is the minuend, B is subtrahend, C is the borrow produced by the previous stage, D is the difference output and C' is the borrow output.

Truth Table

Inputs			Output
A	B	C	(A-B-C) C
0	0	0	0 0
0	0	1	1 1
0	1	0	1 1
0	1	1	0 1
1	0	0	1 0
1	0	1	0 0

1	1	0	0 0
1	1	1	1 1

Circuit Diagram

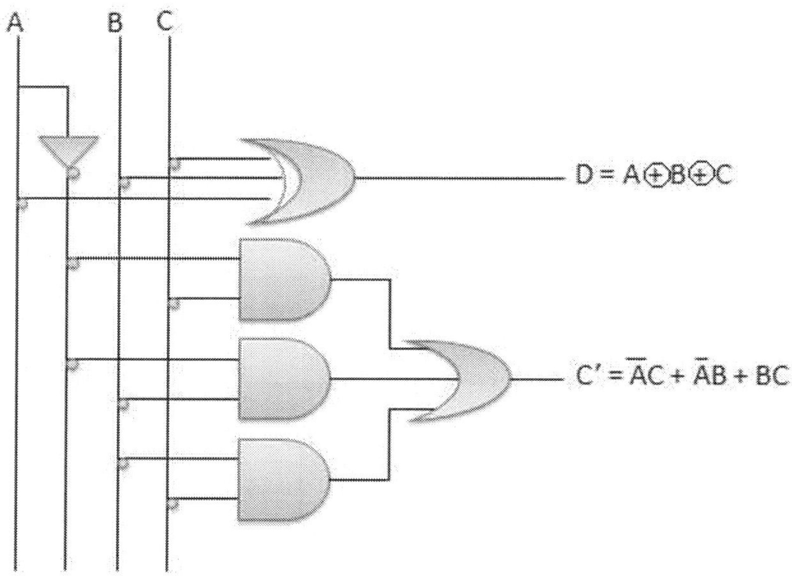

Multiplexers

Multiplexer is a special type of combinational circuit. There are n-data inputs, one output and m select inputs with 2m = n. It is a digital circuit which selects one of the n data inputs and routes it to the output. The selection of one of the n inputs is done by the selected inputs. Depending on the digital code applied at the selected inputs, one out of n data sources is selected and transmitted to the single output Y. E is called the strobe or enable input which is useful for the cascading. It is generally an active low terminal that means it will perform the required operation when it is low.

Block Diagram

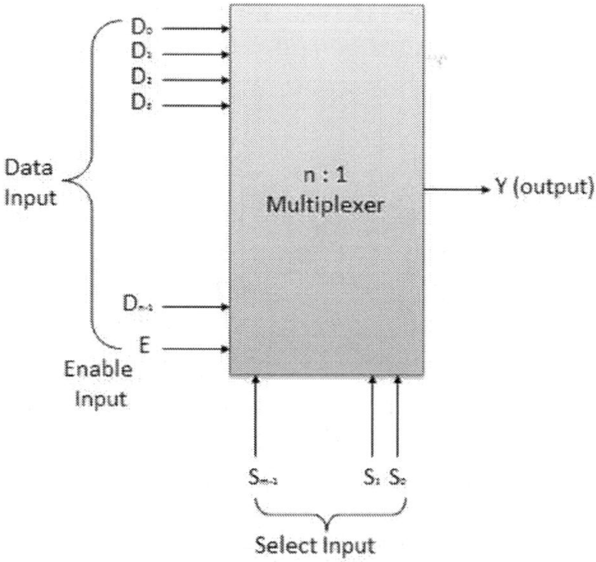

Multiplexers come in multiple variations

- 2:1 multiplexer
- 4:1 multiplexer
- 16:1 multiplexer
- 32:1 multiplexer

Truth Table

Enable	Select	Output
E	S	Y
0	X	0
1	0	D_0
1	1	D_1
X=Don't care		

4-to-1 Channel De-Multiplexer

The 4-to-1 multiplexer has 4 input bit, 2 control bits, and 1 output bit. The four input bits are D_0, D_1, D_2 and D_3. Only one of this is transmitted to the output y. The output depends on the value of AB which is the control input. The control input determines which of the input data bit is transmitted to the output.

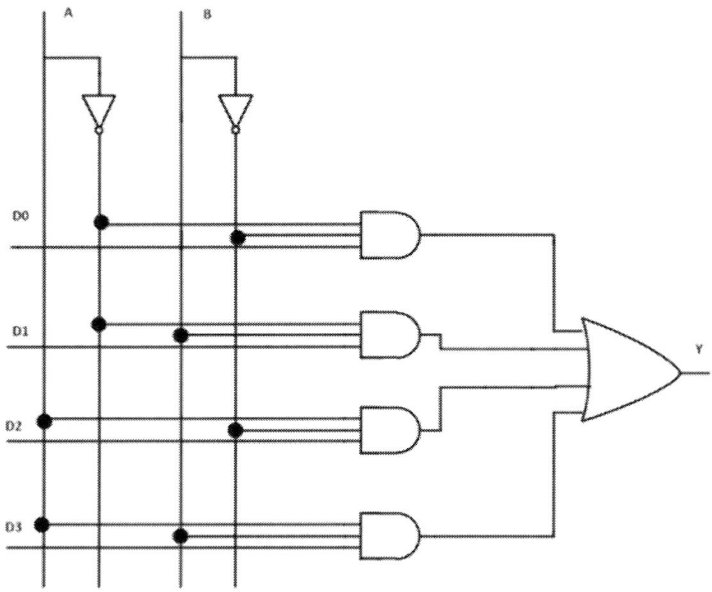

Applications of Multiplexer

Multiplexer are used in various fields where multiple data need to be transmitted using a single line. Following are some of the applications of multiplexers -

- *Communication System* – Communication system is a set of system that enables communication like transmission system, relay and tributary station, and communication network. The efficiency of communication system can be increased considerably using multiplexer. Multiplexer allow the process of transmitting different type of data such as audio, video at the same time using a single transmission line.

- *Telephone Network* – In telephone network, multiple audio signals are integrated on a single line for transmission with the help of multiplexers. In this way, multiple audio signals can be isolated and eventually, the desire audio signals reach the intended recipients.
- *Computer Memory* - Multiplexers are used to implement huge amount of memory into the computer, at the same time reduces the number of copper lines required to connect the memory to other parts of the computer circuit.
- *Transmission from the Computer System of a Satellite* – Multiplexer can be used for the transmission of data signals from the computer system of a satellite or spacecraft to the ground system using the GPS (Global Positioning System) satellites.

Demultiplexers

A demultiplexer performs the reverse operation of a multiplexer i.e. it receives one input and distributes it over several outputs. It has only one input, n outputs, m select input. At a time only one output line is selected by the select lines and the input is transmitted to the selected output line.

Demultiplexers come in multiple variations

- 1:2 demultiplexer
- 1:4 demultiplexer
- 1:16 demultiplexer
- 1:32 demultiplexer

Block Diagram

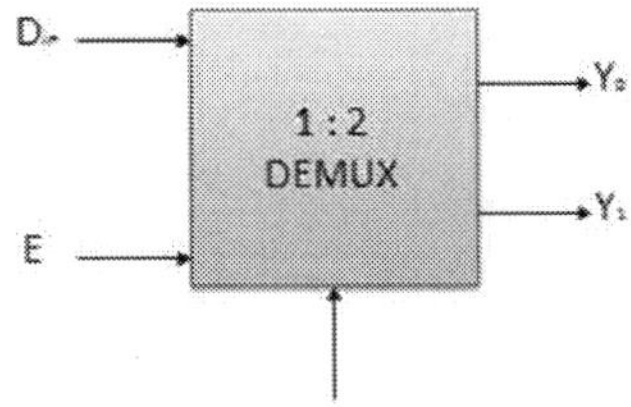

Truth Table

Enable	Select	Output
E	S	Y0 Y1
0	X	0 0
1	0	0 Din
1	1	Dn 0
X=Don't care		

1- to-4 Demultiplexer

The 1-to-4 demultiplexer has 1 input bit, 2 control bit, and 4 output bits. An example of 1-to-4 demultiplexer is IC74155. The 1-to-4 demultiplexer is shown in figure below-

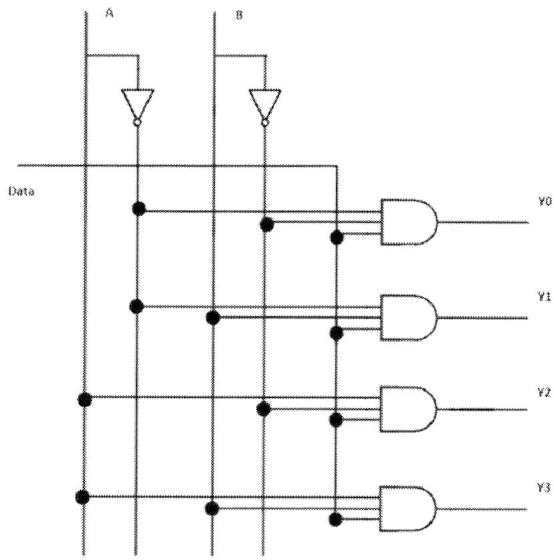

The input bit is labelled as Data D. This data bit is transmitted to the data bit of the output lines. This depends on the value of AB, the control input.

When AB = 01, the upper second AND gate is enabled while other AND gates are disabled. Therefore, only data bit D is transmitted to the output, giving Y1 = Data.

Decoder

A decoder is a combinational circuit. It has n input and to a maximum m = 2n outputs. Decoder is identical to a demultiplexer without any data input. It performs operations which are exactly opposite to those of an encoder.

Block Diagram

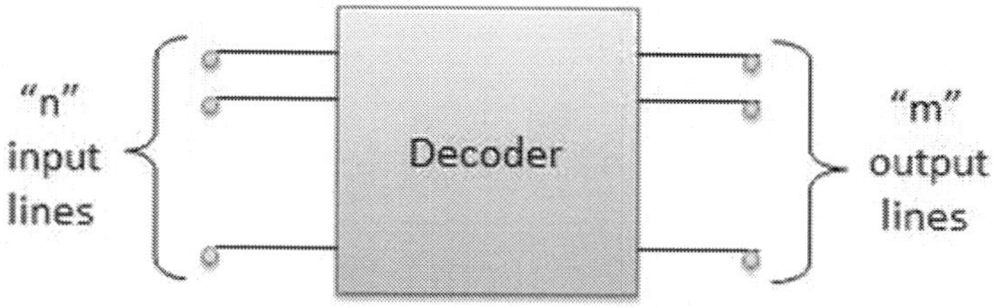

Examples of Decoders are following.

- Code converters
- BCD to seven segment decoders
- Nixie tube decoders
- Relay actuato

Encoder

Encoder is a combinational circuit which is designed to perform the inverse operation of the decoder. An encoder has n number of input lines and m number of output lines. An encoder produces an m bit binary code corresponding to the digital input number. The encoder accepts an n input digital word and converts it into an m bit another digital word.

Block Diagram

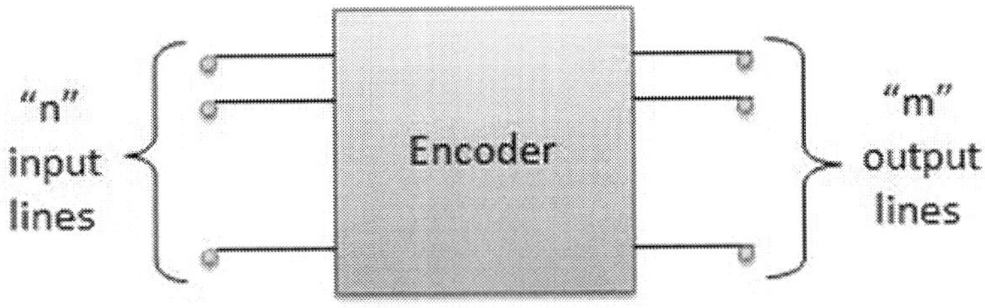

Examples of Encoders are following.

- Priority encoders
- Decimal to BCD encoder
- Octal to binary encoder
- Hexadecimal to binary encoder

Priority Encoder

This is a special type of encoder. Priority is given to the input lines. If two or more input line is 1 at the same time, then the input line with highest priority will be considered. There are four inputs D_0, D_1, D_2, D_3 and two outputs Y_0, Y_1. Out of the four inputs D_3 has the highest priority and D_0 has the lowest priority. That means if $D_3 = 1$ then $Y_1\ Y_1 = 11$ irrespective of the other inputs. Similarly if $D_3 = 0$ and $D_2 = 1$ then $Y_1 Y_0 = 10$ irrespective of the other inputs.

4 Sequential Circuit

Combinational circuits and systems produce an output based on input variables only. Sequential circuits use current input variables and previous input variables by storing the information and putting back into the circuit on the next clock (activation) cycle.

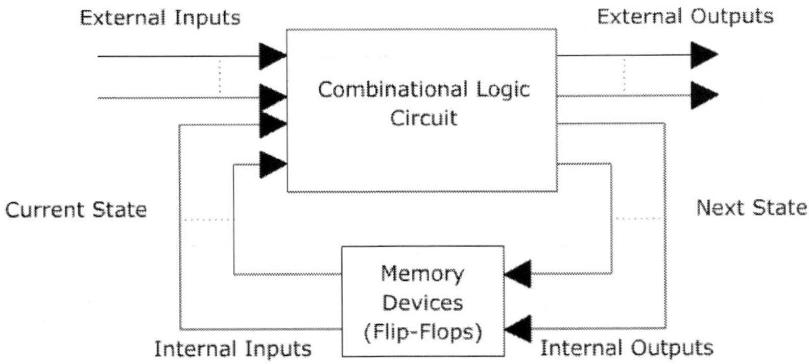

The figure above shows a theoretical view of how sequential circuits are made up from combinational logic and some storage elements.

Flip Flop

Flip flop is a sequential circuit which generally samples its inputs and changes its outputs only at particular instants of time and not continuously. Flip flop is said to be edge sensitive or edge triggered rather than being level triggered like latches.

S-R Flip Flop

It is basically S-R latch using NAND gates with an additional **enable** input. It is also called as level triggered SR-FF. For this circuit in output will take place if and only if the enable input (E) is made active. In short this circuit will operate as an S-R latch if E= 1 but there is no change in the output if E = 0.

Block Diagram

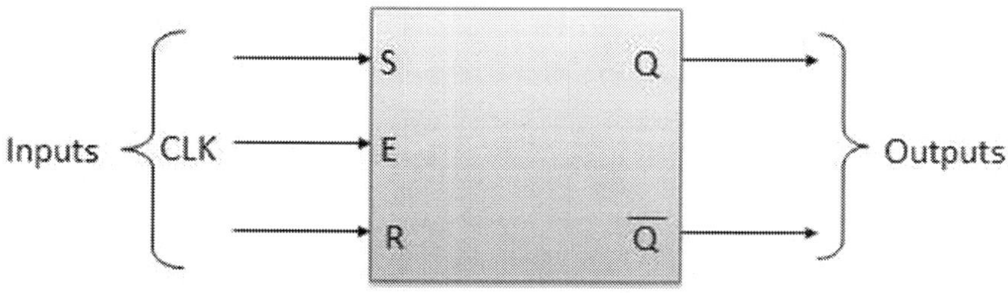

Circuit Diagram

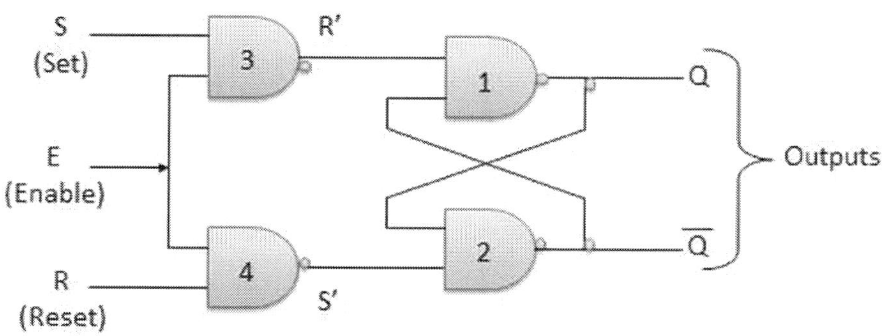

Truth Table

Input			Output		Comments
E	S	R	Q_{n+1}	$\overline{Q}_{n+1}$	
1	0	0	Q_n	$\overline{Q}_n$	No change
1	0	1	0	1	Rset
1	1	0	1	0	Set
1	1	1	x	x	Interminate

J-K Flip-Flop

A modified version of the *SR* flip-flop which eliminates the unstable oscillation and indeterminate behaviour is the *JK* flip-flop.

Circuit Diagram

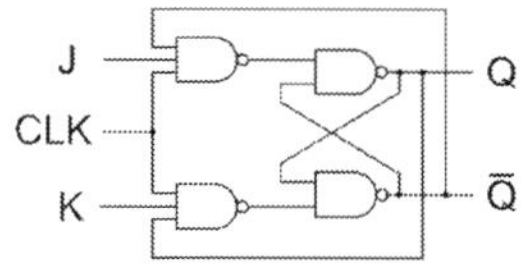

Truth Table

CLOCK	J	K	$\overline{SET}$	$\overline{RESET}$	Q	$\overline{Q}$
-	-	-	0	1	1	0
-	-	-	1	0	0	1
⌝⌞	0	0	1	1	Q	$\overline{Q}$
⌝⌞	1	0	1	1	1	0
⌝⌞	0	1	1	1	0	1
⌝⌞	1	1	1	1	$\overline{Q}$	Q

D-Flip-flop

Delay Flip Flop or D Flip Flop is the simple gated S-R latch with a NAND inverter connected between S and R inputs. It has only one input. The input data is appearing at the output after some time. Due to this data delay between i/p and o/p, it is called delay flip flop. S and R will be the complements of each other due to NAND inverter. Hence S = R = 0 or S = R = 1, these input condition will never appear. This problem is avoid by SR = 00 and SR = 1 conditions.

Circuit Diagram

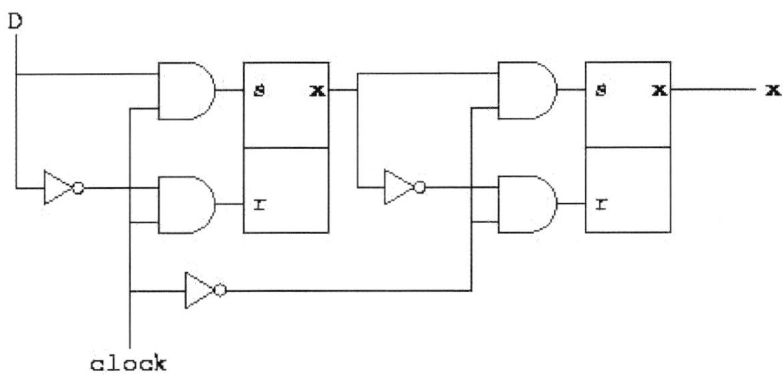

Truth Table

$\overline{SET}$	$\overline{RESET}$	D	CK	Q	$\overline{Q}$
0	1	-	-	1	0
1	0	-	-	0	1
0	0	-	-	1	1
1	1	1	↑	1	0
1	1	0	↑	0	1

Toggle Flip Flop/T Flip Flop

Toggleflipflopisbasically a JK flip flop with J and K terminals permanently connected together. It has only input denoted by **T** is shown in the Symbol Diagram. The symbol for positive edge triggered T flip flop is shown in the Block Diagram.

Symbol Diagram

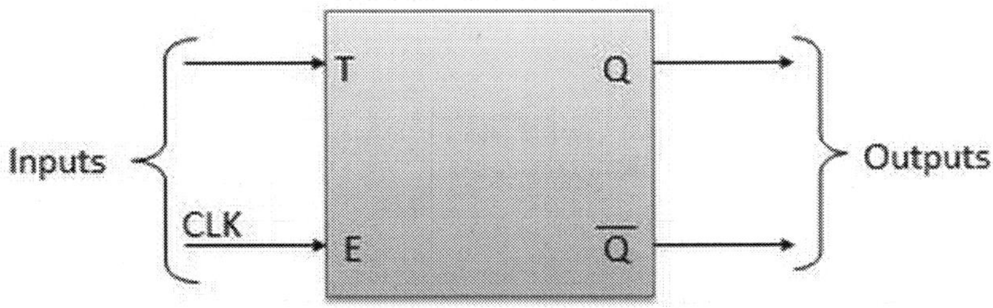

Block Diagram

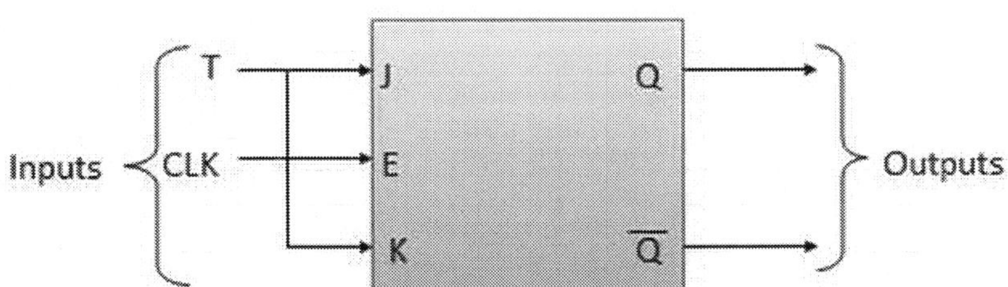

Truth Table

T	$\overline{\text{Preset}}$	$\overline{\text{Clear}}$	Q	Q
↑	1	1	$\bar{Q}_0$	Q_0
0	1	1	Q_0	$\bar{Q}_0$
1	1	1	Q_0	$\bar{Q}_0$
X	0	1	1	0
X	1	0	0	1

Conversion of one Flip-Flop to another Flip-Flop

- SR-FF to JK-FF : $S = J\bar{Q}_n$ and $R = KQ_n$
- SR-FF to D-FF : $S = D$ and $R = \bar{D}$
- SR-FF to T-FF : $S = T\bar{Q}$ and $R = TQ$
- JK-FF to SR-FF : $J = S$ and $K = R$
- JK-FF to D-FF : $J = D$ and $K = \bar{D}$
- JK-FF to T-FF : $J = K = T$
- D-FF to SR-FF : $D = S + \bar{R}Q_n$
- D-FF to JK-FF : $D = J\bar{Q} + \bar{K}Q$
- D-FF to T-FF : $D = T \oplus Q$
- T-FF to JK-FF : $T = J\bar{Q} + KQ$
- T-FF to SR-FF : $T = S\bar{Q} + RQ$
- T-FF to D-FF : $T = D \oplus Q$

Toggle Mode of Operation

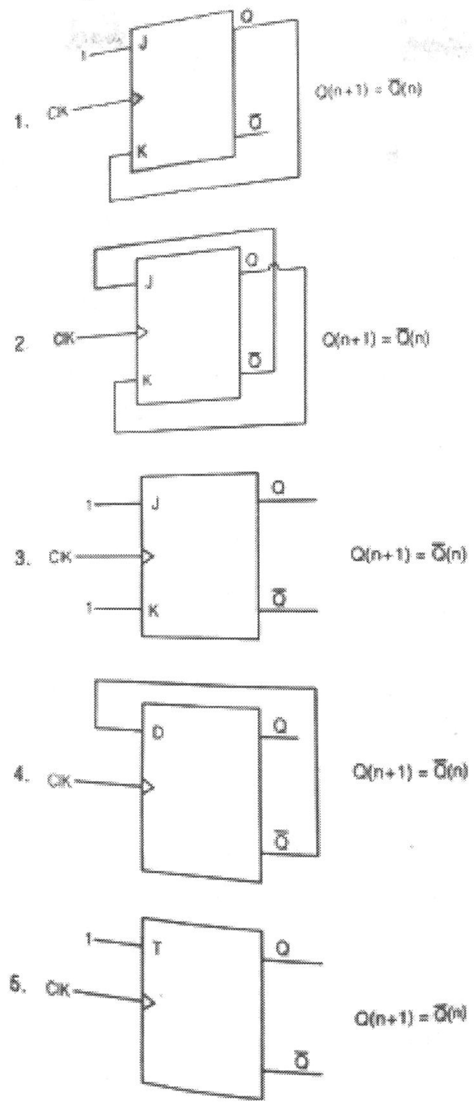

Shift Registers

Shift registers are a type of sequential logic circuit, mainly for storage of digital data. They are a group of flip-flops connected in a chain so that the output from one flip-flop becomes the input of the next flip-flop.

The Shift Register is another type of sequential logic circuit that can be used for the storage or the transfer of data in the form of binary numbers. This sequential device loads the data present on its inputs and then moves or "shifts" it to its output once every clock cycle, hence the name "shift register".

4-bit Right Shift Register

A shift register is a clocked sequential circuit in which stored the binary word bits shift either towards left or towards right (towards higher place value or lower place value) on each successive clock transition.

4-bit Right Shift Register (n + 1)th clock transition after nth clock defined the present state

- Serial input ▯ Q A;
- Q A ▯ Q B;
- Q B ▯ QC ;
- Q C ▯ QD ;
- Q D = Serial out;
- When output bits from left to right are Q A, Q B, QC and Q D.

4-bit Left Shift Register

- In this above SISO register MSB data is applied to the LSB FF (D-FF).
- To enter n bit data in serial from we require '*n*' clock pulse.
- To exit or getting output of '*n*' bit data as serially we require (*n*-1) clock pulse.

Serial Input Parallel Output

- In such types of operations, the data is entered serially and taken out in parallel fashion.
- Data is loaded bit by bit. The outputs are disabled as long as the data is loading.

- As soon as the data loading gets completed, all the flip-flops contain their required data, the outputs are enabled so that all the loaded data is made available over all the output lines at the same time.
- 4 clock cycles are required to load a four bit word. Hence the speed of operation of SIPO mode is same as that of SISO mode.

Parallel Input Serial Output (PISO)

- Data bits are entered in parallel fashion.
- The circuit shown below is a four bit parallel input serial output register.
- Output of previous Flip Flop is connected to the input of the next one via a combinational circuit.
- The binary input word B_0, B_1, B_2, B_3 is applied though the same combinational circuit.
- There are two modes in which this circuit can work namely shift mode or load mode.

Parallel Input Parallel Output (PIPO)

In this mode, the 4 bit binary input B_0, B_1, B_2, B_3 is applied to the data inputs D_0, D_1, D_2, D_3 respectively of the four flip-flops. As soon as a negative clock edge is applied, the input binary bits will be loaded into the flip-flops simultaneously. The loaded bits will appear simultaneously to the output side. Only clock pulse is essential to load all the bits.

Counters

Depending on clock pulse applied counters are of two types:

	Asynchronous	Synchronous
	The logic circuit of this type of counters is simple to design and we feed output of one FF to clock of next FF	The circuit diagram for type of counter becomes difficult as number of states increase in the counter

Propagation Time	Propagation time delay of this type of counter is: Tpd=N*(Delay of 1 FF) Which is quite high N is number of FFs	Propagation time delay of this type of counter is: Tpd=(Delay of 1 FF) + delay of 1 gate Inclusion of delay of 1 gate would be illustrated when we design higher counter
Maximum Operating Frequency	And hence operating frequency is Low	And hence operating frequency is higher

Modulus Counter (MOD-N Counter)

The 2-bit ripple counter is called as MOD-4 counter and 3-bit ripple counter is called as MOD-8 counter. So in general, an n-bit ripple counter is called as modulo-N counter. Where, MOD number = 2n.

Type of Modulus

2-bit up or down (MOD-4)

3-bit up or down (MOD-8)

4-bit up or down (MOD-16)

UP/DOWN Counter

In the up/down counter, when up counter and down counter combined together to obtain an UP/DOWN counter. A mode control (M) input is also provided to select either up or down mode. A combinational circuit is required to be designed and used between each pair of flip-flop in order to achieve the up/down operation.

UP/DOWN Ripple Counters

In the UP/DOWN ripple counter all the FFs operate in the toggle mode. So either T flip-flops or JK flip-flops are to be used. The LSB flip-flop receives clock directly. But the clock to every other FF is obtained from (Q = Q bar) output of the previous FF.

- **UP Counting mode (M = 0)** - The Q output of the preceding FF is connected to the clock of the next stage if up counting is to be achieved. For this mode, the mode select input M is at logic 0 (M = 0).
- **DOWN counting mode (M = 1)** - If M = 1, then the Q bar output of the preceding FF is connected to the next FF. This will operate the counter in the counting mode.

Decade Counter

A decade counter is the one which goes through 10 unique combinations of outputs and then resets as the clock proceeds. We may use some sort of a feedback in a 4-bit binary counter to skip any six of the sixteen possible output states from 0000 to 1111 to get to a decade counter. A decade counter does not necessarily count from 0000 to 1001 it could count as 0000,0001, 0010, 1000, 1001, 1010, 1011, 1110, 1111, 0000, 0001 and so on.

Synchronous Counter

A synchronous counter, in contrast to an asynchronous counter, is one whose output bits change state simultaneously, with no ripple. The only way we can build such a counter circuit from J-K flip-flops is to connect all the clock inputs together, so that each and every flip-flop receives the exact same clock pulse at the exact same time:

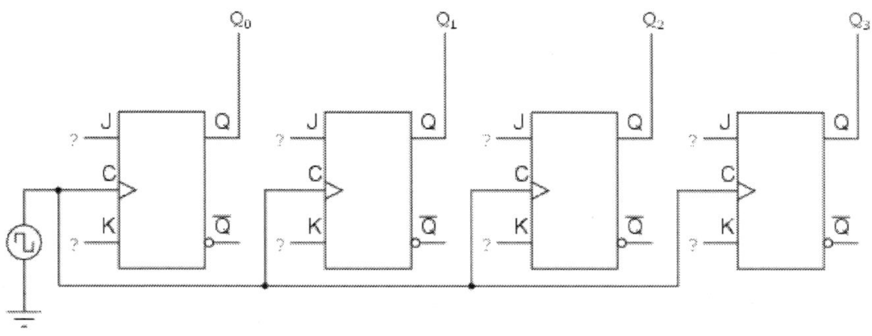

Self-Starting Ring Counters

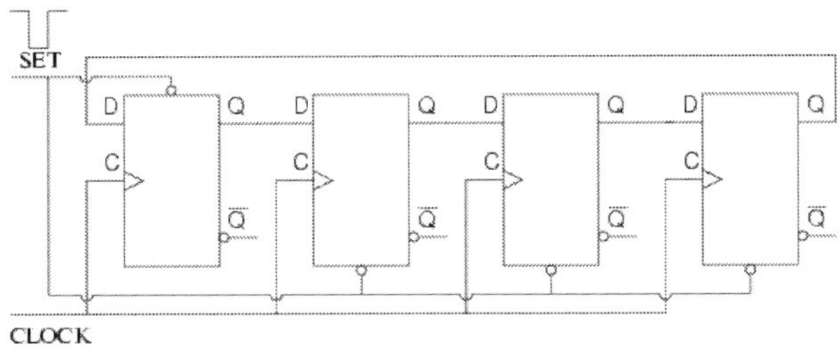

Set one stage, clear three stages

Johnson Counters

The switch-tail ring counter, also known as the Johnson counter, overcomes some of the limitations of the ring counter. Like a ring counter a Johnson counter is a shift register fed back on its' self. It requires half the stages of a comparable ring counter for a given division ratio. If the complement output of a ring counter is fed back to the input instead of the true output, a Johnson counter results. The difference between a ring counter and a Johnson counter is which output of the last stage is fed back (Q or Q'). Carefully compare the feedback connection below to the previous ring counter.

Synchronous Series Carry Counter

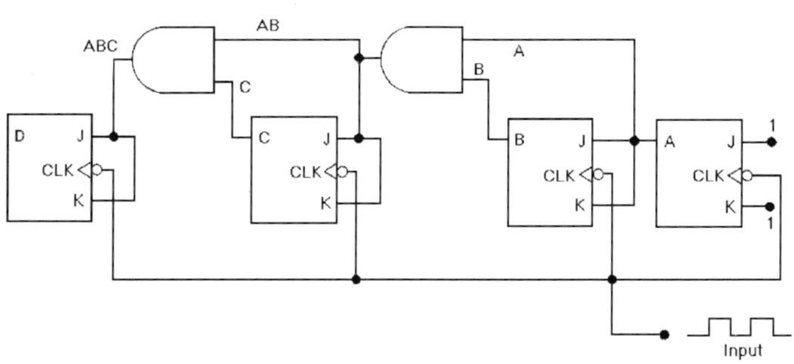

Synchronous Parallel Carry Counter

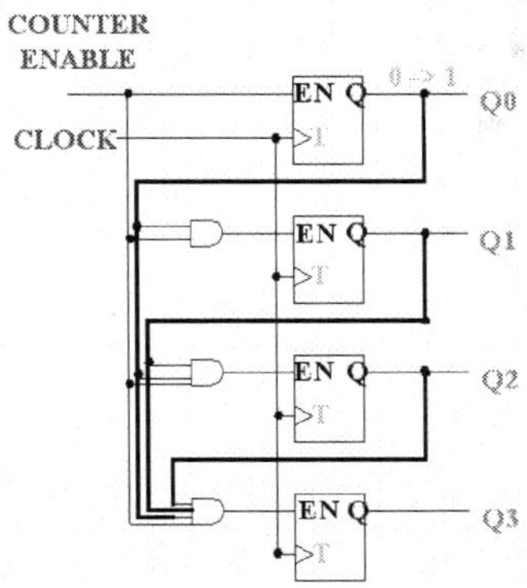

Digital Number System

A digital system can understand positional number system only where there are only a few symbols called digits and these symbols represent different values depending on the position they occupy in the number.

A value of each digit in a number can be determined using

- The digit
- The position of the digit in the number
- The base of the number system (where base is defined as the total number of digits available in the number system).

Weighted Number System

A number D consists of n digits with each digit has a particular position.

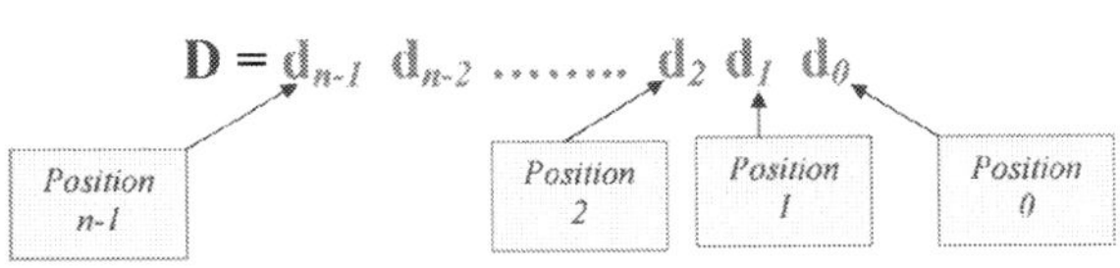

- Every digit position is associated with a fixed weight.
- If the weight associated with the ith position is w_i, then the value of D is given by:

$$D = d_{n-1} w_{n-1} + d_{n-2} w_{n-2} + \ldots + d_2 w_2 + d_1 w_1 + d_0 w_0$$

Un-Weighted Number System

These codes are not positionally weighted i.e. each position within the binary equivalent of the number is not assigned a fixed value. Thus, un-weighted codes do not obey positional weighting principal.

Grey code is an example of un-weighted codes. In grey code, computation not only depends on the bit under consideration but also on the neighboring bits. Due to which, unlike weighted codes, the binary equivalent of a number may return different values on each computation Excess-3 code is also an example of un-weighted code.

Codes

Code is a symbolic representation of discrete information, a wide variety of binary codes is used in digital systems.

Binary coded decimal code

In this code each decimal digit is represented by a 4-bit binary number. BCD is a way to express each of the decimal digits with a binary code. In the BCD, with four bits we can represent sixteen numbers (0000 to 1111). But in BCD code only first ten of these are used (0000 to 1001). The remaining six code combinations i.e. 1010 to 1111 are invalid in BCD.

Decimal	0	1	2	3	4	5	6	7	8	9
BCD	0000	0001	0010	0011	0100	0101	0110	0111	1000	1001

Advantages of BCD Codes

- It is very similar to decimal system.
- We need to remember binary equivalent of decimal numbers 0 to 9 only.

Eccess-3 code

The Excess-3 code is also called as XS-3 code. It is non-weighted code used to express decimal numbers. The Excess-3 code words are derived from the 8421 BCD code words adding (0011)2 or (3)10 to each code word in 8421. The excess-3 codes are obtained as follows

Decimal Number → 8421 BCD —Add 0011→ Excess-3

Example

Decimal	BCD 8 4 2 1	Excess-3 BCD + 0011
0	0 0 0 0	0 0 1 1
1	0 0 0 1	0 1 0 0
2	0 0 1 0	0 1 0 1
3	0 0 1 1	0 1 1 0
4	0 1 0 0	0 1 1 1
5	0 1 0 1	1 0 0 0
6	0 1 1 0	1 0 0 1
7	0 1 1 1	1 0 1 0
8	1 0 0 0	1 0 1 1
9	1 0 0 1	1 1 0 0

Gray code

It is the non-weighted code and it is not arithmetic codes. That means there are no specific weights assigned to the bit position. It has a very special feature that has only one bit will change, each time the decimal number is incremented as shown in fig. As only one bit changes at a time, the gray code is called as a unit distance code. The gray code is a cyclic code. Gray code cannot be used for arithmetic operation.

Application of Gray Code

- Gray code is popularly used in the shaft position encoders.
- A shaft position encoder produces a code word which represents the angular position of the shaft.

Binary-to-Gray Conversion

It is a very simple process. There are several steps to do this types of conversions. Steps given below elaborate on the idea on this type of conversion.

- The M.S.B. of the gray code will be exactly equal to the first bit of the given binary number.
- Now the second bit of the code will be exclusive-or of the first and second bit of the given binary number, i.e. if both the bits are same the result will be 0 and if they are different the result will be 1.
- The third bit of gray code will be equal to the exclusive-or of the second and third bit of the given binary number. Thus the Binary to gray code conversion goes on. One example given below can make your idea clear on this type of conversion.

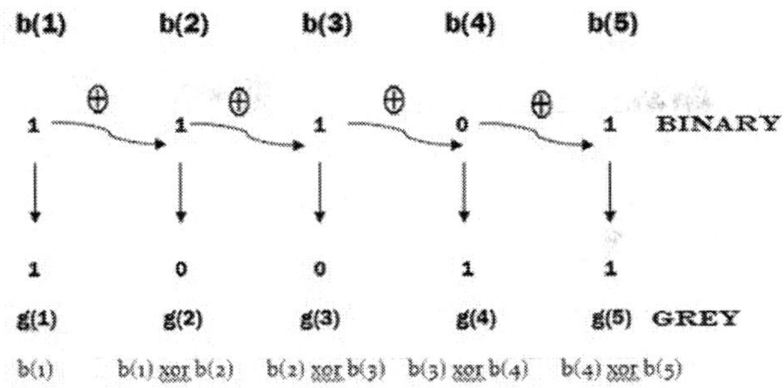

Gray-to -Binary Conversion

Follow the below steps to convert Gray Code to Binary

- Most significant bit (G_1) is same as the most significant bit in Binary Code ($G_1 = B_1$)
- The next number can be obtain by taking Exclusive OR operation between the previous binary bit, and the current gray code bit and write down the value.
- Repeat the Above Step until you find B_n.

Example

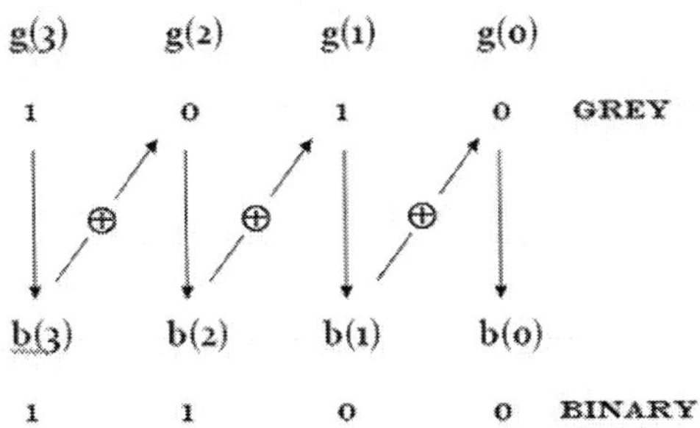

i.e $b(3) = g(3)$

$b(2) = b(3) \oplus g(3)$

$b(1) = b(2) \oplus g(1)$

$b(0) = b(1) \oplus g(0)$

5 Number Representation and Computer Arithmetic

In digital control systems we will need to understand the ways in which these systems represent numbers. We traditionally use the decimal numbering system but computers use binary and when we program and try to understand what the computing system is doing we use hexadecimal and octal systems. The systems work the same but use a different number of characters to represent numbers.

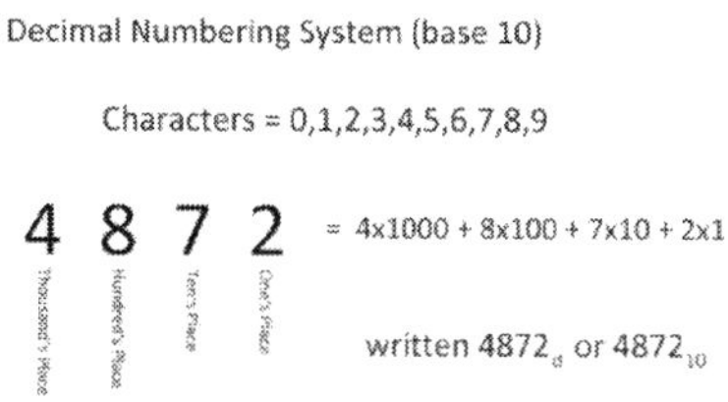

Binary Arithmetic

Binary arithmetic is essential part of all the digital computers and many other digital system.

1's complement addition

? Same as 2's complement accept that instead of discarding the last carry, it is added to the n-bit sum in the right-most position ("end-around" carry).

(a) & (b) same as 2's complement

(c) Pos + Neg numbers, Neg > Pos

+5 0101

-6 1001

-1 1110 (correct answer)

(d) Pos + Neg numbers, Pos > Neg

-5 1010

+6 0110

(1) 0000

1 (end-around carry)

+1 0001 (correct; no overflow)

2's complement addition

Here are some examples of eight-bit, twos complement binary addition. In each case, we compute the sum, and note if there was an overflow. If there was a carry out, the extra bit is shown on the next line. (It's falling into the bit bucket, where it will never be heard from again.) You can also look at the rules for determining overflow.

- -39 + 92 = 53:

```
[1] 1       1   1
    1   1   0   1   1   0   0   1
+   0   1   0   1   1   1   0   0
---------------------------------
    0   0   1   1   0   1   0   1
```

Carryout without overflow. Sum is correct.

- 104 + 45 = 149:

```
    1   1       1
    0   1   1   0   1   0   0   0
+   0   0   1   0   1   1   0   1
---------------------------------
    1   0   0   1   0   1   0   1
```

Overflow, no carryout. Sum is not correct.

- 10 + -3 = 7:

```
[1] 1   1   1   1
    0   0   0   0   1   0   1   0
+   1   1   1   1   1   1   0   1
---------------------------------
    0   0   0   0   0   1   1   1
```

Carryout without overflow. Sum is correct.

- -19 + -7 = -26:

```
[1] 1   1   1   1           1
    1   1   1   0   1   1   0   1
+   1   1   1   1   1   0   0   1
---------------------------------
    1   1   1   0   0   1   1   0
```

Carryout without overflow. Sum is correct.

- -75 + 59 = -16:

```
        1   1   1   1   1   1
    1   0   1   1   0   1   0   1
+   0   0   1   1   1   0   1   1
---------------------------------
    1   1   1   1   0   0   0   0
```

No overflow nor carryout.

- 127 + 1 = 128:

```
    1   1   1   1   1   1   1
    0   1   1   1   1   1   1   1
+   0   0   0   0   0   0   0   1
---------------------------------
    1   0   0   0   0   0   0   0
```

Overflow, no carryout. Sum is not correct.

Over flow

One caveat with signed binary numbers is that of overflow, where the answer to an addition or subtraction problem exceeds the magnitude which can be represented with the allotted number of bits. Remember that the place of the sign bit is fixed from the beginning of the problem. With the last example problem, we used five binary bits to represent the magnitude of the number, and the left-most (sixth) bit as the negative-weight, or sign, bit. With five bits to represent magnitude, we have a representation range of 2^5, or thirty-two integer steps from 0 to maximum.

Floating Point Presentation

A floating-point number (or real number) can represent a very large (1.23 × 10^88) or a very small (1.23 × 10^-88) value. It could also represent very large negative number (-1.23 × 10^88) and very small negative number (-1.23 × 10^88), as well as zero, as illustrated:

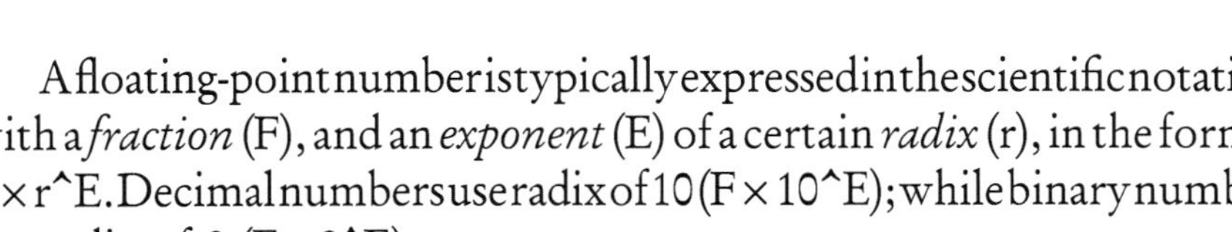

Floating-point Numbers (Decimal)

A floating-point number is typically expressed in the scientific notation, with a *fraction* (F), and an *exponent* (E) of a certain *radix* (r), in the form of F × r^E. Decimal numbers use radix of 10 (F × 10^E); while binary numbers use radix of 2 (F × 2^E).

Representation of floating point number is not unique. For example, the number 55.66 can be represented as 5.566 × 10^1, 0.5566 × 10^2, 0.05566 × 10^3, and so on. The fractional part can be *normalized*. In the normalized form, there is only a single non-zero digit before the radix point. For example, decimal number 123.4567 can be normalized as 1.234567 × 10^2; binary number 1010.1011B can be normalized as 1.0101011B × 2^3.

It is important to note that floating-point numbers suffer from *loss of precision* when represented with a fixed number of bits (e.g., 32-bit or 64-bit). This is because there are *infinite* number of real numbers (even within a small range of says 0.0 to 0.1). On the other hand, a *n*-bit binary pattern can represent a *finite* 2^*n* distinct numbers. Hence, not all the real numbers can be represented. The nearest approximation will be used instead, resulted in loss of accuracy.

It is also important to note that floating number arithmetic is very much less efficient than integer arithmetic. It could be speed up with a so-called dedicated *floating-point co-processor*. Hence, use integers if your application does not require floating-point numbers.

Fixed Point Presentation

- Uses the two numbers from 0 to 1
- Every column represents a power of 2

Memory

A memory is just like a human brain. It is used to store data and instruction. Computer memory is the storage space in computer where data is to be processed and instructions required for processing are stored.

Memory is primarily of two types:

- **Internal Memory** - cache memory and primary/main memory
- **External Memory** - magnetic disk / optical disk etc.

Serial Access Memory

Sequential access means the system must search the storage device from the beginning of the memory address until it finds the required piece of data. Memory device which supports such access is called a Sequential Access Memory or Serial Access Memory. Magnetic tape is an example of serial access memory.

Direct Access Memory

Direct access memory or Random Access Memory, refers to condition in which a system can go directly to the information that the user wants. Memory device which supports such access is called a Direct Access Memory. Magnetic disk, optical disks are an examples of direct access memory.

Difference between RAM and ROM

	RAM	**ROM**
Definition	Random Access Memory or RAM is a form of data storage that can be accessed randomly at any time, in any order and from any physical location...allowing quick access and manipulations	Read Only Memory or ROM is also a form of data storage that cannot be easily altered or reprogrammed. Stores instructions that are not necessary for rebooting up to make the computer operate when it is switched off. They are hardwired.
Stands For	Random Access Memory	Read Only Memory

Use	RAM allows the computers to read data quickly to run applications. It allows reading and writing.	ROM stores the program required to initially boot the computer. It only allows reading.
Volatility	RAM is volatile i.e. its contents are lost when the device is powered off.	It is non-volatile i.e. its contents are retained even when the device is powered off.
Types	The two main types of RAM and dynamic RAM.	The types of ROM include PROM, EPROM and EEPROM.

RAM

A RAM constitutes the internal memory of the CPU for storing data, program and program result. It is read/write memory. It is called random access memory (RAM).

RAM is volatile, i.e. data stored in it is lost when we switch off the computer or if there is a power failure. Hence a backup uninterruptible power system (UPS) is often used with computers. RAM is small, both in terms of its physical size and in the amount of data it can hold.

Static RAM (SRAM)

The word static indicates that the memory retains its contents as long as power remains applied. However, data is lost when the power gets down due to volatile nature. SRAM chips use a matrix of 6-transistors and no capacitors. Transistors do not require power to prevent leakage, so SRAM need not have to be refreshed on a regular basis.

Dynamic RAM (DRAM)

DRAM, unlike SRAM, must be continually refreshed in order for it to maintain the data. This is done by placing the memory on a refresh circuit that rewrites the data several hundred times per second. DRAM is used for most system memory because it is cheap and small. All DRAMs are made up of memory cells. These cells are composed of one capacitor and one transistor.

A Handbook on Computer Science

3

Computer Organization and Architecture

CONTENTS

1 Machine Instructions and Addressing Modes

Computer Architecture and Organization is the study of internal working, structuring and implementation of a computer system. Architecture in computer system, same as anywhere else, refers to the externally visual attributes of the system. Externally visual attributes, here in computer science, mean the way a system is visible to the logic of programs. Organization of computer system is the way of practical implementation which results in realization of architectural specifications of a computer system.

Machine Instructions

Operation commands (program) written in the native code (machine code) of a machine (such as a computer or robot) that it can recognize and execute.

- Zero address instructions: NOP
- One address instructions: PUSH, POP
- Two address instruction: ADD, MULT, SUB

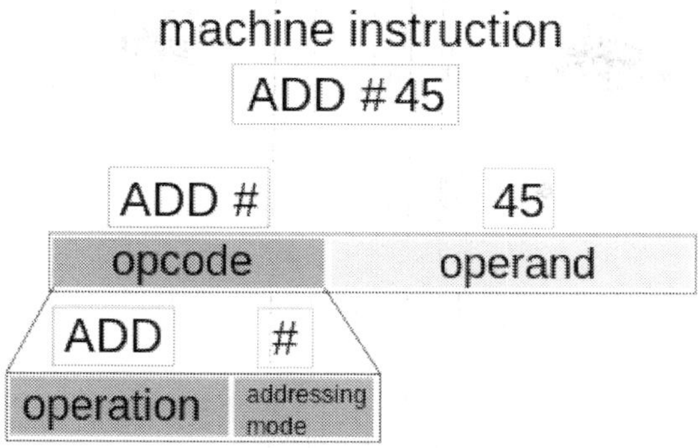

Load and Store Instructions

Load/store Instructions only allows memory to be accessed by load and store operations, and all values for an operation need to be loaded from memory and be present in registers. Following the operation, the result needs to be stored back to memory.

Addressing Modes

The term addressing modes refers to the way in which the operand of an instruction is specified. Information contained in the instruction code is the value of the operand or the address of the result/operand. Following are the main addressing modes that are used on various platforms and architectures.

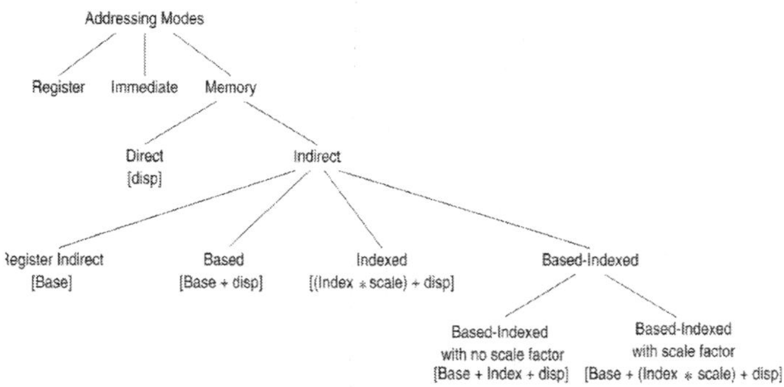

Sequential Control Flow Addressing Mode

Sequential control flow addressing mode is describe as follows:

Register addressing mode

Register mode is similar to direct mode. The key difference between the two modes is that the address field of the instruction refers to a register rather than a memory location.

- Operands are located in registers
- It is the most efficient addressing mode

Immediate Addressing Mode

The immediate mode is the simplest form of addressing. The operand is part of the instruction and therefore no memory reference, other than the instruction, is required to retrieve the operand. This fast mode is used to define constants or set initial variable values. Immediate mode has a limited range because it is restricted to the size of the address field, which for most instruction sets is small compared to word length.

- Operand is stored as part of the instruction
- This mode is used mostly for constants
- It imposes several restrictions
- Efficient as the data comes with the instructions

Auto Indexed Addressing Mode

- This mode is used to access the linear array element.
- The base address is maintained in the base register.
- Step size is dependency on the amount of the data to be accessed from the memory.

Data=[EA]=[[base register]+[step size]]

Memory Addressing Modes

- Pentium offers several addressing modes to access operands located in memory
- Primary reason: To efficiently support high-level language constructs and data structures
- Available addressing modes depend on the address size used
- 16-bit modes (shown before)
- same as those supported
- 32-bit modes (shown before)
- supported by Pentium
- more flexible set

Direct Memory Addressing

When operands are specified in memory addressing mode, direct access to main memory, usually to the data segment, is required. This way of addressing results in slower processing of data. To locate the exact location of data in memory, we need the segment start address, which is typically found in the DS register and an offset value. This offset value is also called **effective address.**

In direct addressing mode, the offset value is specified directly as part of the instruction, usually indicated by the variable name. The assembler calculates the offset value and maintains a symbol table, which stores the offset values of all the variables used in the program.

Indirect Memory Addressing

This addressing mode utilizes the computer's ability of Segment: Offset addressing. Generally, the base registers EBX, EBP (or BX, BP) and the index registers (DI, SI), coded within square brackets for memory references, and are used for this purpose. Indirect addressing is generally used for variables containing several elements like, arrays. Starting address of the array is stored in, say, the EBX register.

2 ALU and Data Path, CPU Control Design

Arithmetic logic unit (ALU)

Arithmetic logic unit is a digital circuit used to perform arithmetic and logic operations. It represents the fundamental building block of the central processing unit of a computer. Modern CPUs contain very powerful and complex ALUs. In addition to ALUs, modern CPUs contain a control unit. Most of the operations of a CPU are performed by one or more ALUs, which load data from input registers. A register is a small amount of storage available as part of a CPU. The control unit tells the ALU what operation to perform on that data and the ALU stores the result in an output register. The control unit moves the data between these registers, the ALU and memory.

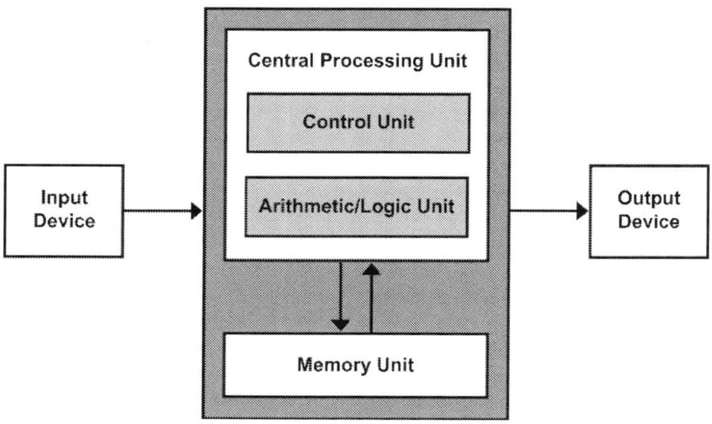

Data path

A data path is a collection of functional units, as arithmetic logic units or multipliers that perform data processing operations, registers, and buses. Along with the control unit it composes the central processing unit (CPU).

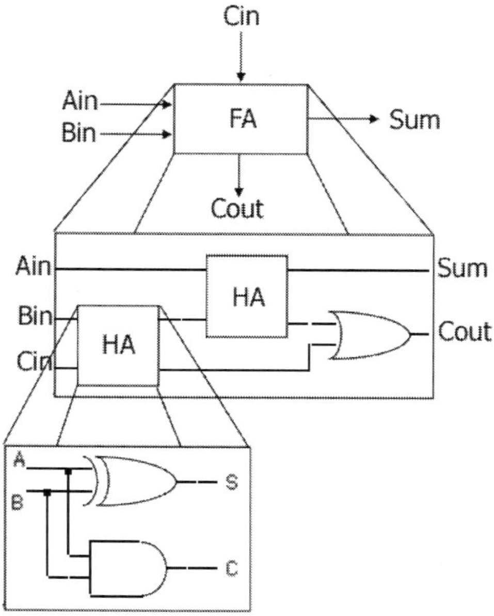

- Elements that process data and addresses in the CPU
- We will build a MIPS data path incrementally
- considering only a subset of instructions

CPU Registers

In computer architecture, a processor register is a very fast computer memory used to speed the execution of computer programs by providing quick access to commonly use values-typically, the values being in the midst of a calculation at a given point in time.

These registers are the top of the memory hierarchy, and are the fastest way for the system to manipulate data. In a very simple microprocessor, it consists of a single memory location, usually called an accumulator. Registers are built from fast multi-ported memory cell. They must be able to drive its data onto an internal bus in a single clock cycle. The result of ALU operation is stored here and could be re-used in a subsequent operation or saved into memory.

- **Memory Address Register (MAR)**: It stores address of data or instructions to be fetched from memory.
- **Memory Buffer Register (MBR):** It stores instruction and data received from the memory and sent from the memory.
- **Instruction Register (IR):** Instructions are stored in instruction register. When one instruction is completed, next instruction is fetched in memory for processing.
- **Program Counter (PC):** It counts instructions.

CPU Control Design

CPU-Control is a small yet powerful software solution designed to boost performance of multi-core systems, setting up the processes to run on separate processors. The CPU has two major components: the Control Unit and the ALU. If the design did include an instruction pre-fetch unit, that unit would independently fetch instructions and place them in an instruction queue for use by the execute unit, which might then fetch and execute an instruction in a single step.

Design of Control Unit

To execute an instruction, the control unit of the CPU must generate the required control signal in the proper sequence. As for example, during the fetch phase, CPU has to generate PCout signal along with other required signal in the first clock pulse.

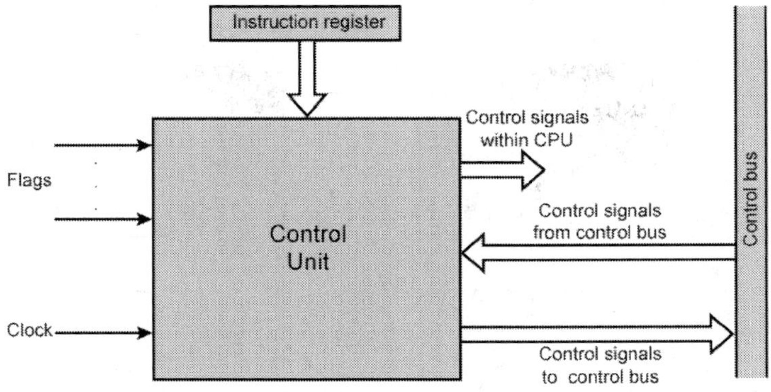

In the second clock pulse CPU has to generate PCin signal along with other required signals. So, during fetch phase, the proper sequence for generating the signal to retrieve from and store to PC is PCout and PCin. To generate the control signal in proper signal, a write variety of techniques exists. Most of these techniques, however, fall into one of the two categories.

- Hardwired control
- Micro programmed Control

Hardwired Control Unit

In this hardwired control techniques the control signals are generated by means of hardwired circuit. The main object of control unit is to generate the control signal in proper sequence.

Consider the sequence of control signal required to execute the add instruction that is explained in previous lecture. It is obvious that eight non-overlapping time slots are required for proper execution of the instruction represented by this sequence.

Hence the required control signals are uniquely determined by the following

- Contents of the control counter
- Contents of instruction register
- Contents of the condition code and other status flags.

Similarly, the Boolean logic function for add signal is

Add = T1 + T6.ADD_MD + T5.BR + ...

These logic functions can be implemented by a two level combinational circuit of AND and OR gates.

Similarly, the End control signal is generated by the logic function:

End = T8.ADD_MD + M7.BR + (T7.N + T4.Nbar).BRN + ...

Micro-program Control Unit

Control unit (CU) design focused on hardwired control units - i.e., ones where the control functions for the various components were synthesized using combinational logic. In this document, we will consider an alternate design technique: the micro programmed CU.

3 Memory and I/O Interface

Memory

In computing, memory refers to the devices used to store information for use in a computer. The term primary memory is used for storage systems which function at high-speed (i.e. RAM), as a distinction from secondary memory, which provides program and data storage that is slow to access but offer higher memory capacity. If needed, primary memory can be stored in secondary memory, through a memory management technique called "virtual memory". An archaic synonym for memory is store.

The term "memory", meaning primary memory is often associated with addressable semiconductor memory, i.e. integrated circuits consisting of silicon-based transistors, used for example as primary memory but also other purposes in computers and other digital electronic devices. There are two main types of semiconductor memory: volatile and non-volatile. Examples of non-volatile memory are flash memory (sometimes used as secondary, sometimes primary computer memory) and ROM/PROM/EPROM/EEPROM memory (used for firmware such as boot programs). Examples of volatile memory are primary memory (typically dynamic RAM, DRAM), and fast CPU cache memory (typically static RAM, SRAM, which is fast but energy-consuming and offer lower memory capacity per area unit than DRAM).

Most semiconductor memory is organized into memory cells or bistable flip-flops, each storing one bit (0 or 1). Flash memory organization includes both one bit per memory cell and multiple bits per cell (called MLC, Multiple Level Cell). The memory cells are grouped into words of fixed word length, for example 1, 2, 4, 8, 16, 32, 64 or 128 bit. Each word can be accessed by a binary address of N bit, making it possible to store 2 raised by N words in the memory. This implies that processor registers normally are not considered as memory, since they only store one word and do not include an addressing mechanism.

The term storage is often used to describe secondary memory such as tape, magnetic disks and optical discs (CD-ROM and DVD-ROM).

Memory Interface

Memory interface is a bus protocol for communication from an integrated circuit, such as a microprocessor, to an external memory device located on a circuit board. The memory is referred to as external because it is not contained within the internal circuitry of the integrated circuit and thus is externally located on the circuit board.

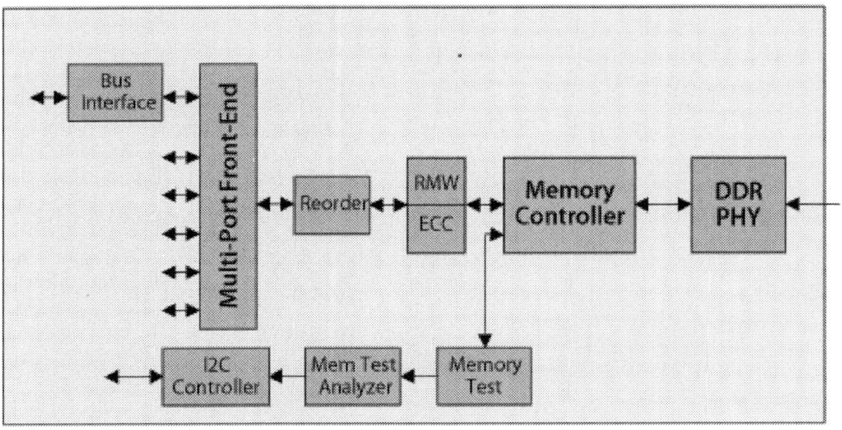

Input and Output Interface

Provides a method for transferring information between internal storage (such as memory and CPU registers) and external I/O devices

- Resolves the differences between the computer and peripheral devices

- Peripherals - Electromechanical Devices
- CPU or Memory - Electronic Device
- Data Transfer Rate
- Peripherals - Usually slower
- CPU or Memory - Usually faster than peripherals
- Some kinds of Synchronization mechanism may be needed
- Unit of Information
- Peripherals – Byte, Block, ...
- CPU or Memory – Word

Input Device

- Keyboard
- Optical input devices
    - Card Reader
    - Paper Tape Reader
    - Bar code reader
    - Digitizer
    - Optical Mark Reader
- Magnetic Input Devices
    - Magnetic Stripe Reader
- Screen Input Devices
    - Touch Screen
    - Light Pen
    - Mouse
- Analog Input Devices

Output Devices

- Card Puncher, Paper Tape Puncher
- CRT
- Printer (Impact, Ink Jet, Laser, Dot Matrix)
- Plotter

- Analog
- Voice

I/O Interface Module

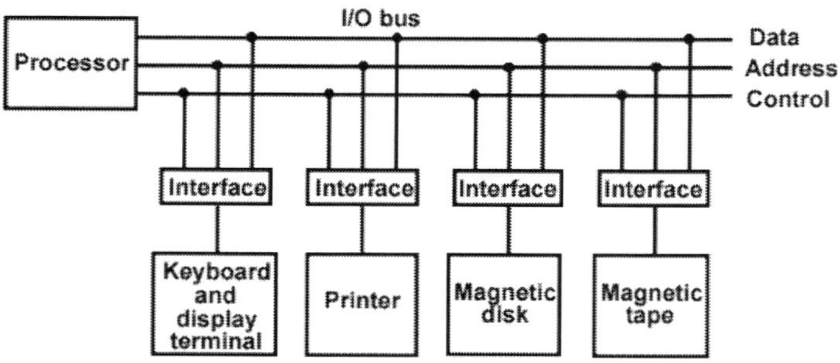

Each peripheral has an interface module associated with it Interface

- Decodes the device address (device code)
- Decodes the commands (operation)
- Provides signals for the peripheral controller
- Synchronizes the data flow and supervises the transfer rate between peripheral and CPU or Memory

Interrupted

The CPU issues commands to the I/O module then proceeds with its normal work until interrupted by I/O device on completion of its work.

For input, the device interrupts the CPU when new data has arrived and is ready to be retrieved by the system processor. The actual actions to perform depend on whether the device uses I/O ports, memory mapping.

Direct Memory Access (DMA)

Direct Memory Access (DMA) means CPU grants I/O module authority to read from or write to memory without involvement. DMA module controls exchange of data between main memory and the I/O device. Because of DMA device can transfer data directly to and from memory, rather than using the CPU as an intermediary, and can thus relieve congestion on the bus. CPU is only involved at the beginning and end of the transfer and interrupted only after entire block has been transferred.

4 Instruction Pipelining

The instruction pipeline represents the stages in which an instruction is moved through the processor, including its being fetched, perhaps buffered, and then executed.

- Instruction fetch
- Instruction decode and register fetch
- Execute
- Memory access
- Register write back

Instruction Processing

The first step in applying pipelining techniques to instruction processing is to divide the task into steps that may be performed with independent hardware. The most obvious division is between the FETCH cycle (fetch and interpret instructions) and the EXECUTE cycle (access operands and perform operation). If these two activities are to run simultaneously, they must use independent registers and processing circuits, including independent access to memory

Non-linear Pipelines

More sophisticated instruction pipelines can sometimes be nonlinear or no sequential. One *example* is branch processing in which the pipeline has two forks to process two possible paths at once. Sequential processing can be relaxed by a pipeline which allows a later instruction to enter when a previous one is stalled by a data conflict. This, of course, introduces much more difficult timing and consistency problems.

5 Cache Memory and Main Memory, Secondary Storage

Cache Memory

A small, high speed memory close to the CPU

- Each line of cache memory can be "occupied" or "empty"
- "Occupied" lines map to a memory location
- Hardwarecachemanagementmechanism(potentiallywithsoftware hints)
- Typically used for both programs and data

Also, by extension, other specialized hardware or software buffers

- TLB for mapping physical to virtual memory addresses
- Disk sector storage
- Network machine name to IP address translation
- Read and write buffers

Works because of locality

- (Does not work when there isn't locality)

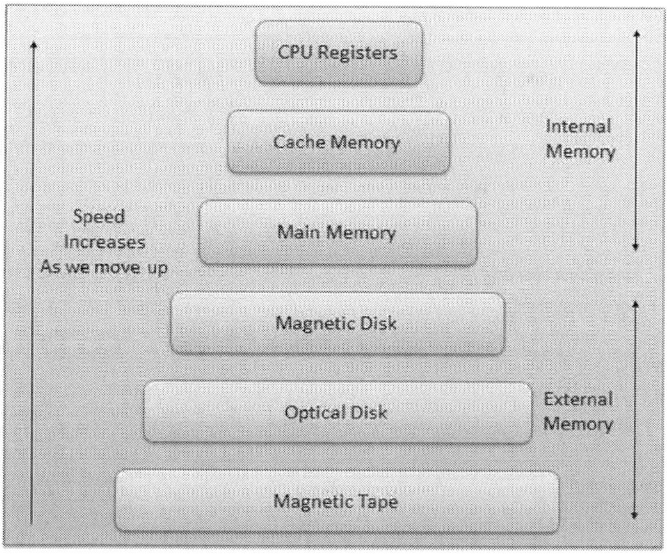

Main Memory

The main memory of the computer is also known as RAM, standing for Random Access Memory. It is constructed from integrated circuits and needs to have electrical power in order to maintain its information. When power is lost, the information is lost too! It can be directly accessed by the CPU. Main memory is where programs and data are kept when the processor is actively using them. When programs and data become active, they are copied from secondary memory into main memory where the processor can interact with them. A copy remains in secondary memory.

Secondary Memory

Secondary memory is where programs and data are kept on a long-term basis. Common secondary storage devices are the hard disk and optical disks.

- The hard disk has enormous storage capacity compared to main memory.
- The hard disk is usually contained inside the case of a computer.

- The hard disk is used for long-term storage of programs and data.
- Data and programs on the hard disk are organized into files.
- A **file** is a collection of data on the disk that has a name.

Secondary Storage

Secondary storage does not lose the data when the device is powered down—it is non-volatile. Per unit, it is typically also an order of magnitude less expensive than primary storage. Consequently, modern computer systems typically have an order of magnitude more secondary storage than primary storage and data is kept for a longer time there.

A Handbook on Computer Science

4

Programming and Data Structures

CONTENTS

1 Programming in C

Data Types

Char: 8 bits

int: 16 bits or 32 bits

float: 4 bytes

double: 8 bytes

void: Generic pointer

Operator Precedence Table

Precedence	Operator	Description	Associativity
1	++ --	Suffix/postfix increment and decrement	Left-to-right
	()	Function call	
	[]	Array subscripting	
	.	Structure and union member access	
	->	Structure and union member access through pointer	
	(type){*list*}	Compound literal(C99)	

2	++ --	Prefix increment and decrement	Right-to-left
	+ –	Unary plus and minus	
	! ~	Logical NOT and bitwise NOT	
	(*type*)	Type cast	
	*	Indirection (dereference)	
	&	Address-of	
	sizeof	Size-of	
	_Alignof	Alignmentrequirement(C11)	
3	* / %	Multiplication,division,and remainder	Left-to-right
4	+ –	Addition and subtraction	
5	<< >>	Bitwise left shift and right shift	
6	< <=	For relational operators < and ≤ respectively	
	> >=	For relational operators > and ≥ respectively	
7	== !=	For relational = and ≠ respectively	
8	&	Bitwise AND	
9	^	Bitwise XOR (exclusive or)	
10	|	Bitwise OR (inclusive or)	
11	&&	Logical AND	
12	||	Logical OR	
13	?:	Ternary conditional	Right-to-Left
14	=	Simple assignment	
	+= –=	Assignment by sum and difference	
	*= /= %=	Assignment by product, quotient, and remainder	
	<<=>>=	Assignment by bitwise left shift and right shift	
	&= ^= |=	Assignment by bitwise AND, XOR, and OR	
15	,	Comma	Left-to-right

Storage Classes

A storage class defines the scope (visibility) and life time of variables and/ or functions within a C Program.

There are following storage classes which can be used in a C Program:

- auto
- register
- static
- extern

auto - Storage Class

auto is the default storage class for all local variables.

```
{
int Count;
auto int Month;
}
```

The example defines two variables with the same storage class. auto can only be used within functions, i.e. local variables.

register - Storage Class

register is used to define local variables that should be stored in a register instead of RAM. This means that the variable has a maximum size equal to the register size (usually one word) and can't have the unary '&' operator applied to it (as it does not have a memory location).

```
{
register int  Miles;
}
```

Register should only be used for variables that require quick access - such as counters. It should also be noted that defining 'register' goes not mean that the variable will be stored in a register. It means that it MIGHT be stored in a register - depending on hardware and implementation restrictions.

static - Storage Class

static is the default storage class for global variables. The two variables (count and road) both have a static storage class.

```
    static int Count;
int Road;

{
   printf("%d\n", Road);
}
```

static variables can be 'seen' within all functions in this source file. At link time, the static variables defined here will not be seen by the object modules that are brought in.

extern - Storage Class

extern is used to give a reference of a global variable that is visible to ALL the program files. When you use 'extern' the variable cannot be initialized as all it does is point the variable name at a storage location that has been previously defined.

When you have multiple files and you define a global variable or function which will be used in other files also, then *extern* will be used in another file to give reference of defined variable or function. Just for understanding *extern* is used to declare a global variable or function in another file.

File 1: main.c

```
int count=5;

main()
{
 write_extern();
}
```

Format Specifier's

- %c char single character
- %d (%i) int signed integer
- %e (%E) float or double exponential format
- %f float or double signed decimal
- %g (%G) float or double use %f or %e as required
- %o int unsigned octal value
- %p pointer address stored in pointer
- %s array of char sequence of characters
- %u int unsigned decimal
- %x (%X) int unsigned hex value

Operators

- Assignment operators: =
- Arithmetic operators: +, -, *, /
- Relational operators: >, >=,<, <=, ==, !=
- Logical operators: &&, ||
- Bitwise operators: &, ^, <<, !, ~

Control Statements

- if statement
- Nested if statement

- Conditional Operator
- Switch statement
- For statement
- While statement
- Do- while statement
- Break statement
- Continue statement

Pointer

A pointer is a variable whose value is the address of another variable, i.e., direct address of the memory location. Like any variable or constant, you must declare a pointer before you can use it to store any variable address. The general form of a pointer variable declaration is:

type *var-name;

Array

Array can store a fixed-size sequential collection of elements of the same type. An array is used to store a collection of data, but it is often more useful to think of an array as a collection of variables of the same type.

2 Function and Recursion

A function is a rule which relates the values of one variable quantity to the values of another variable quantity, and does so in such a way that the value of the second variable quantity is uniquely determined by (i.e. is a function of) the value of the first variable quantity.

Function Prototype Declaration

Functionprototypedeclarationisnecessaryinordertoprovideinformation to the compiler about function, about return type, parameter list and function name etc.

- Ourprogramstartsfrommainfunction.Eachandeveryfunctionis called directly or indirectly through main function
- Like variable we also need to declare function before using it in program.
- In C, declaration of function is called as prototype declaration
- Function declaration is also called as function prototype

There are some of the important notable things related to prototype declaration -

- It tells name of function, return type of function and argument list related information to the compiler
- Prototype declaration always ends with semicolon.
- Parameter list is optional.
- Default return type is integer.

Syntax

return_type function_name (type arg1, type arg2......);

prototype declaration comprised of three parts i.e name of the function,return type and parameter list

Factorial Function

```
#include <stdio.h>
int main(){
int c, n, fact = 1;
printf("Enter a number to calculate it's factorial\n");
scanf("%d", &n);
for (c = 1; c <= n; c++)
fact = fact * c;
printf("Factorial of %d = %d\n", n, fact);
return 0;}
```

Tower-of-Hanoi

```
#include <stdio.h>
void towers(int, char, char, char);
int main()
{
int num;
printf("Enter the number of disks : ");
scanf("%d", &num);
printf("The sequence of moves involved in the Tower of Hanoi are :\n");
towers(num, 'A', 'C', 'B');
return 0; }
void towers(int num, char frompeg, char topeg, char auxpeg){
```

```
if (num == 1){
printf("\n Move disk 1 from peg %c to peg %c", frompeg, topeg);
return; }
towers(num - 1, frompeg, auxpeg, topeg);
printf("\n Move disk %d from peg %c to peg %c", num, frompeg, topeg);
towers(num - 1, auxpeg, topeg, frompeg);
```

Examples of prototype Declaration

Function with two integer arguments and integer as return type is represented using syntax

int sum(int,int);

Function with integer argument and integer as return type is represented using syntax

int square(int);

In the example we have written function with no argument and no return type

void display (void);

In example we have declared function with no argument and integer as return type

int getValue(void);

Positioning Function Declaration

If function definition is written after main then and then only we write prototype declaration in global declaration section

If function definition is written the main function then ,no need to write prototype declaration

Need of Prototype Declaration

Program Execution always starts from main, but during lexical analysis (1st Phase of Compiler) token generation starts from left to right and from top to bottom.

During code generation phase of compiler it may face issue of backward reference.

If we write prototype declaration then -

- Prototype declaration tells compiler that we are going to define this function somewhere in the program.
- Compiler will have prior information about function.
- As compiler have prior information, during function calling compiler looks forward in the program for the function definition.

If we don't write prototype declaration then -

- Compiler don't have any reference of Function.
- Compiler don't have prior information of that function.
- Compiler gets confused and interpret it as unknown reference and throws error.

Technically, a recursive function is a function that makes a call to itself. To prevent infinite recursion, you need an if-else statement (of some sort) where one branch makes a recursive call, and the other branch does not. The branch without a recursive call is usually the base case (base cases do not make recursive calls to the function).

Functions can also be mutually recursive. For example, function f() can call function g() and function g() can call function f(). This is still considered recursion because a function can eventually call itself. In this case, f() indirectly calls itself.

Functions can be tail-recursive. In a tail-recursive function, none of the recursive call do additional work after the recursive call is complete (additional work includes printing, etc), except to return the value of the recursive call.

The following is typical of a tail-recursive function return.

return rec_func(x, y); // no work after recursive call, just return the value of call

The following is NOT tail-recursive.

return rec_func(x, y) + 3; // work after recursive call, add 3 to result because once rec_func is done, it must add 3, and then return that value. Hence additional work. Hence, not tail-recursive.

It's common, in tail-recursive functions, to have one of the parameters be pass-by-reference (though this is not necessary), which is used to accumulate the answer. Once the base case is reached, you simply return the parameter value, which has the answer. Thus, tail-recursive functions often require an additional parameter, where non tail-recursive functions do not.

Recursion Function

Recursion is the process of repeating items in a self-similar way. Same applies in programming languages as well where if a programming allows you to call a function inside the same function that is called recursive call of the function as follows.

The C programming language supports recursion, i.e., a function to call itself. But while using recursion, programmers need to be careful to define an exit condition from the function; otherwise it will go in infinite loop.

A recursive function is a function that calls itself during its execution. This enables the function to repeat itself several times, outputting the result and the end of each iteration. It is an example of a recursive function.

```
function Count (integer N)
if (N < = 0) return "Must be a Positive Integer";
if (N > 9) return "Counting Completed";
else return Count (N+1);
end function
```

The function Count() uses recursion to count from any number between 1 and 9, to the number 10. For example, Count(1) would return 2,3,4,5,6,7,8,9,10. Count(7) would return 8,9,10. The result could be used as a roundabout way to subtract the number from 10.

```
void recursion()
```

```
{
  recursion(); /* function calls itself */
}
int main()
{
recursion();
}
```

Recursive functions are common in computer science because they allow programmers to write efficient programs using a minimal amount of code. The downside is that they can cause infinite loops and other unexpected results if not written properly. For example, in the example, the function is terminated if the number is 0 or less or greater than 9. If proper cases are not included in the function to stop the execution, the recursion will repeat forever, causing the program to crash, or worse yet, hang the entire computer system.

Advantages and Disadvantages of Recursion

Recursion is more elegant and requires few variables which make program clean. Recursion can be used to replace complex nesting code by dividing the problem into same problem of its sub-type.

In other hand, it is hard to think the logic of a recursive function. It is also difficult to debug the code containing recursion.

When to Use Recursion?

Some people think recursion is so neat, they would like to use it all the time. In general, recursion should be used when you know the number of recursive calls isn't excessive. That number depends somewhat on how much memory you have. Usually, 1000 recursive calls should be fine. Stack sizes can now be several megabytes of memory, which allows recursion to go fairly deep without causing a core dump.

Sometimes recursion is used because it produces a cleaner answer compared to the iterative version. For example, nearly all code written for tree-like structures is recursive. Many sorting algorithms are more naturally written recursively as well.

What Makes Recursion Work

Recursion works only when a problem has a recursive structure. This means that the problem's solution is similar for a large input size as well as a small input size. If reducing the input size causes the solution to look different, then it will be hard to use recursion. However, for the same reason, it can be hard to use loops too. Loops also depend on doing the same thing over and over, but on, say, a different index of an array, or a different node in a linked list.

3 Parameter Passing

In C Programming we have different ways of parameter passing schemes such as Call by Value and Call by Reference. Function is good programming style in which we can write reusable code that can be called whenever require. Whenever we call a function then sequence of executable statements gets executed. We can pass some of the information to the function for processing called argument.

All our languages so far this quarter have had the same semantics for function calls:

- Evaluate the function value and arguments.
- Bind the argument names to the argument values. (For OO languages, this includes the self-receiver argument, and usually its instance variables.)
- Evaluate the function body in the environment produced in step 2.

This is called call by value parameter passing, because the parameter names are bound to the values of the arguments.

This is not the only way to design the semantics of function calls, although it is probably the "best". There are several other ways to design parameter passing; some are used by popular languages today, but others are mostly of historical interest:

Call by Reference

- Evaluate the procedure value, and evaluate the arguments to locations.
- Bind the argument names to references to the argument locations.

- Evaluatetheprocedurebodyintheenvironmentproducedinstep2.

Call by Name

- Evaluate the procedure value. Do not evaluate the arguments.
- Bind the argument names to expressions that will be re-evaluated every time the argument is referenced.
- Evaluatetheprocedurebodyintheenvironmentproducedinstep2. Whereveryourefertoaparametername,re-evaluatetheexpression.

Call by Result

- Evaluatetheprocedurevalue.Evaluateonlythelocationtostorethe arguments,nottheargumentsthemselves.(Forexample,ifyoupass the array subscript expression a[0], simply compute the location
- Bind the argument name(s) to fresh empty location(s).
- Evaluatetheprocedurebodyintheenvironmentproducedinstep2.
- Copythefinalresultsfromthelocationsproducedinstep2,intothe locations produced in step 1.

The intuition behind this mode is that the procedure is producing output in its parameters --- so instead of evaluating the arguments fully, simplyfigureouttheirlocations,andcopytheresultsoutafterthefunction runs.

Call by Value Result

- Evaluate the procedure value and arguments, remembering the locations of the argument values.
- Bind the argument names to the argument values.
- Evaluatetheprocedurebodyintheenvironmentproducedinstep2.
- Copy the final results into the locations remembered in step 1.

The intuition behind this mode is that the procedure is copying argumentvaluesintothecalleeandcopyingresultvaluesbacktothecaller.

Example

```
#include <stdio.h>
void call_by_value(int x) {
printf("Inside call_by_value x = %d before adding 10.\n", x);
x += 10;
printf("Inside call_by_value x = %d after adding 10.\n", x); }
int main() {
int a=10;
printf("a = %d before function call_by_value.\n", a);
call_by_value(a);
printf("a = %d after function call_by_value.\n", a);
return 0; }
```

Output

```
a = 10 before function call_by_value.
Inside call_by_value x = 10 before adding 10.
Inside call_by_value x = 20 after adding 10.
a = 10 after function call_by_value.
```

Example

```
#include <stdio.h>
void call_by_reference(int *y) {
printf("Inside call_by_reference y = %d before adding 10.\n", *y);
 (*y) += 10;
printf("Inside call_by_reference y = %d after adding 10.\n", *y); }
int main() {
int b=10;
printf("b = %d before function call_by_reference.\n", b);
call_by_reference(&b);
printf("b = %d after function call_by_reference.\n", b);
return 0; }
```

Output

b = 10 before function call_by_reference.
Inside call_by_reference y = 10 before adding 10.
Inside call_by_reference y = 20 after adding 10.
b = 20 after function call_by_reference.

4 Scope and Binding

Scope

A scope in any programming is a region of the program where a defined variable can have its existence and beyond that variable cannot be accessed.

Static Scoping

With static scope, a variable always refers to its top-level environment. This is a property of the program text and unrelated to the runtime call stack. Static scoping also makes it much easier to make modular code and reason about it, since its binding structure can be understood in isolation.

Dynamic Scoping

Dynamic scoping was used in early dialects of Lisp, and some older interpreted languages such as SNOBOL and APL. It is available as an option in Common Lisp. Using this scoping rule, we first look for a local definition of a variable. If it isn't found, we look up the calling stack for a definition. If dynamic scoping were used, the output would be:

in main program -- n = 100

in laurel -- m = 50

in laurel -- n = 1

in hardy -- n = 1 ;; NOTE DIFFERENCE -- here hardy is called from laurel

in hardy -- n = 100 ;; here hardy is called from the main program

Binding

Binding means connecting the function call to a function implementation.

Static binding is done at compile time when a function is called in order to match it with the definition.

Dynamic binding is at run time where we can specify that the compiler matches a function call with the correct function definition at run time. Virtual keyword is used if the function needs to be dynamically bounded.

5 Abstract Data Types, Array, and Linked List

An abstract data type (ADT) is an object with a generic description independent of implementation details. This description includes a specification of the components from which the object is made and also the behavioral details of the object. Instances of abstract objects include mathematical objects (like numbers, polynomials, integrals, vectors), physical objects (like pulleys, floating bodies, missiles), animate objects (dogs, Pterodactyls, Indians) and objects (like poverty, honesty, inflation) that are abstract even in the natural language sense.

Examples

Integers: An integer is an abstract data type having the standard mathematical meaning. In order that integers may be useful, we also need to specify operations (arithmetic operations, gcd, square root etc.) and relations (ordering, congruence etc.) on integers.

Primitive Data Type

- Primitive data type is one that fits the base architecture of the underlying computer such as int, float, and pointer, and all of the variations, thereof such as char short long unsigned float double and etc., is primitive data type.
- Primitive data are only single values, they have not special capabilities.

- The examples of Primitive data types are given byte, short, int, long, float, double, char etc.
- The integer real's, logic data character data pointer and reference are primitive data structures data structures that normally are directly operated upon by machine level instructions are known as primitive structure and data type.

Non- Primitive Data type

- A non-primitive data type is something else such as an array structure or class is known as the non-primitive data type.
- The data type that are derived from primary data types are known as non-primitive data type.
- The non-primitive data types are used to store the group of values.
- Examples of non-primitive data types are Array, structure, union, link list, stacks, queue etc.

Data structures based on storage criteria:

Linear Data Structures: - In which insertion and deletion is possible in linear fashion .example:- arrays, linked lists.

Nonlinear Data Structures:-In which it is not possible. Example: - trees, stacks.

Linked Lists

Linked list is one of the fundamental data structures in C. Linked lists are a way to store data with structures so that the programmer can automatically create a new place to store data whenever necessary. Linked list is a dynamic data structure whose length can be increased or decreased at run time.

Linked list is created using following elements –

No	Element	Explanation
1	Node	Linked list is collection of number of nodes

2	Address Field in Node	Address field in node is used to keep address of next node
3	Data Field in Node	Data field in node is used to hold data inside linked list.

- An array is a static data structure. This means the length of array cannot be altered at run time. While, a linked list is a dynamic data structure.
- In an array, all the elements are kept at consecutive memory locations while in a linked list the elements (or nodes) may be kept at any location but still connected to each other.

Linked Lists are arranged in Memory

Linked list basically consists of memory blocks that are located at random memory locations. Now, one would ask how are they connected or how they can be traversed?

```
struct test_struct {
int val;
struct test_struct *next; };
```

How a Node is created?

A node is created by allocating memory to a structure in the following way:

```
struct test_struct *ptr = (struct test_struct*)malloc(sizeof(struct test_
struct));
```

Once a node is created, then it can be assigned the value (that it is created to hold) and its next pointer is assigned the address of next node. If no next node exists (or if it's the last node) then as already discussed, a NULL is assigned. This can be done in following way:

```
...
...
ptr->val = val;
ptr->next = NULL;
```

...

...

Remember that:

- The first node is always made accessible through a global 'head' pointer. This pointer is adjusted when first node is deleted.
- Similarly there is a 'curr' pointer that contains the last node in the list. This is also adjusted when last node is deleted.
- Whenever a node is added to linked list, it is always checked if the linked list is empty then add it as the first node.

Array

C Array is a collection of variables belongings to the same data type. You can store group of data of same data type in an array.

- Array might be belonging to any of the data types
- Array size must be a constant value.
- Always, Contiguous (adjacent) memory locations are used to store array elements in memory.
- It is a best practice to initialize an array to zero or null while declaring, if we don't assign any values to array.

Example

int a[10]; // integer array

char b[10]; // character array i.e. string

There are three types of arrays in C,

- Single Dimensional Array.
- Two dimensional Array &
- Multi-Dimensional Array.

Single Dimensional Arrays

data_type array_name[size];

Two Dimensional Arrays

Two dimensional array is nothing but array of array.

data_type array_name[row][column];

Operations on Arrays

Operations on arrays, the comparison of two distinct arrays with the same content results in FALSE. The behavior of comparison is explained when we note that the comparison is a comparison of addresses, not contents.

```
#include <stdio.h>
int main(void) {
int a[2] = {1,2}; /* The aggregates like {1,2} are literals for arrays */
int b[2] = {2,3};
int i;
/* It is legal to use subscripts on arrays, both on the left and on
* the right hand side of assignments. */
for(i=0;i<2;i++)
a[i]=b[i];
/* It is not legal to assign arrays, like in a=b; */
/* The comparison of two distinct arrays with the same content
* results in FALSE. We print "They are not equal"
if(a==b)
printf("They are equal\n");
else
printf("They are not equal\n");
/* The following comparison results in TRUE. */
if(a==a)
printf("Of course a is equal to a\n");
else
printf("No, a is not equal to a\n");
```

```
/* The behavior of comparison is explained when we note that the comparison is a comparison of addresses, not contents.*/
/* We cannot print out an array as a single unit. We have to print out
* its elements one at a time*/
for(i=0;i<2;i++)
printf("a[%1d] = %3d\n", i, a[i]); }
```

6 Stacks and Queues

Stack is a specialized data storage structure (Abstract data type). Unlike, arrays access of elements in a stack is restricted. It has two main functions push and pop. Insertion in a stack is done using push function and removal from a stack is done using pop function.

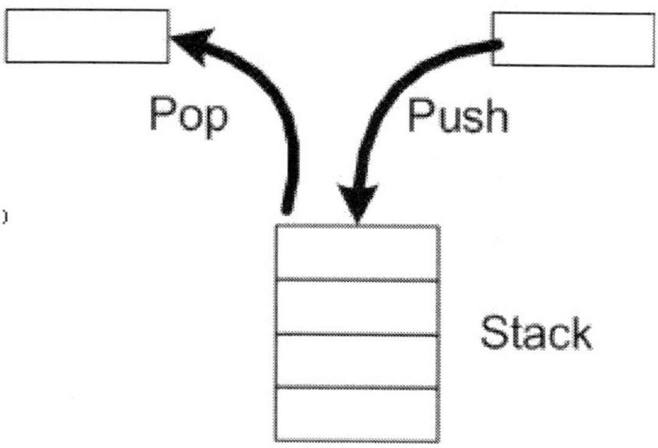

Application of Stack

- Expression Evolution
- Expression conversion
  a. Infix to Postfix.
  b. Infix to Prefix.
  c. Postfix to Infix.
  d. Prefix to Infix.
- Parsing

- Simulation of recursion
- Function call

Stack Operations

StackPush():

Now, pushing onto the stack requires the stack itself as well as something to push. So, its prototype will look like:

void StackPush(stackT *stackP, stackElementT element);

The function should place an element at the correct position in the contents array and update the top. However, before the element is placed in the array, we should make sure the array is not already full...Here is the body of the function:

```
void StackPush(stackT *stackP, stackElementT element)
{
 if (StackIsFull(stackP)) {
  fprintf(stderr, "Can't push element on stack: stack is full.\n");
  exit(1);  /* Exit, returning error code. */
 }

 /* Put information in array; update top. */

 stackP->contents[++stackP->top] = element;
}
```

Note how we used the prefix ++ operator. It increments the top index before it is used as an index in the array (i.e., where to place the new element).

Also note how we just reuse the StackIsFull() function to test for fullness.

StackPop():

Finally, popping from a stack only requires a stack parameter, but the value popped is typically returned. So, its prototype will look like:

stackElementT StackPop(stackT *stackP);

The function should return the element at the top and update the top. Again, before an element is removed, we should make sure the array is not empty....Here is the body of the function:

```
stackElementT StackPop(stackT *stackP)
{
  if (StackIsEmpty(stackP)) {
    fprintf(stderr, "Can't pop element from stack: stack is empty.\n");
    exit(1);  /* Exit, returning error code. */
  }

  return stackP->contents[stackP->top--];
}
```

Queue

It is first in first out. Queue is a specialized data storage structure (Abstract data type). Unlike, arrays access of elements in a Queue is restricted. It has two main operations enqueue and dequeue. Insertion in a queue is done using enqueue function and removal from a queue is done using dequeue function.

One side insertion (Rear). other side deletion (front)

Queue Operations: enqueuea Dequeue( ). Is empty

Double ended queue: Insertion and deletion can be on both side book

Input restricted queue: Restriction only on lip not or deinoni insertion.
Output restricted queue: Deletion on one side and no win

Priorityqueue: Ascendingpriorityqueue/Descendingprioritizingcanbe implemented using two stacks.

Enqueue Operation for QUEUE

QUEUE[0:n-1]isanarray, 'front' storesthesubscriptvalueoftheelement of the queue 'rear' stores the subscript value of the last element the queue. Irony and 'rear' are initialized to -1

7 Tree, BSTs and Binary Heaps

Tree is a widely used abstract data type (ADT) or data structure implementing this ADT that simulates a hierarchical tree structure, with a root value and subtrees of children with a parent node, represented as a set of linked nodes.

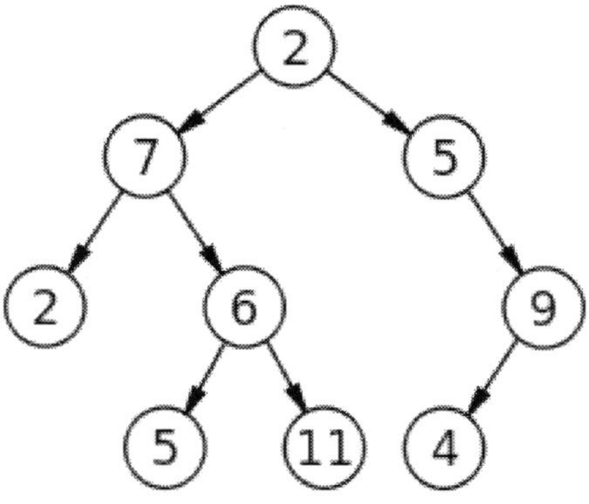

Terminologies used in Trees

Root – The top node in a tree.

Parent – The converse notion of child.

Siblings – Nodes with the same parent.

Descendant – a node reachable by repeated proceeding from parent to child.

Ancestor – a node reachable by repeated proceeding from child to parent.

Leaf - a node with no children.

Internal node - a node with at least one child.

External node - a node with no children.

Degree - number of sub trees of a node.

Edge - connection between one node to another.

Path - a sequence of nodes and edges connecting a node with a descendant.

Level - The level of a node is defined by 1 + the number of connections between the node and the root.

Height of tree - The height of a tree is the number of edges on the longest downward path between the root and a leaf.

Height of node - The height of a node is the number of edges on the longest downward path between that node and a leaf.

Depth - The depth of a node is the number of edges from the node to the tree's root node.

Forest - A forest is a set of $n \geq 0$ disjoint trees.

Binary Search Tree

Binary Search tree is a binary tree in which each internal node x stores an element such that the element stored in the left subtree of x are less than or equal to x and elements stored in the right subtree of x are greater than or equal to x. This is called binary-search-tree property.

A Handbook on
Computer Science

1

Algorithms

CONTENTS

1 Analysis Asymptotic Notation

ALGORITHM

An algorithm (pronounced AL-go-rith-um) is a procedure or formula for solving a problem.

Asymptotic Notations

Asymptotic notations are used to describe the limiting behavior of a function when the argument tends towards a particular value (often infinity), usually in terms of simpler functions. In computational complexity theory, big O notation is used to classify algorithms by how they respond (e.g., in their processing time or working space requirements) to changes in input size.

Big O Notation

Big O notation is used in Computer Science to describe the performance or complexity of an algorithm. Big O specifically describes the worst-case scenario, and can be used to describe the execution time required or the space used (e.g. in memory or on disk) by an algorithm.

```
bool IsFirstElementNull(String[] strings)
{
    if(strings[0] == null)
    {
        return true;
```

```
        }
        return false;
}
```

Big-Ω (Big-Omega) Notation

Sometimes, we want to say that an algorithm takes at least a certain amount of time, without providing an upper bound. We use big-Ω notation; that's the Greek letter "omega."

If a running time is Ω(f(n)) then for large enough n, the running time is at least k f(n) for some constant k. Here's how to think of a running time that is Ω(f(n)):

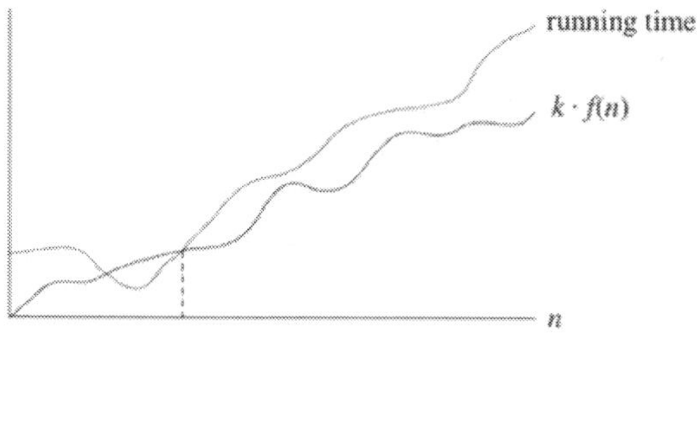

Big-θ (Big-Theta) Notation

Big-Theta notation is one which is used to denote the algorithmic complexity of a code/Algorithm which has the same order for best and worst case efficiency.

Very simple example is Merge Sort:

Its best case as well as worst case order is n log n. So it is correct to say that its order is Θ(n logn).

On the other hand Big Oh - O deals only with worst case efficiency and has nothing to do with best case.

Similarly, Big Omega - Ω deals with only best case efficiency.

Little-o

Little-oislikeBig-Obutsloppy.Big-Oandtheactualalgorithmperformance will actually become nearly identical as you head out to infinity. Little-o is just some function that will always be bigger than the actual performance. Example: o(n^7) is a valid little-o for a function that might actually have linear or O(n) performance.

Little-Omega

Little-Omega is just the opposite. w(1) [constant time] would be a valid littleomegaforthesamefunctionthatmightactuallyexihbitBigOmega(n) performance.

- Big-O -- asymptotic upper bound (inclusive)
- little-o -- asymptotic upper bound (exclusive)
- Theta -- asymptotic tight bound (Big-O and Big-Omega)
- Big-Omega -- asymptotic lower bound (inclusive)

Best/worst/average case runtimes are specific values (can be asymptotic) that describe the shortest possible runtime, longest possible runtime, and expected runtime.

Specific examples are as:

- Big-O: 10n is O(n), O(0.001*n^1.1), NOT O(999n^0.9)
- little-o: 10n is o(0.001*n^1.1), NOT o(999n)
- Theta: 10n is Theta(n), Θ(0.1n), Θ(10n)
- Big-Omega: 10n is Ω(n), Ω(999n^0.9), NOT Ω(0.001*n^1.1)

Algorithm Complexities

Constant	O(1)
Logarithmic	O(log(N))
Linear	O(N)
Quadratic	O(n^2)

Cubic	$O(n^3)$
Exponential	$O(2^n)$, $O(N!)$, $O(n^k)$, ...

Properties of Asymptotics

- Reflexivity

  $f(n) = O(f(n))$

  $f(n) = \Omega(f(n))$

  $f(n) = \Theta(f(n))$

- Transitivity

  $f(n) = \Theta(g(n))$ *and*

  $g(n) = \Theta(h(n))\Theta(f(n))$

- Transpose Symmetry

  $f(n) = O(g(n))$

  if and only if

  $g(n) = \Omega(f(n))$

Properties of Logarithms

1. $\log_a (xy) = \log_a x + \log_a y$
2. $\log_a x = \log_a x - \log_a yy$
3. $\log_x x = 1$
4. $\log_a 1 = 0$
5. $\log_a (x^n) = n(\log_a x)$
6. $\log_a x = 1\log_x a$
7. $\log_a x = \log_b x = \log x.\log_b a\log a$

Algebraic Properties of the Logarithm Function

- log(A*B) = log(A) + log(B) [additive property]
- log(A/B) = log(A) - log(B) [subtractive property]
- log(A^B) = B*log(A)
- A^log(B) = B^log(A)
- $\log_P(A) = \log_Q(A)/\log_Q(P)$ [change of base formula]
- log(1) = 0
- $A^\wedge \log_A(B) = B$
- $\log_A(A) = 1$
- log(1/A) = -log(A)

Logarithm Derivatives

$$[\ln(x)]' = 1/x[\log A(x)]' = 1/(x * \ln(A))$$

$$[x * \ln(x)]' = 1 + \ln(x)[\ln(x)^2]' = 2 * \ln(x)/x$$

$$[\ln(\ln(x))]' = 1/(x * \ln(x))$$

$$[1/\ln(x)]' = -1/(x * \ln(x)^2)$$

$$[\ln(x)^m]' = (m/x) * \ln(x)^{(m-1)}$$

$$[\ln(m - x)]' = -1/(m - x)$$

$$[\ln(m * x)]' = 1/x[\ln(x^m)]' = m/x$$

$$[\ln(m^x)]' = \ln(m)$$

$$[\ln(m * x + b)]' = m/(m * x + b)$$

$$[\ln(\cos(x))]' = -\tan(x)$$

Asymptotic Analysis

When analyzing the running time or space usage of programs, we usually try to estimate the time or space as function of the input size. For example, when analyzing the worst case running time of a function that sorts a list of numbers, we will be concerned with how long it takes as a function of the length of the input list. For example, we say the standard insertion sort takes time T(n) where0

$T(n) = c * n^2 + k$ for some constants c and k. In contrast, merge sort takes time $T'(n) = c' * n * \log_2(n) + k'$.

Since we are really measuring growth rates, we usually ignore:

- all but the "largest" term, and
- any constant multipliers

So for example

- $\lambda n.0.4n^5 + 3n^3 + 253$ behaves asymptotically like n^5
- $\lambda n.6.22 n \log n + \frac{n}{7}$ behaves asymptotically like nlogn

The justification for doing this is

- The difference between 6n and 3n isn't meaningful when looking at algorithms abstractly, since getting a computer that is twice as fast makes the former look like the latter.
- The difference between 2n and 2n + 8 is insignificant as n gets larger and larger.
- If you are comparing the growth rates of, say, $O(g) = def \{ f \mid \exists cN. \forall n > N. | f(n) | \leq c | g(n) | \}$ the former will always eventually overtake the latter no matter how big you make k.

How can we formalize this? That is, how do we formalize things like "the set of all quadratic functions" or the "set of all cubic functions" or "the set of all logarithmic functions"?

Big-O: Asymptotic Upper Bounds

A function f is in O(g) whenever there exist constants c and N such that for every n > N, f(n) is bounded by a constant times g(n). Formally:

$$O(g) = def\{f \mid \exists cN.\forall n > N. \mid f(n) \mid \leq c \mid g(n) \mid\}$$

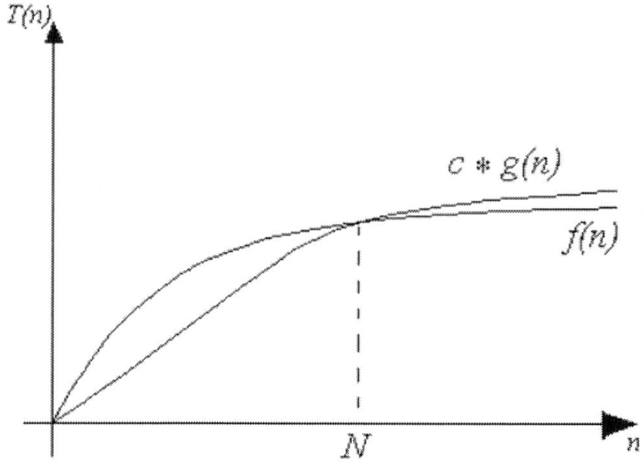

This means that O(g) is the set of all functions for which g is an asymptotic upper bound of f.

Examples

- $\lambda n.0.4n^5 + 3n^3 + 253 \in O(\lambda n.n^5)$
- $\lambda n.6.22n\log n + \frac{n}{7} \in O(\lambda n.n\log n)$

Notation

By convention, people usually drop the lambdas when writing expressions involving Big-O, so you will see things like $O(n^2)$.

Big-Ω: Asymptotic Lower Bounds

There is a Big-Ω notation for lower bounds.

A function f is in Ω(g) whenever there exist constants c and N such that for every n > N, f(n) is bounded by a constant times g(n)

$$\Omega(g) = \text{def}\{f \mid \exists c N. \forall n > N. \mid f(n) \mid \geq c \mid g(n) \mid \}$$

Lower bounds are useful because they say that an algorithm requires at least so much time. For example, you can say that printing an array is $O(n^2)$ because n^2 really is an upper bound, it's just not a very tight one! But saying printing an array is Ω(n) means it requires at least linear time which is more accurate. Of course just about everything is Ω(1).

Big-Θ

When the lower and upper bounds are the same, we can use Big-Theta notation.

$$\Theta(g) = \text{def}\{f \mid \exists c_1 c_2 N. \forall n > N. c_1 \mid g(n) \mid \leq \mid f(n) \mid \leq c_2 \mid g(n) \mid \}$$

Less-Common Complexity Functions

There are also little-oh and little-omega.

$$o(g) = \text{def}\{f \mid \lim_{x \to \infty} f(x) / g(x) = 0\}$$

$$\omega(g) = \text{def}\{f \mid \lim_{x \to \infty} f(x) / g(x) = \infty\}$$

Purpose of Asymptotic Analysis

- To estimate how long a program will run.
- To estimate the largest input that can reasonably be given to the program.
- To compare the efficiency of different algorithms.
- To help focus on the parts of code that are executed the largest number of times.
- To choose an algorithm for an application.

Recurrence Relation

A recurrence relation is an equation that recursively defines a sequence or multidimensional array of values, once one or more initial terms are given: each further term of the sequence or array is defined as a function of the preceding terms.

There are mainly three ways for solving recurrences.

Substitution Method: We make a guess for the solution and then we use mathematical induction to prove the guess is correct or incorrect.

For example consider the recurrence $T(n) = 2T(n/2) + n$

We guess the solution as $T(n) = O(nLogn)$. Now we use induction to prove our guess.

We need to prove that $T(n) <= cnLogn$. We can assume that it is true for values smaller than n.

$$
\begin{aligned}
T(n) &= 2T(n/2) + n \\
&<= cn/2Log(n/2) + n \\
&= cnLogn - cnLog2 + n \\
&= cnLogn - cn + n \\
&<= cnLogn
\end{aligned}
$$

Recurrence Tree Method: In this method, we draw a recurrence tree and calculate the time taken by every level of tree. Finally, we sum the work done at all levels. To draw the recurrence tree, we start from the given recurrence and keep drawing till we find a pattern among levels. The pattern is typically an arithmetic or geometric series.

For example consider the recurrence relation

$$T(n) = T(n/4) + T(n/2) + cn^2$$

```
        cn2

     /        \

T(n/4)       T(n/2)
```

If we further break down the expression T(n/4) and T(n/2), we get following recursion tree.

```
               cn2

          /             \

    c(n2)/16        c(n2)/4

   /       \          /      \

T(n/16)     T(n/8)  T(n/8)    T(n/4)
```

Breaking down further gives us following

```
                    cn2

              /              \

        c(n2)/16               c(n2)/4

        /         \             /          \

c(n2)/256    c(n2)/64   c(n2)/64     c(n2)/16

 /     \        /     \     /     \         /    \
```

To know the value of T(n), we need to calculate sum of tree nodes level by level. If we sum the tree level by level, we get the following series

$$T(n) = c(n^2 + 5(n^2)/16 + 25(n^2)/256) + ...$$

The series is geometrical progression with ratio 5/16.

To get an upper bound, we can sum the infinite series.

We get the sum as $(n^2)/(1 - 5/16)$ which is $O(n^2)$

Master Method

Master Method is a direct way to get the solution. The master method works only for following type of recurrences or for recurrences that can be transformed to following type.

$T(n) = aT(n/b) + f(n)$ where $a >= 1$ and $b > 1$

There are following three cases:

- If $f(n) =$ [Tex]$\Theta(n^c)$[/Tex]where $c <$ [Tex]$\log_b a$[/Tex]then $T(n) =$ [Tex]$\Theta(n^{\log_b a})$[/Tex]
- If $f(n) =$ [Tex]$\Theta(n^c)$[/Tex]where $c =$ [Tex]$\log_b a$[/Tex]then $T(n) =$ [Tex]$\Theta(n^c \log n)$[/Tex]
- If $f(n) =$ [Tex]$\Theta(n^c)$[/Tex]where $c >$ [Tex]$\log_b a$[/Tex]then $T(n) =$ [Tex]$\Theta(f(n))$[/Tex]

2 Divide and Conquer

Divide-and-conquerisatop-downtechniquefordesigningalgorithmsthat consists of dividing the problem into smaller sub-problems hoping that the solutions of the sub-problems are easier to find and then composing the partial solutions into the solution of the original problem.

Little more formally, divide-and-conquer paradigm consists of following major phases:

- Breaking the problem into several sub-problems that are similar to the original problem but smaller in size,
- Solve the sub-problem recursively (successively and independently), and then
- Combine these solutions to sub-problems to create a solution to the original problem.

1) Binary Search is a searching algorithm. In each step, the algorithm compares the input element x with the value of the middle element in array. If the values match, return the index of middle. Otherwise, if x is less than the middle element, then the algorithm recurs for left side of middle element, else recurs for right side of middle element.

5	2	4	7	1	3	2	6

1	2	2	3	4	5	6	7

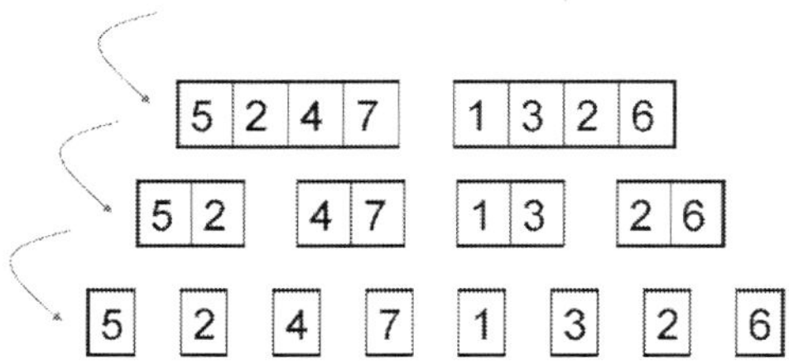

2) Quicksortisasortingalgorithm.Thealgorithmpicksapivotelement, rearrangesthearrayelementsinsuchawaythatallelementssmaller than the picked pivot element move to left side of pivot, and all greaterelementsmovetorightside.Finally,thealgorithmrecursively sorts the sub arrays on left and right of pivot element.

   For randomly chosen pivots, the expected running time of the algorithm satisfies the recurrence equation

$$T(n) = \begin{cases} 2T(n/2)+O(n) & \text{if } n>1 \\ 0 & \text{if } n=1 \end{cases}$$

3) Merge Sort is also a sorting algorithm. The algorithm divides the arrayintwohalves;recursivelysortsthemandfinallymergesthetwo sorted halves.

   The time complexity of the algorithm satisfies the recurrence equation

$$T(n) = \begin{cases} 2T(n/2)+O(n) & \text{if } n>1 \\ 0 & \text{if } n=1 \end{cases}$$

4) Closest Pair of Points the problem is to find the closest pair of points in a set of points in x-y plane. The problem can be solved in O(n^2) time by calculating distances of every pair of points and comparing the distances to find the minimum. The Divide and Conquer algorithm solves the problem in O (nLogn) time.

5) Strassen's Algorithm is an efficient algorithm to multiply two matrices. A simple method to multiply two matrices need 3 nested loopsandisO(n^3).Strassen'salgorithmmultipliestwomatricesin O(n^2.8974) time.

6) Cooley-Tukey Fast Fourier Transform (FFT) algorithm is the most common algorithm for FFT. It is a divide and conquer algorithm which works in O(nlogn) time.

Matrix Multiplication

Suppose we are dealing with integers that have hundreds of bits. Such integers are too big to fit into one memory word. Need to design an algorithm for multiplication. The naive algorithm for addition takes O(n) steps if the integers are n bits each. For multiplication, the elementary algorithm takes $O(n^2)$

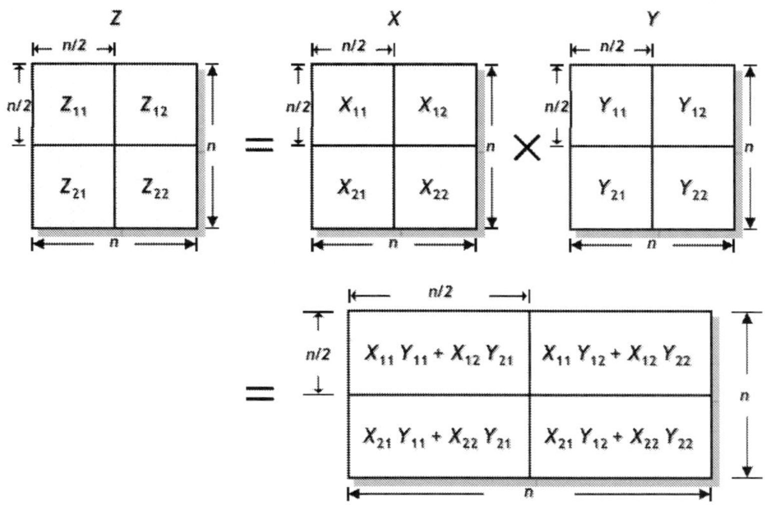

Strassen's Algorithms for Matrix Multiplication

In 1968 Volker Strassen came up with a recursive MM algorithm that runs asymptotically faster than the classical $O(n^3)$ algorithm.

The Strassen's method of matrix multiplication is a typical divide and conquer algorithm. We've seen so far some divide and conquer algorithms like merge sort and the Karatsuba's fast multiplication of large numbers.

Howeverlet'sgetagainonwhat'sbehindthedivideandconquerapproach.

In each level of recursion the algorithm uses:

- 7 recursive matrix multiplications (instead to 8), and
- 18 matrix additions (instead of 4).

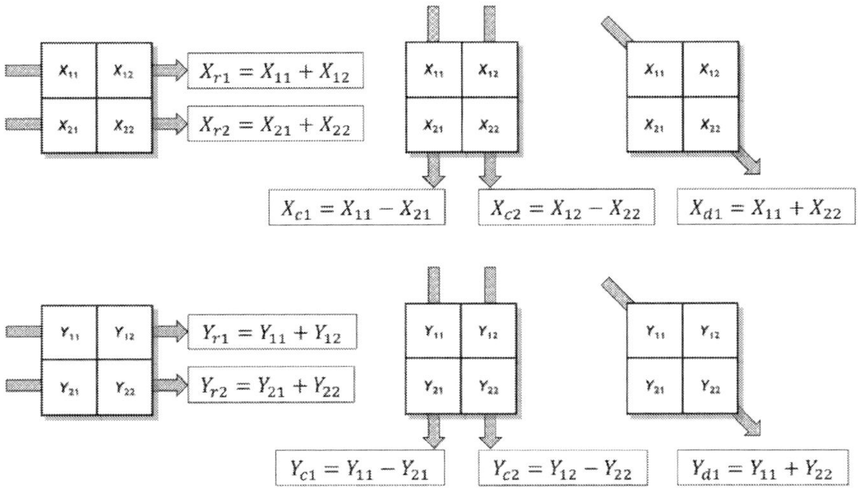

Power of Element

This algorithm generates, for each subset in the power set, the power set of that subset.

Thealgorithmusesavectorcontainingasmanyelementsastheoriginal set, and counts in base 3 from all zeroes to all twos.

This can then be interpreted for each element as follows:

- 0 - Not present in the subset
- 1 - Present in the subset and in this subset of it
- 2 - Present in the subset, but not this subset of it

Power Set Power set P(S) of a set S is the set of all subsets of S. For example S = {a, b, c} then P(s) = {{}, {a}, {b}, {c}, {a, b}, {a, c}, {b, c}, {a, b, c}}.

If S has n elements in it then P(s) will have 2^n elements

Algorithm

Input: Set[], set_size

1. Get the size of power set

   powet_set_size = pow(2, set_size)

2 Loop for counter from 0 to pow_set_size

   (a) Loop for i = 0 to set_size

   (i) If ith bit in counter is set

   Print ith element from set for this subset

   (b) Print separator for subsets i.e., newline

3 Greedy Approach

A greedy algorithm is a mathematical process that looks for simple, easy-to-implement solutions to complex, multi-step problems by deciding which step will provide the most obvious benefit.

Optimal Merge Pattern (Huffman Coding)

A Huffman code is a particular type of optimal prefix code that is commonly used for lossless data compression.

The time complexity of the Huffman algorithm is O(nlogn). Using a heap to store the weight of each tree, each iteration requires O(logn) time to determine the cheapest weight and insert the new weight. There are O(n) iterations, one for each item.

Example: Huffman Code

Let A = $\{a_1 \ldots a_5\}$, P (a_i) = {0.2, 0.4, 0.2, 0.1, 0.1}.

Symbol	Step 1	Step 2	Step 3	Step 4	Codeword
a_2	0.4	0.4	0.4	0.6 0	1
a_1	0.2	0.2	0.4 0	0.4 1	01
a_3	0.2	0.2 0	0.2 1		000
a_4	0.1 0	0.2 1			0010
a_5	0.1 1				0011

Combine last two symbols with lowest probabilities, and use one bit (last bit in code word) to differentiate between them!

Optimal Merge Pattern

We have a set of files of various sizes to be merged. In what order and combinations should we merge them? The solution to this problem is basically the same as the Huffman algorithm - a merge tree is constructed with the largest file at its root.

A greedy attempt to obtain an optimal merge pattern is easy to formulate. Since merging an n record file and an m record file requires possibly n + m records moves, the obvious choice for a selection criterion is: at each step merge the two smallest size files together.

Fractional Knapsack Problem

Greedy Algorithm – It obtains the solution of a problem by making a sequence of choices. At each decision point, the best possible choice is made.

The basic idea is to calculate for each item the ratio of value/weight, and sort them according to this ratio. Then take the items with the highest ratios and add them until we cannot add the next item as whole. Finally add as much as you can of the next item.

Job Sequencing With Deadline

Step 1: Sort p[i] into non-increasing order. After sorting p[1]> = p[2]> =p[3]> =p[i.]

Step 2: Add the next job i to the solution set if i can be completed by its deadline.

Assign i to time slot [r-1, r], where r is the largest integer such that 1 < = r < = d[i] and [r-1, r] is free.

Step 3: Stop if all jobs are examined. Otherwise, go to step 2.

Time complexity: O(n^2)

Minimum Cost Spanning Tree

An edge-weighted graph is a graph where we associate weights or costs with each edge. A minimum spanning tree (MST) of an edge-weighted graph is a spanning tree whose weight (the sum of the weights of its edges) is no larger than the weight of any other spanning tree.

Let $G = (V, E)$ be a connected graph in which each edge $(u, v) \in E$ has an associated cost $C(u, v)$.

- A Spanning Tree for G is a sub graph of G that it is a free tree connecting all vertices in V. The cost of a spanning tree is the sum of costs on its edges.
- An MST of G is a spanning tree of G having a minimum cost.

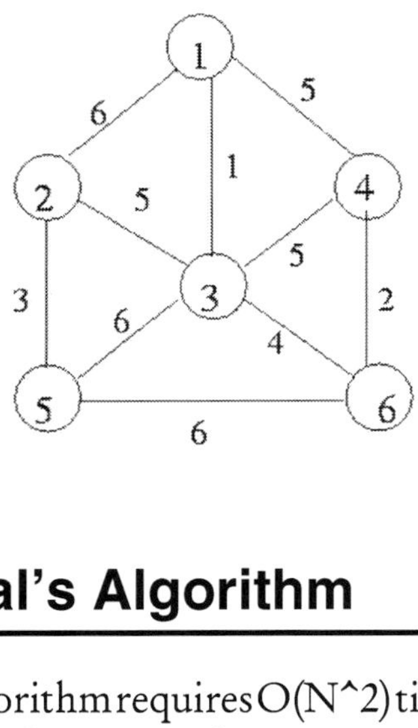

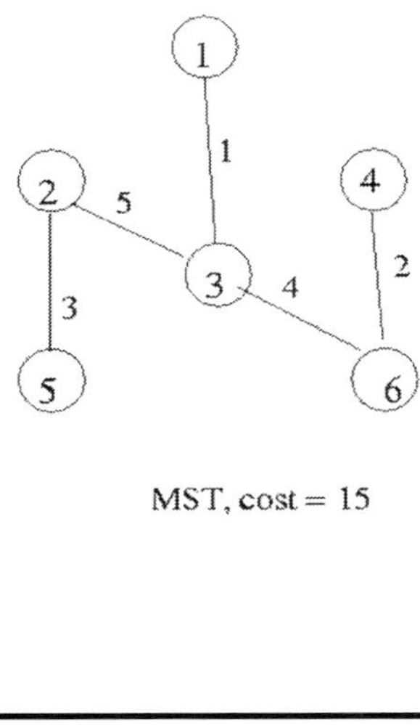

MST, cost = 15

Kruskal's Algorithm

Prim's algorithm requires O(N^2) time. We can do better using Kruskal's algorithm if E < < N^2.

Kruskal's algorithm constructs a MCST incrementally.

Initially, each node is in its own MCST, consisting of that node and no edges.

At each step in the algorithm, the two MCST's that can be connected together with the least cost are combined, adding the lowest cost edge that links a vertex in one tree with a vertex in another tree.

When there is only one MCST that includes all vertices, the algorithm terminates.

Since we must consider the edges in order of their cost, we must sort them, which requires O(E log E). Merge can be implemented in O(E log E).

Kruskal's algorithm is O(E log E), which is better than Prim's algorithm if the graph is not dense (ie, E < < N^2).

Single Source Shortest Path (Dijkstra's Algorithm)

Djikstra's algorithm solves the problem of finding the shortest path from a point in a graph (the source) to a destination. It turns out that one can find the shortest paths from a given source to all points in a graph in the same time; hence this problem is sometimes called the single-source shortest paths problem.

This problem is related to the spanning tree one. The graph representing all the paths from one vertex to all the others must be a spanning tree - it must include all vertices. There will also be no cycles as a cycle would define more than one path from the selected vertex to at least one other vertex. For a graph,

G = (V, E) where

- V is a set of vertices and
- E is a set of edges.

Dijkstra's algorithm keeps two sets of vertices:

- S the set of vertices whose shortest paths from the source have already been determined and
- V-S the remaining vertices.

The other data structures needed are:

- d array of best estimates of shortest path to each vertex
- pi an array of predecessors for each vertex

The basic mode of operation is:

- Initialise d and pi,
- Set S to empty,
- While there are still vertices in V-S,

  Sort the vertices in V-S according to the current best estimate of their distance from the source,

  Add u, the closest vertex in V-S, to S,

  Relax all the vertices still in V-S connected to u

DIJKSTRA (G, w, s)

- INITIALIZE SINGLE-SOURCE (G, s)
- S ← { }// S will ultimately contains vertices of final shortest-path weights from s
- Initialize priority queue Q i.e., Q ← V[G]
- while priority queue Q is not empty do
- *u* ← EXTRACT_MIN(Q) // Pull out new vertex
- S ← S È {*u*} // Perform relaxation for each vertex *v* adjacent to u
- for each vertex v in Adj[u] do
- Relax (*u*, *v*, *w*)

Bellman-Ford Algorithm

Bellman-Ford algorithm solves the single-source shortest-path problem in the general case in which edges of a given digraph can have negative weight as long as G contains no negative cycles.

This algorithm, like Dijkstra's algorithm uses the notion of edge relaxation but does not use with greedy method. Again, it uses d[u] as an upper bound on the distance d[u, v] from u to v.

The algorithm progressively decreases an estimate d[v] on the weight of the shortest path from the source vertex s to each vertex v in V until it achieve the actual shortest-path. The algorithm returns Boolean TRUE if the given digraph contains no negative cycles that are reachable from source vertex s otherwise it returns Boolean False.

BELLMAN-FORD (G, w, s)

- INITIALIZE-SINGLE-SOURCE (G, s)
- for each vertex i = 1 to V[G] - 1 do
- for each edge (u, v) in E[G] do
- RELAX (u, v, w)
- For each edge (u, v) in E[G] do
- if d[u] + w(u, v) < d[v] then
- return FALSE
- return TRUE

Analysis

- The initialization in line 1 takes $\Theta(v)$ time
- For loop of lines 2-4 takes O(E) time and For-loop of line 5-7 takes O(E) time.

4 Dynamic Programming

Dynamic programming is a method for solving a complex problem by breaking it down into a collection of simpler subproblems. It is applicable to problems exhibiting the properties of overlapping sub problems and optimal substructure. When applicable, the method takes far less time than other methods that don't take advantage of the sub problem overlap.

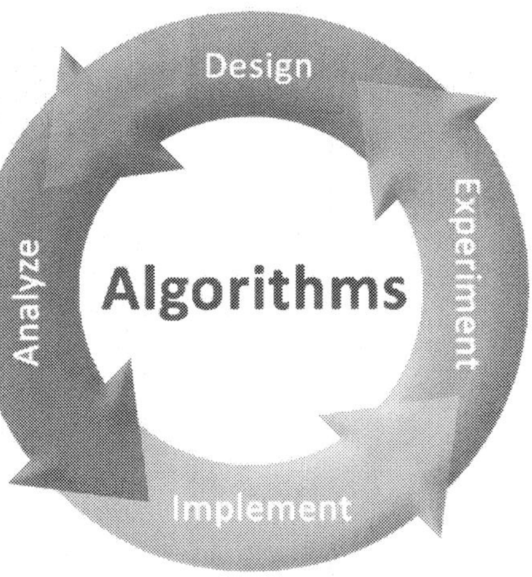

Longest Common Subsequence

The longest common subsequence (or LCS) of groups A and B is the longest group of elements from A and B that are common between the two groups and in the same order in each group. For example, the sequences "1234" and "1224533324" have an LCS of "1234":

Recursive Solution

So we want to solve the longest common subsequence problem by dynamic programming. To do this, we first need a recursive solution. The dynamic programming idea doesn't tell us how to find this; it just gives us a way of making the solution more efficient once we have.

```
    int lcs_length(char * A, char * B)
{
    if (*A == '\0' || *B == '\0') return 0;
    else if (*A == *B) return 1 + lcs_length(A+1, B+1);
    else return max(lcs_length(A+1,B), lcs_length(A,B+1));
}
```

1/0 Knapsack Problem

The knapsack problem or rucksack problem is a problem in combinatorial optimization: Given a set of items, each with a mass and a value, determine the number of each item to include in a collection so that the total weight is less than or equal to a given limit and the total value is as large as possible.

If we limit the x_i to only 1 or 0 (take it or leave it), this results in the 0/1 Knapsack problem.

$$x_1, x_2, \ldots\ldots x_n, \text{ such that :}$$

$$\begin{cases} \text{maximize: } \sum_{i=1}^{n} p_i . x_i \\ \text{subject to: } \sum_{i=1}^{n} w_i . x_i \leq m \\ \qquad x_i \in \{0,1\}, 1 \leq i \leq n \end{cases}$$

```
FOR w= 0 TO W
  DO c[0,w] = 0
FOR i = 1 to n
  DO c[i, 0] = 0
   FOR w = 1 TO W
    DO IF f wi ≤ w
      THEN IF vi + c[i − 1, w − wi]
        THEN c[i, w] = vi + c[i − 1, w − wi]
        ELSE c[i, w] = c[i − 1, w]
      ELSE
        c[i, w] = c[i − 1, w]
```

Thisdynamic-0-1-kanpsackalgorithmtakes $\theta(nw)$ times, brokenupas follows: $\theta(nw)$ timestofillthe *c*-table, whichhas $(n + 1).(w + 1)$ entries, each requiring $\theta(1)$ time to compute. $O(n)$ time to trace the solution, because the tracing process starts in row *n* of the table and moves up 1 row at each step.

Travelling Salesman Problem

The Traveling Salesman Problem is one of the most intensively studied problems in computational mathematics. These pages are devoted to the history, applications, and current research of this challenge of finding the shortest route visiting each member of a collection of locations and returning to your starting point.

Naive Solution:

- Consider city 1 as the starting and ending point.
- Generate all (n-1)! Permutations of cities.
- Calculate cost of every permutation and keep track of minimum cost permutation.
- Return the permutation with minimum cost.

Time Complexity: [Tex]\Ω [/Tex] (n!)

TSP is a special case of the travelling purchaser problem.

Matrix-chain Multiplication

The chain matrix multiplication problem involves the question of determining the optimal sequence for performing a series of operations. This general class of problem is important in complier design for code optimization and in databases for query optimization.

```
Mult(i,j) {
   if (i= =j) return A[i];          // Basis
   else {
       k=s[i,j];
       X = Mult(i,k];        // X = A[i]A[k]
       Y = Mult(k+ 1,j];   // Y = A[k+1]A[j]
        return XY;           // multiply matrices X and Y
   }
 }
```

The space complexity of this procedure $O(n^2)$.

Subset Sum Problem

The subset sum problem is an important problem in complexity theory and cryptography.

The Subset Sum problem takes as input a set X = $\{x_1, x_2 \ldots x_n\}$ of n integers and another integer K. The problem is to check if there exists a subset X' of X whose elements sum to K and finds the subset if there is any. For example, if X = {5, 3, 11, 8, 2} and K = 16 then the answer is YES since the subset X' = {5, 11} has a sum of 16. Implement an algorithm for Subset Sum whose run time is at least O(nK).

The complexity is O(nK).

Floyd Warshall All Pair Shortest Path

The Floyd–Warshall algorithm is a graph analysis algorithm for finding shortest paths in a weighted graph with positive or negative edge weights and also for finding transitive closure of a relation R.

$$
\begin{aligned}
&\text{Floyd} - \text{Warshall}(W)\\
&\quad n = W.\text{rows}\\
&\quad D^{(0)} = W\\
&\quad \text{for } k = 1 \text{ to } n\\
&\qquad \text{let } D^{(k)} = \left(d_{ij}^{(k)}\right) \text{ be a new matrix}\\
&\qquad \text{for } i = 1 \text{ to } n\\
&\qquad\quad \text{for } j = 1 \text{ to } n\\
&\qquad\qquad d_{ij}^{(k)} = \min\left(d_{ij}^{(k-1)},\ d_{ij}^{(k-1)} + d_{ij}^{(k-1)}\right)\\
&\qquad \text{return } D^{(n)}
\end{aligned}
$$

The algorithm's running time is clearly $\Theta(n^3)$.

A shortest path does not contain the same vertex more than once.

Optimal Binary Search Tree

An optimal search tree is one in which the probability of occurrence of all keys is equal (or is unknown, in which case we assume it to be equal). Thus we concentrated on balancing the tree so as to make the cost of finding any key at most log n.

```
OPTIMAL – BST(p,q,n)
fori=1ton+1
  do e[i,i–1]=qi–1
        w[i,i–1]=qi–1
for l= 1ton
    dofori=1ton–l+1
            doj=i+l–1
                e[i,j]=â ˆž
                w[i,j]=w[i,j–1]+pj+qj
                forr=itoj
                    dot=e[i,r–1]+e[r+1,j]+w[i,j]
                        if t<e[i,j]
                            thene[i,j]=t
                                root[i,j]=r
returne and root
```

The optimal binary search tree has a time complexity of O(n log n).

5 Graph Traversals, Hashing and Sorting

Graph traversal is the problem of visiting all the nodes in a graph in a particular manner, updating and/or checking their values along the way. Tree traversal is a special case of graph traversal.

The goal of a graph traversal, generally, is to find all nodes reachable from a given set of root nodes. In an undirected graph we follow all edges; in a directed graph we follow only out-edges.

Breadth-First Search

Breadth-first search (BFS) is a graph traversal algorithm that explores nodes in the order of their distance from the roots, where distance is defined as the minimum path length from a root to the node. Its pseudocode looks like this:

```
// let s be the source node
frontier = new Queue()
mark root visited (set root.distance = 0)
frontier.push(root)
while frontier not empty{
    Vertex v = frontier.pop()
    for each successor v' of v{
      if v' unvisited{
        frontier.push(v')
        mark v' visited (v'.distance = v.distance + 1)
      }
    }
}
```

Depth-First Search

In depth-first search, the frontier acts like a last-in first-out stack. The elements are added to the stack one at a time. The one selected and taken off the frontier at any time is the last element that was added. The worst-case asymptotic complexity is often the easiest to show, but it is usually the least useful.

```
dfs(vertex v)
{
visit(v);
for each neighbor w of v
   if w is unvisited
   {
     dfs(w);
      add edge vw to tree T
   }
}
```

Hashing

The mapping between an item and the slot where that item belongs in the hash table is called the hash function. The hash function will take any item in the collection and return an integer in the range of slot names, between 0 and m-1.

Component of Hashing: Hash table, Hash Function, Collisions and Collision Resolution Techniques.

$$\text{Load Factor} = \frac{\text{numbero of elements in hash table}}{\text{Hash table size}}$$

Direct Address Table

If we have a collection of n elements whose keys are unique integers in (1,m), where m > = n, then we can store the items in a direct address table, T[m], where Ti is either empty or contains one of the elements of our collection.

Searching a direct address table is clearly an O(1) operation:

For a key, k, we access T_k,

- If it contains an element, return it,
- If it does not then return a NULL.

There are two constraints here:

- The keys must be unique, and
- The range of the key must be severely bounded.

Types of Hash Function

- *Additive Hash:* Probably the simplest algorithm for hashing a sequence of integral values (such as a string), is to add all of the characters together and then force the range into something suitable for lookup with the remainder of division.
- *XOR Hash:* The XOR hash is another algorithm commonly

suggested by textbooks. Instead of adding together the bytes of an object as the additive hash does, the XOR Hash repeatedly folds the bytes together to produce a seemingly random hash value.

- *Rotating Hash:* The rotating hash is identical to the XOR hash except instead of simply folding each byte of the input into the internal state; it also performs a fold of the internal state before combining it with the each byte of the input.
- *Bernstein Hash:* Dan Bernstein created this algorithm and posted it in a newsgroup. It is known by many as the Chris Torek hash because Chris went a long way toward popularizing it.
- *Shift-Add-XOR Hash:* The shift-add-XOR hash was designed as a string hashing function, but because it is so effective, it works for any data as well with similar efficiency.
- *FNV Hash:* The FNV hash, short for Fowler/Noll/Vo in honor of the creators, is a very powerful algorithm that, not surprisingly, follows the same lines as Bernstein's modified hash with carefully chosen constants.
- *One-at-a-Time Hash:* Bob Jenkins is a well-known authority on designing hash functions for table lookup.
- *JSW Hash:* This is a hash of my own devising that combines a rotating hash with a table of randomly generated numbers.
- *ELF Hash:* The ELF hash function has been around for a while, and it is believed to be one of the better algorithms out there.

Collision Resolution Techniques

- Open Addressing
- Chaining

Collision Resolution Techniques

The key thing in hashing is to find an easy to compute hash function. However, collisions cannot be avoided. Here we discuss three strategies of dealing with collisions, linear probing, quadratic probing and separate chaining.

Open Addressing

Open addressing, or closed hashing, is a method of collision resolution in hash tables. With this method a hash collision is resolved by probing, or searching through alternate locations in the array (the probe sequence) until either the target record is found, or an unused array slot is found, which indicates that there is no such key in the table

Linear Probing: in which the interval between probes is fixed — often at 1.

Disadvantage

- Large clusters tend to build up: if an empty slot is preceded by i filled slots, the probability that the empty slot is the next one to be filled is (i + 1)/M.
- If the preceding slot was empty, the probability is 1/M.

Quadratic Probing: in which the interval between probes increases linearly (hence, the indices are described by a quadratic function). The idea here is to skip regions in the table with possible clusters.

Double Hashing: in which the interval between probes is fixed for each record but is computed by another hash function

In open addressing the load factor L is less than 1.

Good strategy is to keep L < 0.5

If the table is close to full, the search time grows and may become equal to the table size.

Random Probing

Suppose that the hash table has b buckets. In linear open addressing the buckets are examined in the order (f(k) + i) % b, 0 < = i < b, where k is the key of the element being searched for. In random probing a pseudo-random number generator is used to obtain a random sequence R(i), 1 < = i < b where R(1), R(2), ... R(b-1) is a permutation of [1, 2, ..., b-1]. The buckets are examined in the order f(k), (f(k) + R(i)) % b, 1 < = i < b.

When there is a collision, we start a (pseudo) random number generator.

For example;

f(key1)=3

f(key2)=3DD > collision

Then, start the pseudo random number generator and get a number, say 7. Add 3+7=10 and store key2 at location 10.

Chaining

We modify entries of the hash table to hold a key part (and the record) and a link part. When there is a collision, we put the second key to any empty place and set the link part of the first key to point to the second one. Additional storage is needed for link fields.

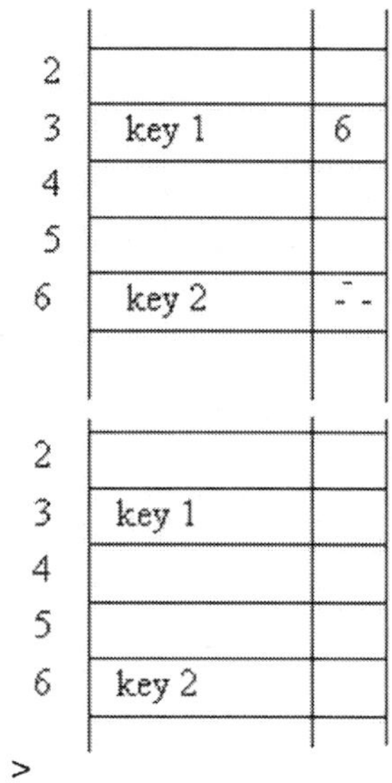

Chaining with Overflow

In this method, we use extra space for colliding items.

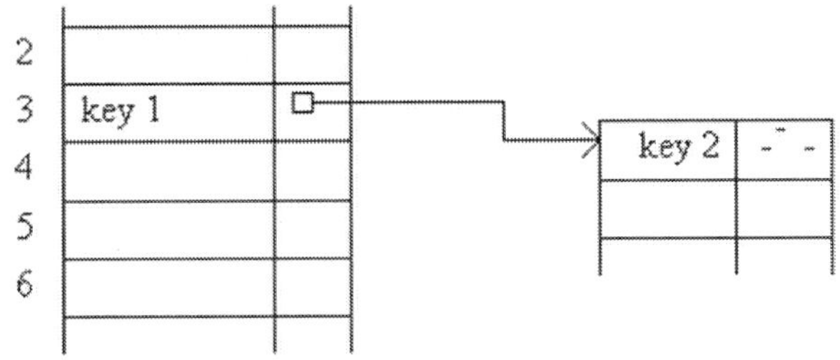

f(key1) = 3 goes into bucket 3

f(key2) = 3 collision, goes into the overflow area

Rehashing

Use a series of hash functions. If there is a collision, take the second hash function and hash again, etc. The probability that two key values will map to the same address with two different hash functions is very low.

Average number of probes (AVP) calculation:

Calculate the probability of collisions, then the expected number of collisions, then average.

1. Linear probing :

$$AVP = \frac{(1 - LF/2)}{1 - LF} \text{ where LF is the Loading factor}$$

2. Random probing :

$$AVP = \frac{1}{LF}\ln(1 - LF)$$

3. Chaining with overflow

$$AVP = 1 + \frac{LF}{0}$$

Searching and Sorting

Insertion Sort:

- Average Case / Worst Case: $\Theta(n^2)$; happens when input is already sorted in descending order

- Best Case: $\Theta(n)$; when input is already sorted
- No. of comparisons: $\Theta(n^2)$ in worst case & $\Theta(n)$ in best case
- No. of swaps: $\Theta(n^2)$ in worst/average case & 0 in Best case

Selection Sort:

- Average Case / Worst Case / Best Case: $\Theta(n^2)$
- No. of comparisons: $\Theta(n^2)$
- No. of swaps: $\Theta(n^2)$ in worst/average case & 0 in best case

Merge Sort:

- Average Case / Worst Case / Best case: $\Theta(nlgn)$; doesn't matter at all whether the input is sorted or not
- No. of comparisons: $\Theta(n+m)$ in worst case & $\Theta(n)$ in best case ; assuming we are merging two array of size n & m where $n<m$
- No. of swaps: No swaps! [but requires extra memory, not in-place sort]

Quick Sort:

- Worst Case: $\Theta(n^2)$; happens input is already sorted
- Best Case: $\Theta(nlogn)$; when pivot divides array in exactly half
- No. of comparisons: $\Theta(n^2)$ in worst case & $\Theta(nlogn)$ in best case
- No. of swaps: $\Theta(n^2)$ in worst case & 0 in best case

Bubble Sort:

- Worst Case: $\Theta(n^2)$
- Best Case: $\Theta(n)$; on already sorted
- No. of comparisons: $\Theta(n^2)$ in worst case & best case
- No. of swaps: $\Theta(n^2)$ in worst case & 0 in best case

Linear Search:

- Worst Case: $\Theta(n)$; search key not present or last element
- Best Case: $\Theta(1)$; first element
- No. of comparisons: $\Theta(n)$ in worst case & 1 in best case

Binary Search:

- Worst case/Average case: $\Theta(logn)$

- Best Case: $\Theta(1)$; when key is middle element
- No. of comparisons: $\Theta(\log n)$ in worst/average case & 1 in best case

6 Complexity Classes: P, NP, NPH and NPC

In computational complexity theory, a complexity class is a set of problems of related resource-based complexity. A typical complexity class has a definition of the form:

The set of problems that can be solved by an abstract machine M using O(f(n)) of resource R, where n is the size of the input.

P Space Problem

In computational complexity theory, PSPACE is the set of all decision problems that can be solved by a Turing machine using a polynomial amount of space.

If we denote by SPACE(t(n)), the set of all problems that can be solved by Turing machines using O(t(n)) space for some function t of the input size n, then we can define PSPACE formally as

$$\text{PSPACE} = \bigcup_{K \in n} \text{SPACE}(N^K).$$

NP (complexity)

NP is one of the most fundamental complexity classes. The abbreviation NP refers to "nondeterministic polynomial time." NP is the set of all decision problems for which the instances where the answer is "yes" have efficiently verifiable proofs of the fact that the answer is indeed "yes".

The complexity class NP can be defined in terms of NTIME as follows:

$$NP = \bigcup_{K \in n} NTIME(N^K).$$

P versus NP Problem

The P versus NP problem is a major unsolved problem in computer science. Informally, it asks whether every problem whose solution can be quickly verified by a computer can also be quickly solved by a computer.

The informal term quickly, used means the existence of an algorithm for the task that runs in polynomial time. The general class of questions for which some algorithm can provide an answer in polynomial time is called "class P" or just "P". For some questions, there is no known way to find an answer quickly, but if one is provided with information showing what the answer is, it is possible to verify the answer quickly. The class of questions for which an answer can be verified in polynomial time is called NP.

Consider the subset sum problem, an example of a problem that is easy to verify, but whose answer may be difficult to compute. Given a set of integers, does some nonempty subset of them sum to 0? For instance, does a subset of the set $\{-2, -3, 15, 14, 7, -10\}$ add up to 0? The answer "yes, because the subset $\{-2, -3, -10, 15\}$ adds up to zero" can be quickly verified with three additions. However, there is no known algorithm to find such a subset in polynomial time (there is one, however, in exponential time, which consists of 2n-n-1 tries), but such an algorithm exists if P = NP; hence this problem is in NP (quickly checkable) but not necessarily in P (quickly solvable).

An answer to the P = NP question would determine whether problems that can be verified in polynomial time, like the subset-sum problem, can also be solved in polynomial time. If it turned out that P $\neq$ NP, it would mean that there are problems in NP (such as NP-complete problems) that are harder to compute than to verify: they could not be solved in polynomial time, but the answer could be verified in polynomial time.

NP-Complete

The computational complexity theory, a decision problem is NP-complete when it is both in NP and NP-hard. The set of NP-complete problems is often denoted by NP-C or NPC. The abbreviation NP refers to "nondeterministic polynomial time".

NP-complete problems are the hardest problems in NP set. A decision problem L is NP-complete if:

- L is in NP (Any given solution for NP-complete problems can be verified quickly, but there is no efficient known solution).
- Every problem in NP is reducible to L in polynomial time.

A problem is NP-Hard if it follows property 2 mentioned, doesn't need to follow property 1. Therefore, NP-Complete set is also a subset of NP-Hard set.

Reduction

Let L_1 and L_2 be two decision problems. Suppose algorithm A_2 solves L_2. That is, if y is an input for L_2 then algorithm A_2 will answer Yes or No depending upon whether y belongs to L_2 or not.

The idea is to find a transformation from L_1 to L_2 so that the algorithm A_2 can be part of an algorithm A_1 to solve L_1.

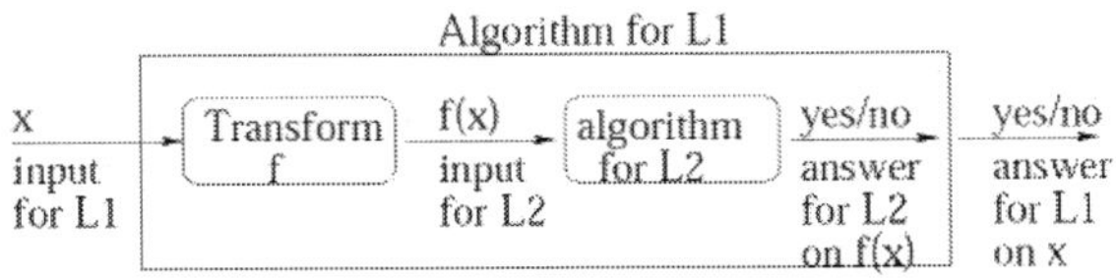

For example, if we have library functions to solve certain problem and if we can reduce a new problem to one of the solved problems, we save a lot of time. Consider the example of a problem where we have to find minimum product path in a given directed graph where product of path is multiplication of weights of edges along the path. If we have code for Dijkstra's algorithm to find shortest path, we can take log of all weights and use Dijkstra's algorithm to find the minimum product path rather than writing a fresh code for this new problem.

A Handbook on Computer Science

6

Theory of Computation

CONTENTS

1 Regular Languages and Finite Automata

INTRODUCTION

Alphabet (Σ): An alphabet is a standard set of symbol.

Example: Σ = {a,b} is alphabet with two symbol a and b.

Binary: Σ = {0,1}

- All lower case letters: Σ = {a,b,c,..z}
- Alphanumeric: Σ = {a-z, A-Z, 0-9}
- DNA molecule letters: Σ = {a,c,g,t}

String: It is traditionally a sequence of characters, either as a literal constant or as some kind of variable. A string or word is a finite sequence of symbols chosen from Σ

Example: abb is a string over Σ = {a,b}

Empty String: It is the special case where the sequence has length zero, so there are no symbols in the string. Empty string is also called null string.

Length of a string:

The length property represents the length of a string.

str.length

Prefix of the string

A prefix of a string S is a substring of S that occurs at the beginning of S

Suffix of the string

A suffix of a string S is a substring that occurs at the end of S.

Power of an Alphabet

Let Σ be an alphabet.

Σk = the set of all strings of length k

$\Sigma^* = \Sigma 0 \cup \Sigma 1 \cup \Sigma 2 \cup \ldots$

$\Sigma^+ = \Sigma 1 \cup \Sigma 2 \cup \Sigma 3 \cup \ldots$

Languages

L is a said to be a language over alphabet Σ, only if $L \subseteq \Sigma^*$ this is because Σ^* is the set of all strings (of all possible length including 0) over the given alphabet Σ

Examples:

1. Let L be the language of all strings consisting of n 0's followed by n 1's:

   L = {□,01,0011,000111,...}

2. Let L be the language of all strings of with equal number of 0's and 1's:

   L = {□, 01,10,0011,1100,0101,1010,1001,...}

Grammars

A grammar on a language L from an alphabet A consists of a finite set N of nonterminal symbols with one symbol specified as the starting one, a finite set Σ of terminal symbols that's disjoint from N (that is, shares no member with N) and is a subset of A, and a finite set P of production rules that transform strings into other strings. I'll give you an example of a grammar that produces the language L = ab*(c|a)b.

The grammar G has nonterminals N = {S, Q, R} (where S is the starting symbol), terminals ∑ = {a, b, c} = A and production rules given by

S ▯ aQ

Q ▯ bQ

Q ▯ cR

Q ▯ aR

R ▯ b

Automation

Automation act as a recognizer or accepter.

Automatons are abstract models of machines that perform computations on an input by moving through a series of states or configurations.

Formal Language

Formal language is a set of strings of symbols that may be constrained by rules that are specific to it.

Every formal language can be generated by equivalent grammar and ne accepted by the equivalent automaton.

Chomsky hierarchy

Chomsky hierarchy is a containment hierarchy of classes of formal grammars.

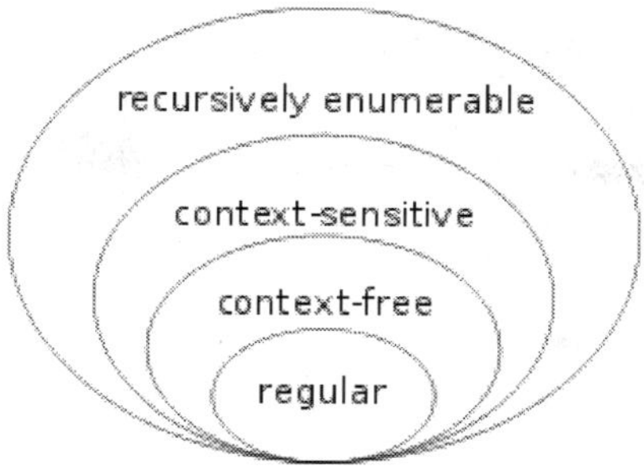

Type of Automation

Finite Automata

A finite automaton (FA) is a simple idealized machine used to recognize patterns within input taken from some character set (or alphabet) C. The job of an FA is to accept or reject an input depending on whether the pattern defined by the FA occurs in the input.

Type of Finite Automata

- Deterministic finite automaton (DFA)
- Non-deterministic finite automaton (NDFA)

L(DFA) = L(NDFA)

Pushdown Automation

Pushdown automaton (PDA) is a type of automaton that employs a stack. Pushdown automata are used in theories about what can be computed by machines.

Type of Pushdown Automation

- Deterministic pushdown automation (DPA)
- Non-deterministic pushdown automaton (NDPA)

L(DPA) < L(NDPA)

Linear Bounded Automaton (LBA)

Linear bounded automaton is a restricted form of Turing machine.

Nondeterministic Turing machine that satisfies the following three conditions:

- Its input alphabet includes two special symbols, serving as left and right endmarkers.
- Its transitions may not print other symbols over the endmarkers.
- Its transitions may neither move to the left of the left endmarkers nor to the right of the right endmarkers.

Turing Machine

Turing machine is a hypothetical device that manipulates symbols on a strip of tape according to a table of rules.

Types of Turing Machine

- Deterministic Turing machine (DTM)
- Non-deterministic Turing machine (NDTM)

L(DTM) = L(NDTM)

Types of Grammars

The Chomsky Hierarchy comprises four types of languages and their associated grammars and machines.

Language	Grammar	Machine	Example	
Type 3	Regular languages	Regular grammars Right-linear grammars Left-linear grammars	Finite-state automata	a*

Type 2	Context-free languages	Context-free grammars	Push-down automata	a^nb^n
Type 1	Context-sensitive languages	Context-sensitive grammars	Linear-bound automata	$a^nb^nc^n$
Type 0	Recursive languages Recursively enumerable languages	Unrestricted grammars	Turing machines	any computable function

The types of languages form a strict hierarchy: regular languages Ì context-free languages Ì context-sensitive languages Ì recursive languages Recursively enumerable languages.

The distinction between languages can be seen by examining the structure of the grammar rules of their grammar, or the nature of the automata which can be used to identify them.

Type 3 - Regular Languages

As we have discussed, a regular language is one which can be represented by a regular grammar, described using a regular expression, or accepted using an FSA.

There are two kinds of regular grammar:

Right-linear (right-regular), with rules of the form

A □□ B or A □□ ,

Where A and B are single non-terminal symbols, □ is a terminal symbol Parse trees with these grammars are right-branching.

Left-linear (left-regular), with rules of the form

A □ B □ or A □□

Parse trees with these grammars are left-branching.

Examples of regular languages are pattern matching languages (regular expressions).

Type 2 - Context-Free Languages

A Context-Free Grammar (CFG) is one whose production rules are of the form:

A □ □

where A is any single non-terminal, and □ is any combination of terminals and non-terminals.

The minimal automaton that recognizes context-free languages is a push-down automaton. It uses stack when expanding the non-terminal symbols with the right-hand side of the corresponding grammar rule.

Examples of CFLs are some simple programming languages.

Type 1 - Context-Sensitive Languages

Context-Sensitive grammars may have more than one symbol on the left-hand-side of their grammar rules, provided that at least one of them is a non-terminal and the number of symbols on the left-hand-side does not exceed the number of symbols on the right-hand-side.

Their rules have the form:

□ A □□ □ □ □

where A is a single non-terminal symbol, and□□□are any combination of terminals and non-terminals.

Since we allow more than one symbol on the left-hand-side, we refer to those symbols other than the one we are replacing as the context of the replacement.

The automaton which recognizes a context-sensitive language is called a linear-bounded automaton: an FSA with a memory to store symbols in a list.

Since the number of the symbols on the left-hand side is always smaller or equal to the number of the symbols on the right-hand side, the length of each derivation string is increased when applying a grammar rule. This length is bound by the length of the input string. Thus a linear-bound automaton always needs a finite list as its store

Examples of context-sensitive languages are most programming languages.

Type 0 - Unrestricted (Free) Languages

Unrestrictedgrammarshavenorestrictionsontheirgrammarrules,except that there must be at least one non-terminal on the left-hand-side. The rules have the form

▯ ▯ ▯

where ▯ and ▯ are arbitrary strings of terminal and non-terminal symbols and ▯ ¹ ▯ (the empty string).

Thetypeofautomatawhichcanrecognizesuchalanguageisa Turing machine, with an infinitely long memory.

Examples of unrestricted languages are almost all natural languages.

Theorem: A language is generated by an unrestricted grammar if and only if it is recursively enumerable.

Equivalence of Language, Automata and Grammar

(1) Regular Language (Type-3 language or finite state language

Finite Automaton [DFA = NFA = e-NFA]

Regular Grammar (Type-3 grammar)

≅

Left linear Grammar

≅

Right linear Grammar

≅

Regular Expression

(ii) Context Free language (Type-21anguvel Pushdown Automata (NPDA or PDA)

Context Free Grammar

(iii) CSG a LBA -a CSL (Typed language)

(iv) REG 2 TM_ REL (Type-0 language) •

Expressive Power of Automata:

Expressive class or set of languages accepted by the particular FA < GPDA < PDA < LBA < TM. FA is less powerful machine and TM is more powerful than any other

(i) Type 3 class c Type 2 class c Type 1 Gass c TO*

(ii) FA a TM with read only tape a TM with um: TM with finite tape a PDA with finite stack

(iii) PDA a FA with stack

(iv) TM a PDA with additional stack a FA with two

Applications of Automata:

(i) Finite automata can be used in the following cases:

(a) To design a lexical analysis of a compiler

(b) To recognize the pattern using regular

(c) To design the combination and Sequential circuit mealy machines

(ii) PDA can be used in the following cases:

(a) To design the parsing phase of a compile, (WINS)

(b) To implement stack applications

(c) To evaluate arithmetic expressions

NFA has same power as of DFA

DPDA has less power than NPDA

DIM has same power as of NTM

Mealy and Moore machines have same power mealy machine. Output depends on current state and current input

Moore machine:

Output depends on current state only

Finite automaton does not have infinite memory required for comparison.

Every finite language is regular but converse need not be true.

Language may be infinite but variables, terminals and production rules are finite for every grammar. Regular grammar is either left Hear or right linear or both.

Every NFA can be converted to DFA and then to minimal DFA

If NFA has n-states then the equivalent DFA has at most 2^ states.

Let w be a string of length n Then number of possible substring n(n + 1)/2 + 1 including c is at most Number of prefixes for the given n-length string = (n + 1)

Number of suffixes for the given n-length string = (n + 1)

Finite Automation

Finite Automata

Finite Acceptor (FA without output)

DFA Non-deterministic NFA and i -NFA

Finite Transducer (FA with output)

- Moore Machine
- Mealy Machine

A finite automaton is categorized into two types:

(i) Finite automata with output.

This is of two types Mealy machines and Moore machines.

(a) In Mealy machine the output is associated with transition (state and i/p symbol)

(b) In the Moore machine output is associated with the state

Finite Automata without output: This is of two types DFA or NFA

DFA: It is deterministic finite automata. For every input symbol, in DFA there is an exactly one transition from each mat of automats. It accepts all strings that are Present in the language by halting in a final stage and rejects all strings that are not present in the language by halting in a non-final state NFA: It is non-deterministic finite automata. For every in symbol in NFA there is at least one transition or no transition from each state of finite automata. It accepts all strings that are present in the language by halting in a final state and re • leer, all strings not present in the language either by halting in a final state or by halting in a dead configuration.

-NFA: It is non-deterministic finite automata which include transitions between states.

Model of Finite Automata

Input tape contains a string over the given input alphabet.

Read head is a pointer which reads one input symbol at a time and moves to the next symbol. Finite control contains set of states and a transition function to take an action based on current state and input symbol scanned.

Deterministic Finite Automata (DFA OR FA)

For every input symbol of alphabet there is an exactly one transition from every state of finite automata is called as DFA. The DFA covers transitions for all valid and invalid strings in the given regular language. For every valid string, DFA reaches to one of its final state and for every valid string it reaches to non-final state.

DFA

Deterministicfiniteautomaton(DFA)—alsoknownasdeterministicfinite state machine—is a finite state machine that accepts/rejects finite strings of symbols and only produces a unique computation (or run) of the automaton for each input string.

So a DFA is mathematically represented as a 5-uple

(Q, , , q 0, F)

- a finite set of states (Q)
- a finite set of input symbols called the alphabet ()
- a transition function (: Q ×   Q)

- a start state ($q0 \in Q$)
- a set of accept states ($F \subseteq Q$)

Compound FA

A finite-state machine (FSM) or finite-state automaton (plural: automata), or simply a state machine, is a mathematical model of computation used to design both computer programs and sequential logic circuits. It is conceived as an abstract machine that can be in one of a finite number of states. The machine is in only one state at a time; the state it is in at any given time is called the current state. It can change from one state to another when initiated by a triggering event or condition; this is called a transition. A particular FSM is defined by a list of its states, and the triggering condition for each transition.

The behavior of state machines can be observed in many devices in modern society which perform a predetermined sequence of actions depending on a sequence of events with which they are presented. Simple examples are vending machines which dispense products when the proper combination of coins is deposited, elevators which drop riders off at upper floors before going down, traffic lights which change sequence when cars are waiting, and combination locks which require the input of combination numbers in the proper order.

Finite-state machines can model a large number of problems, among which are electronic design automation, communication protocol design, language parsing and other engineering applications. In biology and artificial intelligence research, state machines or hierarchies of state machines have been used to describe neurological systems. In linguistics, they are used to describe simple parts of the grammars of natural languages.

NFA

Let Q be a finite set and let be a finite set of symbols. Also let be a function from $Q \times \Sigma$ to 2^Q, let q0 be a state in Q and let A be a subset of Q. We call the elements of Q a state, the transition function, q0 the initial state and A the set of accepting states.

Then a nondeterministic finite automaton is a 5-tuple < Q , Σ , q_0, δ , A >

NDFA

A nondeterministic finite automaton (NFA), or nondeterministic finite state machine, needn't obey these restrictions. In particular, every DFA is also an NFA.

Using the subset construction algorithm, each NFA can be translated to an equivalent DFA, i.e. a DFA recognizing the same formal language. Like DFAs, NFAs only recognize regular languages. Sometimes the term NFA is used in a narrower sense, meaning an automaton that properly violates an above restriction i.e. that is not a DFA.

NFAs were introduced in 1959 by Michael O. Rabin and Dana Scott, who also showed their equivalence to DFAs.

NFAs have been generalized in multiple ways, e.g., nondeterministic finite automaton with□-moves, pushdown automaton,□-automaton, and probabilistic automata.

Specification of NFA without Null Moves

They are converting NFA with□-moves to the NFA without□-null moves. I understand that if, there is a □-move between, qi and qj, then all edges from qj have to be repeated from qi. And if the qj is a final state, then qi will also be a final state.

But, if qj does not contain any transition, i.e., there are no edges starting from qj,.

EPSILON NFA (ε-NFA) or NFA

The ε = epsilon. It's just a food for thought. If example is needed consider a DFA that accepts substring 101 at the end of the string. Making a 4 state DFA. Can this model of DFA also be used as NFA and e-NFA

Specification of ε-NFA

It is clear from the diagram above that an NFA does have the same set of states as a DFA, which is the set Q. From this we can also see that there are also still the most important accepting states set, as well as the start state: q• and F.

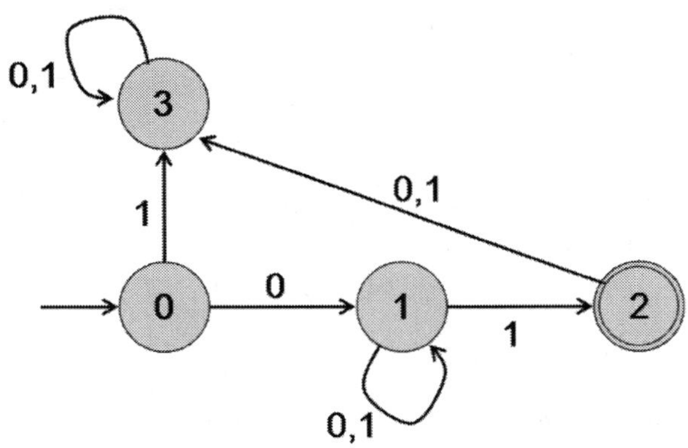

Regular Expressions

Regular languages are languages that can be generated from one-element languages by applying certain standard operations a finite number of times. They are the languages that can be recognized by finite automata. These simple operations include concatenation, union and kleen closure. By the use of these operations regular languages can be represented by an explicit formula.

Regular expressions can be thought of as the algebraic description of a regular language. Regular expression can be defined by the following rules:

- Every letter of the alphabet ∑ is a regular expression.
- Null string ▯ and empty set ▯ are regular expressions.
- If r1 and r2 are regular expressions, then(i) r1, r2(ii) r1r2 (concatenation of r1r2)(iii) r1 + r2 (union of r1 and r2)(iv) r1*, r2* (kleen closure of r1 and r2)are also regular expressions

- If a string can be derived from the rules 1, 2 and 3 then it is also a regular expression.

Equivalences of Languages (or Regular Languages)

Given two regular expressions R and S on an alphabet it is possible to decide their equivalence as follows:

- Build two finite automata MR and MS such that L(R) = L(MR) and L(S) = L(MS)
- BuildanautomatonMsuchthatL(M) = (L(MR) – L(MS)) ∪ (L(MS) – L(MR))
- Test emptiness of L(M) using a reachability algorithm on M

There is another way to decide equivalence. Suppose MR and MS are the minimal DFA (without epsilon-moves) such that L(R) = L(MR) and L(S) = L(MS). If they have a different number of states, then R and S are not equivalent. Otherwise let m be the number of states of the two automata. Isittruethat L(MR) = L(MS) iff $x \in L(MR) : |x| \leq m+1 = x \in L(MS) : |x| \leq m+1$? How to prove that with the Myhill-Nerode theorem?

Closer Properties of Regular Languages

Theregularlanguagesareclosedunderthevariousoperations,thatis,ifthe languages K and L are regular, so is the result of the following operations:

ThesettheoreticBooleanoperations: $K \cup L$, intersection $K \cup L$ and complement $\overline{L}$. from this also relative complement $K - L$ follows.

The regular operations: union $K \cup L$,, concatenation KoL, and Kleene star L^*

The trio operations: string homomorphism, inverse string homomorphism,andintersectionwithregularlanguages.Asaconsequence they are closed under arbitrary finite state transductions, like quotient K / L with a regular language. Even more, regular languages are closed underquotientswitharbitrarylanguages:IfLisregularthenL/Kisregular for any K.

The reverse (or mirror image) L^R

The collection of regular languages over an alphabet ▯ is defined recursively as follows:

- The empty language Ø is a regular language.
- For each a ∈ ▯ (a belongs to ▯), the singleton language {a} is a regular language.
- If A and B are regular languages, then A ∪ B (union), A • B (concatenation), and A* (Kleene star) are regular languages.
- No other languages over ▯ are regular.

Decision Properties of Regular Languages

Wewillconsidersomemoredecisionproblemsrelatedtoregularlanguages as given below.

- Given a FA M, is L(M) empty?
- Given a FAM, is L(M) infinite?
- GiventwoFAsM1andM2,dotheyacceptthesamelanguage?That is, whether L(M1)=L(M2)?

The list is not extensive. We will consider decision algorithm for the above mentioned problem only.

It is interesting to note that we can use the pumping lemma to determine whether the language accepted by a DFA is empty or infinite. The following theorem states this result.

Theorem: If M is a DFA with n states, than the language accepted by M (i.e. L(M)) is

- Non empty if, and only if, M accepts some string w with
- Infinite if, and only if, M accepts some string w such that

It is observed that using the decision algorithm for emptiness and finiteness together with closure properties we can find more decision algorithms. Here is an example.

Example: Given *DFA* s M_1 and M_2. Is $L(M_1) = L(M_2)$?

Solution: Observe that $L(M_1) \subseteq L(M_2)$ and $L(M_1) \cap \overline{L(M_2)} = \phi$

Thus $L(M_1) = L(M_2)$, iff $L(M_1) \subseteq L(M_2)$ and $L(M_2) \subseteq L(M_1)$ This implies that

$L(M_1) = L(M_2)$ *iff* $\left(L(M_1) \cap \overline{L(M_2)}\right) \cup \left(L(M_2) \cap \overline{L(M_1)}\right) = \phi$

Since regular languages are closed under union, intersection and complement, we can construct a *DFA* M_3recognizing the language $\left(L(M_1) \cap \overline{L(M_2)}\right) \cup \left(L(M_2) \cap \overline{L(M_1)}\right)$

If M_3 accepts any string (i.e. $L(M_3) \neq \phi$) then $L(M_1) \neq L(M_2)$) .Otherwise , $L(M_1) = L(M_2)$ (We can use emptiness algorithm to decide if $L(M_3) \neq \phi$)

Moore Machine

In the theory of computation, a Moore machine is a finite-state machine whose output values are determined solely by its current state. This is in contrast to a Mealy machine, whose output values are determined both by its current state and by the values of its inputs.

A Moore machine can be defined as a 6-tuple $(S, S_0, \Sigma, \Lambda, T, G)$ consisting of the following:

- A finite set of states' S
- A start state (also called initial state) S_0 which is an element of S
- A finite set called the input alphabet Σ
- A finite set called the output alphabet Λ
- A transition function $T : S \times \Sigma \rightarrow S$mapping a state and the input alphabet to the next state

An output function $G : S \rightarrow \Lambda$ mapping each state to the output alphabet

A Moore machine can be regarded as a restricted type of finite state transducer.

Mealy Machine

In a machine, the outputs are Function of the present's state and the value of the inputs as shown in figure:

According the outputs Change asynchronously in response to any Change in the output.

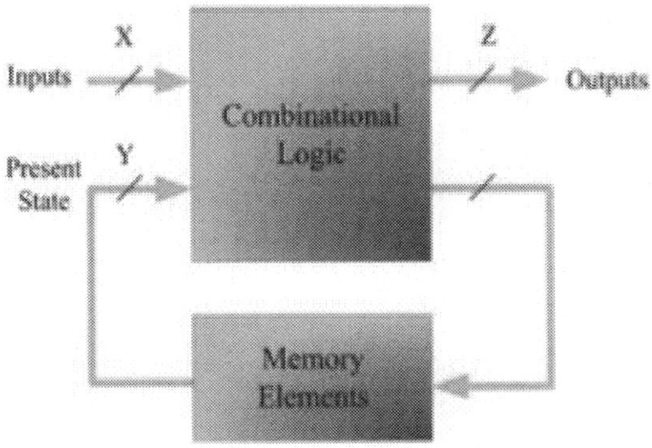

A combinational logic block maps the input at current state into the necessary flip-flop inputs to store appropriate next state just like mealy machine.

2 Pushdown Automata and CFLs

Context-free Grammar

A context-free grammar G is a quadruple (!, ▯,#, $), where

- V is an alphabet
- ▯ (the set of terminals) is a subset of V, its elements represented by lowercase letters
- R (the set of production rules, or just rules) is a finite subset of (V – ▯) × V*
- S (the start symbol) is an element of V – ▯.

Ambiguous Grammars

No ambiguous grammar is LR. Nonetheless, ambiguous grammars are often used in LR parsing.

For instance, compare

$$E \rightarrow E + E \,|\, E * E \,|\, (E)a$$

Unambiguous Grammar

The equivalent unambiguous grammar

$E \to E + T \mid T$

$T \to T * F \mid F$

$F \to (E) \mid a$

Inherently Ambiguous Context Free Languages

A CFG is ambiguous if one or more terminal strings have multiple leftmost derivations from the start symbol. A CFL L is inherently ambiguous if every CFG for L is ambiguous.

$$S \underset{lm}{\Rightarrow} AS \underset{lm}{\Rightarrow} 0A11S \underset{lm}{\Rightarrow} 00111S \underset{lm}{\Rightarrow} 00111$$

Reduced CFG (non-redundant CFG)

There are several ways in which context-free grammars can be simplified.

Consider the CFG G with rules

S □ aBC, B □ b|Cb, C □ c|cC, D □ d

In the grammar with rules

S □ aB, B □ b|BD|cC, C □ cC, D □ d

The symbol C cannot derive a string of terminals. So it and all rules that contain it may be eliminated to get just

S □ aB, B □ b|BD, D □ d

Normal Forms for CFG's

It is often convenient to simplify CFG

$A \to BC \; or$

$A \to a \; or$

$S \to \varepsilon,$

Where A, B and C are nonterminal symbols, *a* is a terminal symbol

A formal grammar is in **Chomsky reduced form** if all of its production rules are of the form:

$A \rightarrow BC$ *or*

$A \rightarrow a,$

- We will see that the algorithm requires the grammar be converted to Chomsky Normal Form.
- A context-free grammar is in Chomsky Normal Form if each rule has one of these forms:

  X □ a

  X □ YZ
- That is, the right-hand side is either a single terminal or two non-terminals.

Greibach Normal Form

A CFG G = (V, T, R, S) is said to be in GNF if every production is of the form A □ a□, where a ∈ T and □ ∈ V*, i.e., □ is a string of zero or more variables.

$$A \rightarrow aA_1A_2......A_n$$

or

$$S \rightarrow \varepsilon$$

Pushdown Automata

A (not necessarily deterministic) PDA*M* can be defined as:

The following is the formal description of the PDA which recognizes the language $\{0^n1^n \mid n \geq 0\}$ by final state:

PDA for $\{0^n1^n \mid n \geq 0\}$ (by final state)

$M = (Q, \Sigma, \Gamma, \delta, p, Z, F)$, where

states: $M = \{p, q, r\}$

input alphabet: $\Sigma = \{0,1\}$

stack alphabet: $\Gamma = \{A, Z\}$

start state: $q_0 = p$

start stack symbol: Z

accepting states: $F = \{r\}$

The transition relation δ consists of the following six instructions:

$(p,0,Z,p,AZ)$, $(p,0,A,p,AA)$, (p,ε,Z,q,Z), (p,ε,A,q,A), $(q,1,A,q,\varepsilon)$, and (q,ε,Z,r,Z).

$$\delta : \left(Q \times \left(\Sigma U \{\varepsilon\}\right) \times \Gamma\right) \rightarrow P\left(Q \times \Gamma^*\right)$$

Acceptance Mechanisms

- Acceptance by final state (university mechanisms)
- Acceptance by empty stack (local mechanisms)
- Acceptance by empty stack and final stack

CFL = PDA by empty stack = PDA final state = PDA by empty stack and final state = CFG

Operation

The operations on push down automata are as follows:

PUSH: Some finite sequence of symbol is pushed into the stack

POP: One symbol at the top of the stack is pooped

BIPASS: do nothing stack contain unchanged while state may be changed

Replace: Replace one symbol at the top of the stack.

Specification

PDA= (Q, Σ, ∞, $q_{0,}$ Z_0 F) etc.

Q is a finite set of states

Σ is a finite set which is called the input alphabet

Γ is a finite set which is called the stack alphabet

δ is a finite subset of $Q \times (\Sigma U \{\varepsilon\}) \times \Gamma \times Q \times \Gamma^*$, the transition relation.

$q_0 \in Q$ is the start state

$Z \in \Gamma$ is the initial stack symbol

$F \subseteq Q$ is the set of accepting states

3 Recursively Enumerable Sets & Turing Machine

Conceptually a Turing machine, like finite automata, consists of a finite control and a tape. At any time it is in one of the finite number of states. The tape has the left end but it extends infinitely to the right. It is also divided into squares and a symbol can be written in each square. However, unlike finite automata, its head is a read-write head and it can move left, right or stay at the same square after a read or write.

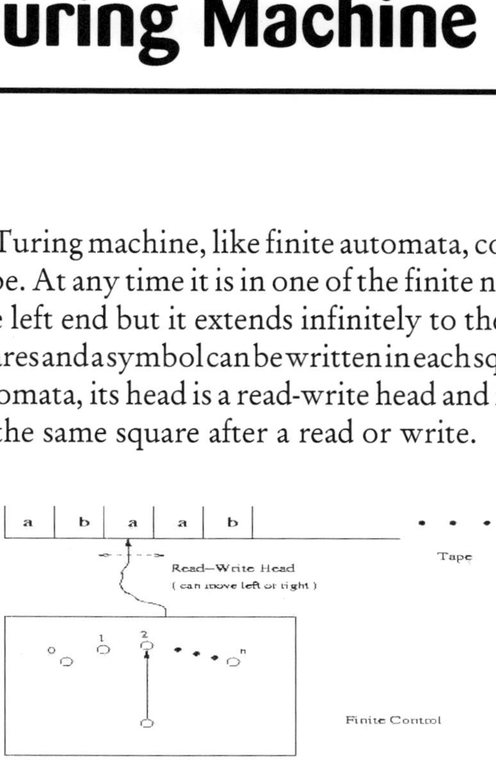

Turing Machine

Given a string of symbols on the tape, a Turing machine starts at the initial state. At any state it reads the symbol under the head either erases it or replaces it with a symbol (possibly the same symbol).

Specification

The Turing machine can be represented as a 7 tuples as follow.

M = ______

Q= Set of states.

Σ = Input alphabet.

Γ = Tape alphabet.

δ = Transititon function; for DTM M $\delta\, Q x \Gamma \rightarrow Q x \Gamma x$ (L.R)

B= Blank Symbl.

F= final States.F $\subseteq Q$

Closure Properties

Recursive languages are closed under the following operations. That is, if L and P are two recursive languages, then the following languages are recursive as well:

- The Kleene star L^*
- The image ▯(L) under an e-free homomorphism ▯
- The concatenation L o P
- The union $L \cup P$

The intersection $L \cap P$

The complement of L

The set difference $L - P$

The last property follows from the fact that the set difference can be expressed in terms of intersection and complement.

Recursive languages

There are two equivalent major definitions for the concept of a recursive language:

- A recursive formal language is a recursive subset in the set of all possible worlds over the alphabet of the language.
- A recursive language is a formal language for which there exists a Turing machine that, when presented with any finite input string, halts and accept if the string is in the language, and halts and rejects otherwise. The turing machine always halts: it is known as a decider and is said to decide the recursive language.

Closure Properties recursive Enumerable languages

If L, L_1 and L_2 are recursively enumerable languages, then so are $L_1 \cup L_2$, L_1L_2, L∗ and L_1 ▯ L_2.

Proof: We consider the concatenation case as an example. Since L_1 and L_2 are recursively enumerable, there are programs pr_1 and pr_2 such that, for all w ∈ Str, w ∈ L_1 iff eval(app(pr 1, str(w))) = norm(const(true)), and for all w ∈ Str, w ∈ L_2 iff eval(app(pr_2, str(w))) = norm(const(true)). (Remember that pr_1 and pr_2 may fail to terminate on some inputs.) To show that L_1L_2 is recursively enumerable, we will construct a program pr such that, for all w ∈ Str, w ∈ L_1L_2 iff eval(app(pr, str(w))) = norm(const(true)).

4 Undecidability

- Does machine M have three states?
- Is starting W a Binary number?
- Does DFA M accept any input?

The Turing machine that decided (solves) a problem answer YES or NO for each instant of the problem.

Formal Languages

1. An alphabet is a finite set of characters, denoted by the Greek symbol ▯ (sigma)

   The alphabet can be the ASCII set, a subset of ASCII, or so ASCII
2. A string over some alphabet is a sequence of symbols drawn from the alphabet

   Example: 01001 is string over the alphabet {0,1}

   The empty or null string ▯ is a special string of length zero

   When ▯ is concatenated with any string s yields s. That is, s▯ = ▯s = s

3. A formal language is a set of strings (possibly infinite) over some alphabet

   Just a set of strings. No specific relationship with a programming language.

   Example: L = {00, 01, 10, 11} is the set of all 2-character strings over ▯ = {0,1}

4. The concatenation of two languages L_1 and L_2 (sets of strings) is:

- ObtainedbyconcatenatingeverystringinL_1witheverystringinL_2
- $L = L_1 L_2 = \{s = s_1 s_2 \mid s_1 \in L_1$ and $s2 \in L_2\}$
- L_1 = {▯, 0, 00}, L_2 = {▯, 1, 11}, $L = L_1 L_2$ = {▯, 1, 11, 0, 01, 011, 00, 001, 0011}

Decidability

In computability theory and computational complexity theory, an undecidable problem is a decision problem for which it is known to be impossible to construct a single algorithm that always leads to a correct yes-or-no answer.

Adecisionproblemisanyarbitraryyes-or-noquestiononaninfiniteset of inputs. Because of this, it is traditional to define the decision problem equivalentlyasthesetofinputsforwhichtheproblemreturnsyes. These inputs can be natural numbers, but also other values of some other kind, such as strings of a formal language. Using some encoding, such as a Gödel numbering, the strings can be encoded as natural numbers. Thus, a decision problem informally phrased in terms of a formal language is alsoequivalent to a set of natural numbers. To keep the formal definition simple, it is phrased in terms of subsets of the natural numbers.

How Many Numbers are there?

But which infinity?! We shall soon be able to conclude that there is more than one kind of infinity. The infinity corresponding to the number of real numbers is much, much greater than the infinity corresponding to the number of integers. To show that two sets have the same number of elements, we need to show that for every element in one set, there is a unique element in the other set, and vice versa. That is, there exists a one-one correspondence between the elements of the two sets. If we can show that no such one-one correspondence exists, then the 2 sets have different number of elements. Technically, we say that the 2 sets have different cardinalities.

To see that the set of integers and the set of real numbers have different cardinalities, assume for the time being that they have the same cardinality. This means that for every real number, there is a unique integer. Then, we can speak of something like the 1st real number, 2nd real number, and so on. Let us list out all the real numbers as in the diagram that follows. We will list out only the real numbers between 0 and 1.

Relationship with Gödel's incompleteness Theorem

The concepts raised by Gödel's incompleteness theorems are very similar to those raised by the halting problem, and the proofs are quite similar. In fact, a weaker form of the First Incompleteness Theorem is an easy consequence of the undesirability of the halting problem. This weaker form differs from the standard statement of the incompleteness theorem by asserting that a complete, consistent and sound axiomatization of all statements about natural numbers is unachievable. The "sound" part is the weakening: it means that we require the axiomatic system in question to prove only true statements about natural numbers. It is important to observe that the statement of the standard form of Gödel's First Incompleteness Theorem is completely unconcerned with the question of truth, but only concerns the issue of whether it can be proven.

The weaker form of the theorem can be proved from the undesirability of the halting problem as follows. Assume that we have a consistent and complete axiomatization of all true first-order logic statements about natural numbers. Then we can build an algorithm that enumerates all these statements. This means that there is an algorithm N(n) that, given a natural number n, computes a true first-order logic statement about natural numbers such that, for all the true statements, there is at least one n such that N(n) yields that statement. Now suppose we want to decide if the algorithm with representation a halts on input i. We know that this statement can be expressed with a first-order logic statement, say H(a, i).

Since the axiomatization is complete it follows that either there is an n such that N(n) = H(a, i) or there is an n' such that N(n') = ¬ H(a, i). So if we iterate over all n until we either find H(a, i) or its negation, we will always halt. This means that this gives us an algorithm to decide the halting problem. Since we know that there cannot be such an algorithm, it follows that the assumption that there is a consistent and complete axiomatization of all true first-order logic statements about natural numbers must be false.

There are two distinct senses of the word "un-decidable" in contemporary use. The first of these is the sense used in relation to Gödel's theorems, that of a statement being neither provable nor refutable in a specified deductive system. The second sense is used in relation to computability theory and applies not to statements but to decision problems, which countable infinite sets are of questions each requiring a yes or no answer. Such a problem is said to be undesirable if there is no computable function that correctly answers every question in the problem set. The connection between these two is that if a decision problem is undecidable (in the recursion theoretical sense) then there is no consistent, effective formal system which proves for every question A in the problem either "the answer to A is yes" or "the answer to A is no".

A Handbook on Computer Science

7

Compiler Design

CONTENTS

1 Lexical Analysis

A compiler is a special type of computer program that translates a human readable text file into a form that the computer can more easily understand. It takes as input a source program typically written in a high-level language and produces an equivalent target program typically in assembly or machine language.

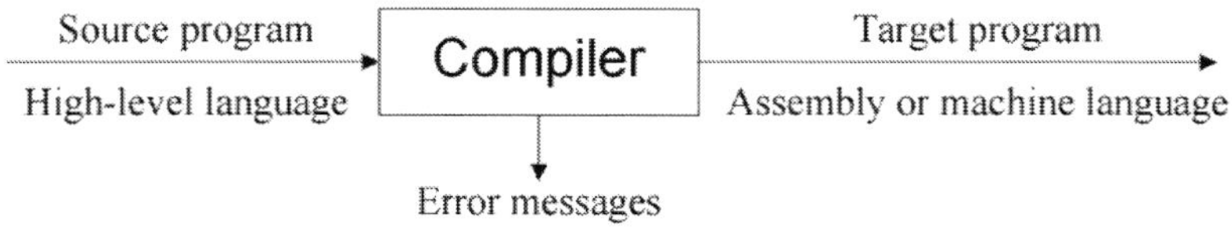

Cross Complier

A compiler that runs on one computer but produces object code for a different type of computer. Cross compilers are used to generate software that can run on computers with a new architecture or on special-purpose devices that cannot host their own compilers.

Complier Parts

Complier have two major parts these are given as follows:

- Analysis Phase
  Lexical analysis
  Syntax analysis
  Semantic analysis
- Synthesis Phase
  Intermediate Code Generation
  Code Optimizer
  Code Generation

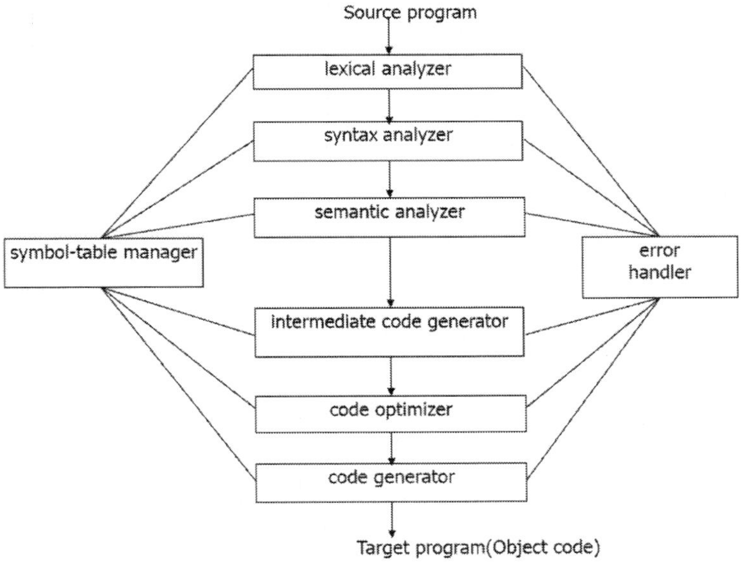

Language Processing System

Language processing system shown as follows:

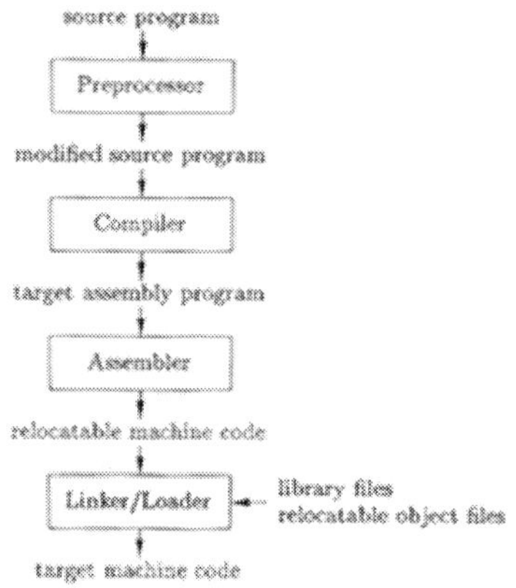

Lexical Analysis

Lexical analysis is the first phase of a compiler. It takes the modified source code from language preprocessors that are written in the form of sentences. The lexical analyzer breaks these syntaxes into a series of tokens, by removing any whitespace or comments in the source code.

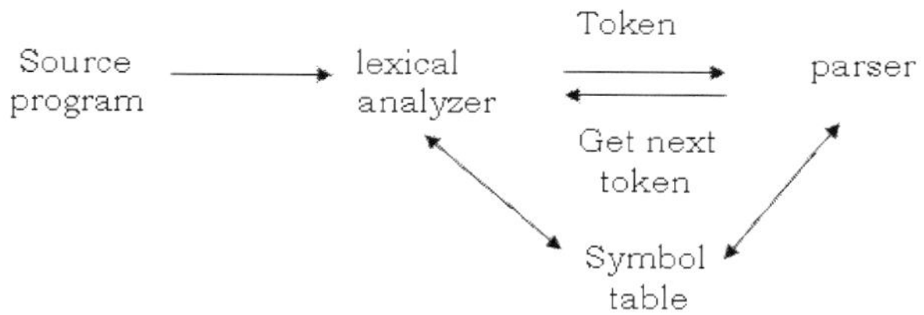

- Input to Lexical Analyzer is "Source Code"
- LexicalAnalysisIdentifiesDifferentLexicalUnitsinaSourceCode.
- Different Lexical Classes or Tokens or Lexemes like Identifiers, Constants, Keywords and Operators
- Lexical Analyzer is also called "Linear Phase" or "Linear Analysis" or "Scanning"
- Individual Token is also Called Lexeme
- Lexical Analyzer's Output is given to Syntax Analysis.

2 Parsing

Parsing or syntax analysis is the second phase of a compiler. The output of lexical analyser is used to create a representation which shows the grammaticalstructureofthetokens. Thesyntaxofprogramminglanguage is described by a context free grammer.

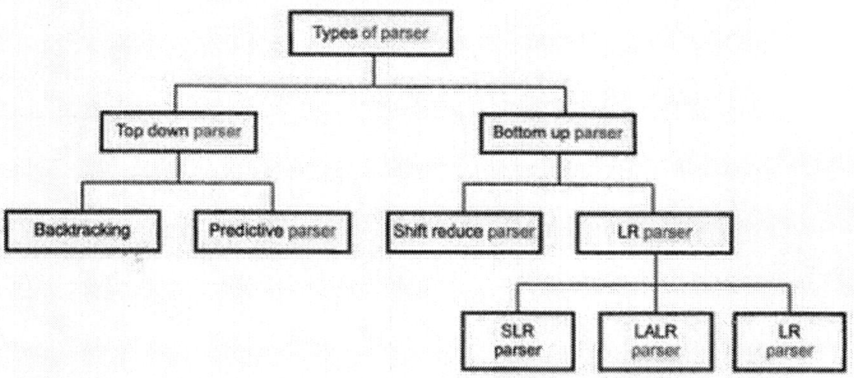

Ambiguous Grammar

A context-free grammar is said to be an ambiguous grammar if there exists a string which can be generated by the grammar in more than one way. It is inherently ambiguous if all context-free grammars generating that language are ambiguous.

Left Recursion

A grammar is left-recursive if there exists a non-terminal symbol A that can derive to a sentential form with itself as the left-most symbol. The grammer: A = > A□ | □isleftrecursive. Topdownparsingtechniquecannot handleleftrecursivegrammers, soweconvertleftrecursivegrammersinto right recursive.

Left Recursive Elimination

$$\text{Left recursive: } A \rightarrow A\alpha \mid \beta \;=>\; \begin{array}{l} A \rightarrow \beta A' \\ A \rightarrow \alpha A \mid \varepsilon. \end{array}$$

Problem with the left recursive grammer is that if such a grammer is used by top down parser, then there is danger of going into infinite loop while string is parsing.

Left Factoring

If more than one grammar production rules has a common prefix string, then the top-down parser cannot make a choice as to which of the production it should take to parse the string in hand.

$$A \rightarrow \alpha\beta_1 \mid \alpha\beta_2 \;=>\; \begin{array}{l} A \rightarrow \alpha A' \\ A \rightarrow \beta_1 \mid \beta_2 \end{array}$$

Parsers

Top-down Parsing

When the parser starts constructing the parse tree from the start symbol and then tries to transform the start symbol to the input, it is called top-down parsing.

Bottom-up Parsing

Bottom-up parsing starts from the leaf nodes of a tree and works in upward direction till it reaches the root node.

Top-down Parsing

Recursive Descent Parsing

It is a common form of top-down parsing. It is called recursive as it uses recursive procedures to process the input. Recursive descent parsing suffers from backtracking.

Predictive Parser

Predictive parser is a recursive descent parser, which has the capability to predict which production is to be used to replace the input string. The predictive parser does not suffer from backtracking.

LL (1) Parse/ Predictive Parser

LL parser is a top-down parser for a subset of context-free languages. LL grammar can be implemented by means of both algorithms namely, recursive-descent or table-driven.

LL parser is denoted as LL (k). The first L in LL (k) is parsing the input from left to right, the second L in LL (k) stands for left-most derivation and k itself represents the number of look aheads. Generally k = 1, so LL (k) may also be written as LL (1).

Configuration of LL (1) Parser

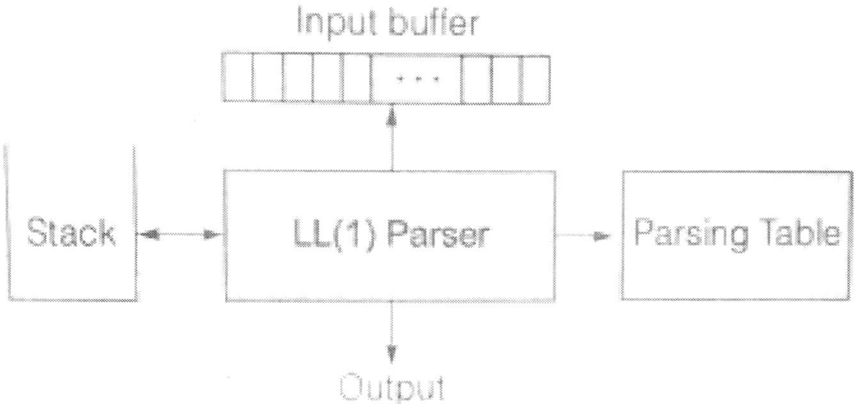

Configuration of LL(1) Parser

LL (1) Parsing Table Configuration

Constructing LL (1) parsing tables using the following algorithm:
For every production $A \rightarrow \alpha$ in the grammar:

1. If α can derive a string starting with *a* i.e., for all *a* in FIRST (α),

   Table [A, *a*] = $A \rightarrow \alpha$
2. If α can derive the empty string ε, then, for all *b* that can follow a string derived from A i.e., for all *b* in FOLLOW (A),

   Table [A, *b*] = $A \rightarrow \alpha$

LL (1) Grammar

LL grammar is a formal grammar that can be parsed by an LL parser. A context-free grammar whose predict sets are always disjoint is said to be LL (1). LL (1) grammars are ideally suited for top-down parsing because it is always possible to correctly predict the expansion of any nonterminal.

Bottom-up Parsing

Bottom up parsers start from the sequence of terminal symbols and work their way back up to the start symbol by repeatedly replacing grammar rules' right hand sides by the corresponding non-terminal. This is the reverse of the derivation process, and is called reduction.

Handle

The part of the input string that matches with RHS of any production is called as handle.

Handle Pruning

A rightmost derivation in reverse can be obtained by handle pruning.

If w is a sentence of the grammar at hand, then w = □n, where □n is the nth right-sentential form of some as yet unknown rightmost derivation.

S = □0 => □1... => □n-1 => □n = w

Shift Reduce Parsing

Shift-reduce parsing attempts to construct a parse tree for an input string beginning at the leaves and working up towards the root.

Shift-reduce parsing uses two unique steps for bottom-up parsing. These steps are known as shift-step and reduce-step.

- *Shift step*: The shift step refers to the advancement of the input pointer to the next input symbol, which is called the shifted symbol. This symbol is pushed onto the stack. The shifted symbol is treated as a single node of the parse tree.
- *Reduce step*: When the parser finds a complete grammar rule (RHS) and replaces it to (LHS), it is known as reduce-step. This occurs when the top of the stack contains a handle. To reduce, a POP function is performed on the stack which pops off the handle and replaces it with LHS non-terminal symbol.

LR Parser

The LR parser is a non-recursive, shift-reduce, bottom-up parser. It uses a wide class of context-free grammar which makes it the most efficient syntax analysis technique. LR parsers are also known as LR(k) parsers, where L stands for left-to-right scanning of the input stream; R stands for the construction of right-most derivation in reverse, and k denotes the number of look ahead symbols to make decisions.

LR (0) Parser

A LR (0) parser of a grammar G is a production of G with a dot at some position of the right side. Thus, production A XYZ yields the four items

A.XYZ

AX.YZ

AXY.Z

AXYZ.

Simple LR Parser

- Works on smallest class of grammar
- Few number of states, hence very small table
- Simple and fast construction

LR (1) Parser

- Works on complete set of LR (1) Grammar
- Generates large table and large number of states
- Slow construction

Canonical LR (1) or LR (1) Parser

Canonical LR (1) parser or LR (1) parser is an LR (k) parser for k = 1, i.e. with a single look ahead terminal. The special attribute of this parser is that all LR (k) parsers with k > 1 can be transformed into a LR (1) parser. It can handle all deterministic context-free languages. In the past this LR (k) parser has been avoided because of its huge memory requirements in favor of less powerful alternatives such as the LALR and the LL (1) parser.

Look ahead LR (1) Parser

(i) It is constructed from CLR (1), if two states are having same production but may contain different look ahead, those two states of CLR(1) are combined into a single states in LALR(1).

(ii) There is no chance of SR conflict but there may be change for RR conflicts in LALR (1) after combining the states of CLR (1) parser.

(iii) Conflicts in CLR (1) and LALR(1)

(a). SR conflict:

A□□. X□, a

B□□., x | y

(b). RR conflict:

A□□.,a | t_1

B□□., a | t_2

(iv). Every LALR(1) grammar is CLR (1) grammar need not be LALR (1).

(v). LALR (1) parser are often used in practice as parsing tables are smaller then CLR (1) parsing.

Parsers Comparison

- OPP < LL(1) < LR(0) < SLR(1) ≤ LALR(1) ≤ CLR(1)
- Numberofstates (SLR(1) = Numberofstates (LALR(1) ≤ Number of states(CLR(1)))

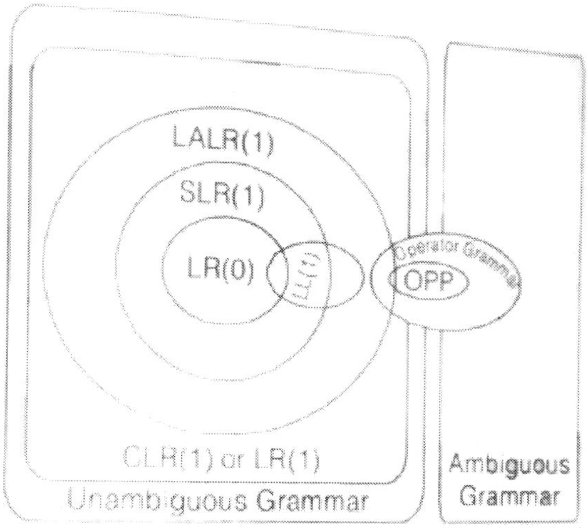

LR(0) ⊂ SLR(0) ⊂ LALR(1) ⊂ LR(1)

LL(1) ⊂ LALR(1) ⊂ CLR(1)

3 Syntax Directed Translation

Syntax-directed translation (SDT) is a method of translating a string into a sequence of actions by attaching one such action to each rule of a grammar. Thus, parsing a string of the grammar produces a sequence of rule applications. SDT provides a simple way to attach semantics to any such syntax.

Parse tree □ SDT □ Annotated parse tree

Example

S□AB	{print (*)}
A□ a	{print (1)}
B□ S	{print (2)}

Types of Attributes

Synthesized Attributes

These attributes get values from the attribute values of their child nodes.

To illustrate, assume the following production:

S □ ABC

If S is taking values from its child nodes (A, B, C), then it is said to be a synthesized attribute, as the values of ABC are synthesized to S.

Inherited Attributes

In contrast to synthesized attributes, inherited attributes can take values from parent and/or siblings. As in the following production,

S ABC

A can get values from S, B and C. B can take values from S, A, and C. Likewise, C can take values from S, A, and B.

Syntax-Directed Definitions

A syntax-directed definition (SDD) is a context-free grammar together with attributes and rules. Attributes are associated with grammar symbols and rules are associated with productions.

S- Attributed SSD

- S-Attributed grammars allow only synthesized attributes
- Semantic action can be placed at right end of the rule
- Follows bottom up approach

  ABC {A. i = f (B. i or C. i)}

L- attributed SSD

- SDT in which attributes are synthesized or restricted to inherit either from 'parent' or 'left siblings',
- Follows DFS and top down approach

Example

A BCD {C. i = f (A. i or B. i)} or {D. i = f (A. i or B. i or C. i)} or {B. i = f (A. i)}

- Every S- attributed SDT is L- attributed SDT.
- Every L- attributed SDT need not be S- attributed SDT.
- SDT follows depth first search notation.

4 Runtime Environment

A program needs memory resources to execute instructions. A program contains names for procedures, identifiers etc., that require mapping with the actual memory location at runtime. Runtime environment is a state of the target machine, which may include software libraries, environment variables, etc., to provide services to the processes running in the system. Runtime support system is a package, mostly generated with the executable program itself and facilitates the process communication between the process and the runtime environment.

Run-time Storage Organization

The machine code of the program is typically located at the lowest part of the layout. Then, after the code, there is a section to keep all the fixed size static data in the program. The dynamically allocated data as well as the static data without a fixed size are created and kept in the heap. The heap grows from low to high addresses.

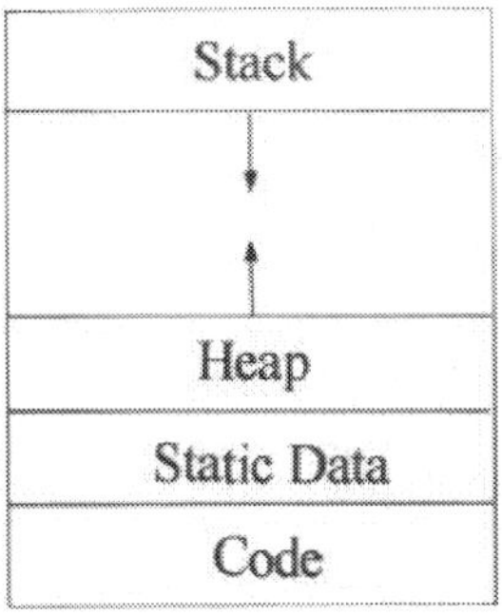

Types of Runtime Environment

Fully Static Runtime Environment

In static runtime environment, the data is stored in fixed memory location during the execution of program. The language that uses static environment will not have the concept of pointer variables and no dynamic memory allocation. They also cannot have recursive functions. All the variables are allocated statically and the location of activation record is also fixed before execution.

Stack based Runtime Environment

The machine that supports for stack allocation for runtime management stores the activation for procedure call in stack rather than static location. This kind of allocation is efficient with the languages that support recursion. Every procedure may have different activation records on the call stack at any time.

Stack based environment requires three pointer

- Pointer to current activation record to access local variables. This pointer is called as current activation pointer (CAP)
- Pointer to previous (caller) activation record (control link)
- Stack pointer (SP) which pointes to top of the stack.

Fully Dynamic Runtime Environment

Functional language such as Lisp, ML etc. uses this style of call stack management. Sailently, here activation records are de-allocated only when all references to them have disappeared and this requires that activation records to dynamically freed at arbitrary times during execution. Memory manager is needed.

The data structure that handles such a management is heap and thus this is also called as heap management.

Activation Records

- The information needed to manage one procedure activation is called an activation record (AR) or frame.
- An activation record is allocated when a procedure is entered and it is deallocated when that procedure is exited.
- It contains temporary data, local data, machine status, optional access link, optional control link, actual parameters and returned value.

Return value
actual parameters
optional control link
optional access link
machine status
local variables
temporaries

5 Intermediate Target Code Generation and Cod Optimization

Intermediate Code

A source code can directly be translated into its target machine code, then why at all we need to translate the source code into an intermediate code which is then translated to its target code? Let us see the reasons why we need an intermediate code.

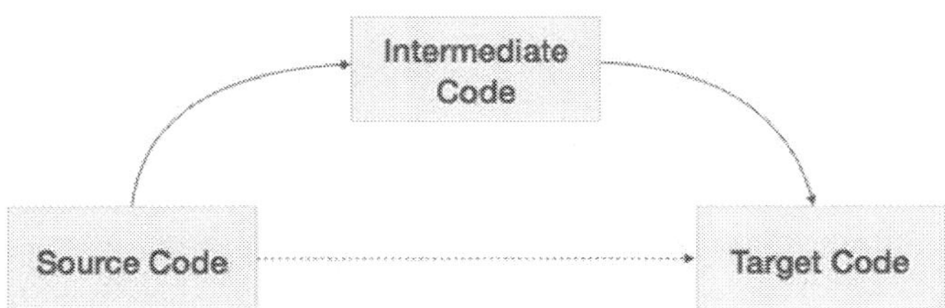

- If a compiler translates the source language to its target machine language without having the option for generating intermediate code, then for each new machine, a full native compiler is required.
- Keeping the analysis portion same for all the compilers.
- The second part of compiler, synthesis, is changed according to the target machine.

- It becomes easier to apply the source code modifications to improve code performance by applying code optimization techniques on the intermediate code.

Intermediate Representation

Intermediate codes can be represented in a variety of ways and they have their own benefits.

- *High Level IR*: High-level intermediate code representation is very close to the source language itself. They can be easily generated from the source code and we can easily apply code modifications to enhance performance. But for target machine optimization, it is less preferred.
- *Low Level IR:* This one is close to the target machine, which makes it suitable for register and memory allocation, instruction set selection, etc. It is good for machine-dependent optimizations.

Intermediate code can be either language specific (e.g., Byte Code for Java) or language independent (three-address code).

Need for Intermediate Code Generation

- Suppose we have n-source languages and m-target languages:
  Without intermediate code
  With intermediate code
- Re-targeting is facilitated; a compiler for a different machine can be created by attaching a back-end for the new machine to an existing front-end.
- A machine independent cod-optimizer can be applied to the intermediate code.
- Intermediate code is simple enough to be easily converted to any target code.
- Complex enough to represent all the complex structure of high level languages

Code Generator

A code generator is expected to have an understanding of the target machine's runtime environment and its instruction set. The code generator should take the following things into consideration to generate the code:

Target language: The code generator has to be aware of the nature of the target language for which the code is to be transformed. That language may facilitate some machine-specific instructions to help the compiler generate the code in a more convenient way.

IR type: Intermediate representation has various forms. It can be in Abstract Syntax Tree (AST) structure, Reverse Polish Notation, or 3-address code.

Selection of instruction: The code generator takes Intermediate Representation as input and converts (maps) it into target machine's instruction set.

Register allocation: Code generator decides what values to keep in the registers. Also, it decides the registers to be used to keep these values.

Ordering of Instructions: At last, the code generator decides the order in which the instruction will be executed.

Code Optimization

Code optimization is a set of methods of code modification to improve code quality and efficiency. A program may be optimized so that it becomes of a smaller size, consumes less memory, executes more rapidly, or performs fewer input/output operations.

The basic requirement optimization methods should comply with is that an optimized program must have the same output and side effects as its non-optimized version. This requirement, however, may be ignored in case the benefit from optimization is estimated to be more important than probable consequences of a change in the program behavior.

In optimization, high-level general programming constructs are replaced by very efficient low-level programming codes. A code optimizing process must follow the three rules given below:

- The output code must not, in any way, change the meaning of the program.
- Optimization should increase the speed of the program and if possible, the program should demand less number of resources.
- Optimization should itself be fast and should not delay the overall compiling process.

Machine Independent Optimizations

Not all optimization techniques are machine-independent. When code is modified to make it more efficient on a particular machine, a machine-dependent optimization is being performed. Machine-dependent optimization uses information about the limits and special features of the target machine to produce code which is shorter or which executes more quickly on the machine.

Loop Optimization

In compiler theory, loop optimization is the process of the increasing execution speed and reducing the overheads associated of loops. It plays an important role in improving cache performance and making effective use of parallel processing capabilities.

Constant Folding

Constant folding is a relatively easy optimization. Programmers generally do not write expressions such as (3 + 5) directly, but these expressions are relatively common after macro expansion and other optimizations such as constant propagation.

Constant Propagation

Constants assigned to a variable can be propagated through the flow graph and substituted at the use of the variable.

Example:

In the code fragment below, the value of x can be propagated to the use of x.

```
x = 3;
y = x + 4;
```

Below is the code fragment after constant propagation and constant folding.

```
x = 3;
y = 7;
```

Some compilers perform constant propagation within basic blocks; some compilers perform constant propagation in more complex control flow.

Some compilers perform constant propagation for integer constants, but not floating-point constants.

Few compilers perform constant propagation through bit field assignments.

Few compilers perform constant propagation for address constants through pointer assignments.

Copy Propagation

In compiler theory, copy propagation is the process of replacing the occurrences of targets of direct assignments with their values. A direct assignment is an instruction of the form x = y, which simply assigns the value of y to x.

From the following code:

```
y = x
z = 3 + y
```

Copy propagation would yield:

```
z = 3 + x
```

Copy propagation often makes use of reaching definitions, use-def. chains and def-use chains when computing which occurrences of the target may be safely replaced. If all upwards exposed uses of the target may be safely modified, the assignment operation may be eliminated.

Copy propagation is a useful "clean up" optimization frequently used after other optimizations have already been run.

Dead Code Elimination

In compiler theory, dead code elimination is a compiler optimization to remove code which does not affect the program results. Removing such code has two benefits: it shrinks program size, an important consideration in some contexts, and it allows the running program to avoid executing irrelevant operations, which reduces its running time. Dead code includes code that can never be executed (unreachable code), and code that only affects dead variables, that is, variables that are irrelevant to the program.

Induction Variable

An induction variable is a variable that gets increased or decreased by a fixed amount on every iteration of a loop, or is a linear function of another induction variable.

For example, in the following loop, i and j are induction variables:

```
for (i=0; i < 10; ++i) {
j = 17 * i;
}
```

A common compiler optimization is to recognize the existence of induction variables and replace them with simpler computations; for example, the code above could be rewritten by the compiler as follows, on the assumption that the addition of a constant will be cheaper than a multiplication.

Strength Reduction

Strength reduction is a compiler optimization where expensive operations are replaced with equivalent but less expensive operations. The classic example of strength reduction converts "strong" multiplications inside a loop into "weaker" additions – something that frequently occurs in array addressing.

Examples of strength reduction include:

- replacing a multiplication within a loop with an addition
- replacing an exponentiation within a loop with a multiplication

Directed Acyclic Graph

Directed Acyclic Graph (DAG) is a tool that depicts the structure of basic blocks, helps to see the flow of values flowing among the basic blocks, and offers optimization too. DAG provides easy transformation on basic blocks. DAG can be understood here:

- Leaf nodes represent identifiers, names or constants.
- Interior nodes represent operators.
- Interior nodes also represent the results of expressions or the identifiers/name where the values are to be stored or assigned.

Example

- $t_0 = a + b$
- $t_1 = t_0 + c$
- $d = t_0 + t_1$

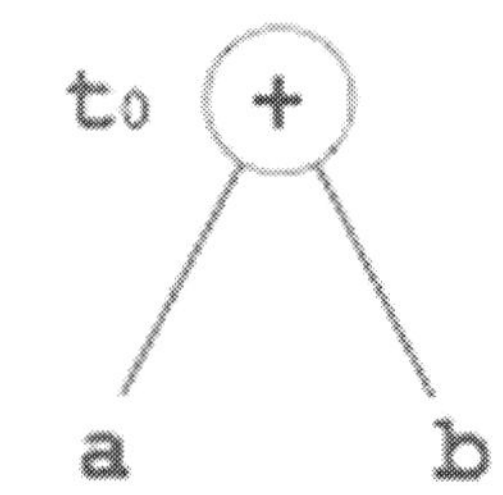

$[t_0 = a + b]$

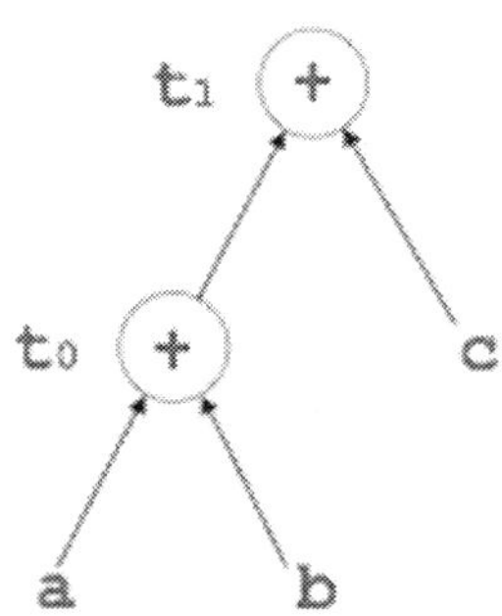

$[t_1 = t_0 + c]$

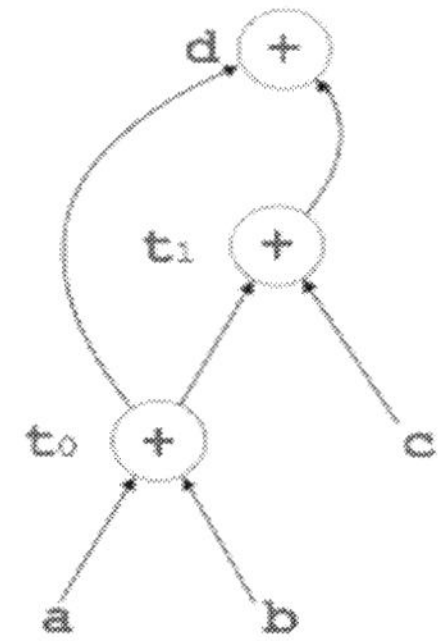

$[d = t_0 + t_1]$

A Handbook on Computer Science

8

Operating System

CONTENTS

1 Processes and Threads

The 1960's definition of an operating system is "the software that controls the hardware". However, today, due to microcode we need a better definition. We see an operating system as the programs that make the hardware useable. In brief, an operating system is the set of programs that controls a computer. Some examples of operating systems are UNIX, Mach, MS-DOS, MS-Windows, Windows/NT, Chicago, OS/2, MacOS, VMS, MVS, and VM.

Controlling the computer involves software at several levels. We will differentiate kernel services, library services, and application-level services, all of which are part of the operating system. Processes run Applications, which are linked together with libraries that perform standard services. The kernel supports the processes by providing a path to the peripheral devices. The kernel responds to service calls from the processes and interrupts from the devices. The core of the operating system is the kernel, a control program that functions in privileged state (an execution context that allows all hardware instructions to be executed), reacting to interrupts from external devices and to service requests and traps from processes. Generally, the kernel is a permanent resident of the computer. It creates and terminates processes and responds to their request for service.

Operating Systems are resource managers. The main resource is computer hardware in the form of processors, storage, input/output devices, communication devices, and data. Some of the operating system functions are: implementing the user interface, sharing hardware among users, allowing users to share data among themselves, preventing users from interfering with one another, scheduling resources among users, facilitating input/output, recovering from errors, accounting for resource usage, facilitating parallel operations, organizing data for secure and rapid access, and handling network communications.

Objectives of Operating Systems

Modern Operating systems generally have following three major goals. Operating systems generally accomplish these goals by running processes in low privilege and providing service calls that invoke the operating system kernel in high-privilege state.

- To hide details of hardware by creating abstraction
- An abstraction is software that hides lower level details and provides a set of higher-level functions. An operating system transforms the physical world of devices, instructions, memory, and time into virtual world that is the result of abstractions built by the operating system. There are several reasons for abstraction.
- First, the code needed to control peripheral devices is not standardized. Operating systems provide subroutines called device drivers that perform operations on behalf of programs for example, input/output operations.
- Second, the operating system introduces new functions as it abstracts the hardware. For instance, operating system introduces the file abstraction so that programs do not have to deal with disks.
- Third, the operating system transforms the computer hardware into multiple virtual computers, each belonging to a different program. Each program that is running is called a process. Each process views the hardware through the lens of abstraction.
- Fourth, the operating system can enforce security through abstraction.
- To allocate resources to processes (Manage resources)
- An operating system controls how processes (the active agents) may access resources (passive entities).
- Provide a pleasant and effective user interface
- The user interacts with the operating systems through the user interface and usually interested in the “look and feel” of the

operating system. The most important components of the user interface are the command interpreter, the file system, on-line help, and application integration. The recent trend has been toward increasingly integrated graphical user interfaces that encompass the activities of multiple processes on networks of computers.

One can view Operating Systems from two points of views: Resource manager and Extended machines. Form Resource manager point of view Operating Systems manage the different parts of the system efficiently and from extended machines point of view Operating Systems provide a virtual machine to users that is more convenient to use. The structurally Operating Systems can be design as a monolithic system, a hierarchy of layers, a virtual machine system, an exokernel, or using the client-server model. The basic concepts of Operating Systems are processes, memory management, I/O management, the file systems, and security.

The notion of process is central to the understanding of operating systems. There are quite a few definitions presented in the literature, but no "perfect" definition has yet appeared.

The term "process" was first used by the designers of the MULTICS in 1960's. Since then, the term process, used somewhat interchangeably with 'task' or 'job'. The process has been given many definitions for instance

- A program in Execution.
- An asynchronous activity.
- The 'animated sprit' of a procedure in execution.
- The entity to which processors are assigned.
- The 'dispatch able' unit.

And many more definitions have given. As we can see from above that there is no universally agreed upon definition, but the definition "Program in Execution" seem to be most frequently used. And this is a concept are will use in the present study of operating systems.

Now that we agreed upon the definition of process, the question is what the relation between process and program is. It is same beast with different name or when this beast is sleeping (not executing) it is called program and when it is executing becomes process. Well, to be very precise. Process is not the same as program. In the following discussion

Foreground processes interact with users. Background processes that stay in background sleeping but suddenly springing to life to handle activity such as email, webpage, printing, and so on. Background processes are called daemons. This call creates an exact clone of the calling process.

A process may create a new process by some create process such as 'fork'. It choose to does so, creating process is called parent process and the created one is called the child processes. Only one parent is needed to create a child process. Note that unlike plants and animals that use sexual representation, a process has only one parent. This creation of process (processes) yields a hierarchical structure of processes like one in the figure. Notice that each child has only one parent but each parent may have many children. After the fork, the two processes, the parent and the child, have the same memory image, the same environment strings and the same open files. After a process is created, both the parent and child have their own distinct address space. If either process changes a word in its address space, the change is not visible to the other process.

Process Control Block

A process in an operating system is represented by a data structure known as a process control block (PCB) or process descriptor. The PCB contains important information about the specific process including

- The current state of the process i.e., whether it is ready, running, waiting, or whatever.
- Unique identification of the process in order to track "which is which" information.
- A pointer to parent process.
- Similarly, a pointer to child process (if it exists).
- The priority of process (a part of CPU scheduling information).
- Pointers to locate memory of processes.
- A register save area.
- The processor it is running on.

The PCB is a certain store that allows the operating systems to locate key information about a process. Thus, the PCB is the data structure that defines a process to the operating systems.

Threads

A thread is a single sequence stream within in a process. Because threads have some of the properties of processes, they are sometimes called lightweight processes. In a process, threads allow multiple executions of streams. In many respect, threads are popular way to improve application through parallelism. The CPU switches rapidly back and forth among the threads giving illusion that the threads are running in parallel. Like a traditional process i.e., process with one thread, a thread can be in any of several states (Running, Blocked, Ready or Terminated). Each thread has its own stack. Since thread will generally call different procedures and thus a different execution history. This is why thread needs its own stack. An operating system that has thread facility, the basic unit of CPU utilization is a thread. A thread has or consists of a program counter (PC), a register set, and a stack space. Threads are not independent of one other like processes as a result threads shares with other threads their code section, data section, OS resources also known as task, such as open files and signals.

Processes vs. Threads

As we mentioned earlier that in many respect threads operate in the same way as that of processes. Some of the similarities and differences are:

Similarities

- Like processes threads share CPU and only one thread active (running) at a time.
- Like processes, threads within a processes, threads within a processes execute sequentially.
- Like processes, thread can create children.
- And like process, if one thread is blocked, another thread can run.

Differences

- Unlike processes, threads are not independent of one another.
- Unlike processes, all threads can access every address in the task .
- Unlike processes, thread is design to assist one other. Note that processes might or might not assist one another because processes may originate from different users.

Why Threads?

Following are some reasons why we use threads in designing operating systems.

- A process with multiple threads makes a great server for example printer server.
- Because threads can share common data, they do not need to use interprocess communication.
- Because of the very nature, threads can take advantage of multiprocessors.

Threads are cheap in the sense that

- They only need a stack and storage for registers therefore, threads are cheap to create.
- Threads use very little resources of an operating system in which they are working. That is, threads do not need new address space, global data, program code or operating system resources.
- Context switching is fast when working with threads. The reason is that we only have to save and/or restore PC, SP and registers.
- But this cheapness does not come free - the biggest drawback is that there is no protection between threads.

Advantages

- The most obvious advantage of this technique is that a user-level threads package can be implemented on an Operating System that does not support threads. Some other advantages are

- User-level threads do not require modification to operating systems.

Simple Representation: Each thread is represented simply by a PC, registers, stack and a small control block, all stored in the user process address space.

Simple Management: This simply means that creating a thread, switching between threads and synchronization between threads can all be done without intervention of the kernel.

Fast and Efficient: Thread switching is not much more expensive than a procedure call.

Disadvantages

- There is a lack of coordination between threads and operating system kernel. Therefore, process as whole gets one time slice irrespective of whether process has one thread or 1000 threads within. It is up to each thread to relinquish control to other threads.
- User-level threads require non-blocking systems call i.e., a multithreaded kernel. Otherwise, entire process will blocked in the kernel, even if there are runnable threads left in the processes. For example, if one thread causes a page fault, the process blocks.

2 IPC, Concurrency, and Synchronization

Since processes frequently need to communicate with other processes therefore, there is a need for a well-structured communication, without using interrupts, among processes.

Race Conditions

In operating systems, processes that are working together share some common storage (main memory, file etc.) that each process can read and write. When two or more processes are reading or writing some shared data and the final result depends on who runs precisely when, are called race conditions. Concurrently executing threads that share data need to synchronize their operations and processing in order to avoid race condition on shared data. Only one 'customer' thread at a time should be allowed to examine and update the shared variable. Race conditions are also possible in Operating Systems. If the ready queue is implemented as a linked list and if the ready queue is being manipulated during the handling of an interrupt, then interrupts must be disabled to prevent another interrupt before the first one completes. If interrupts are not disabled than the linked list could become corrupt.

Critical Section

The key to preventing trouble involving shared storage is find some way to prohibit more than one process from reading and writing the shared data simultaneously. That part of the program where the shared memory is accessed is called the Critical Section. To avoid race conditions and flawed results, one must identify codes in Critical Sections in each thread. The characteristic properties of the code that form a Critical Section are

- Codes that reference one or more variables in a "read-update-write" fashion while any of those variables is possibly being altered by another thread.
- Codes that alter one or more variables that are possibly being referenced in "read-updata-write" fashion by another thread.
- Codes use a data structure while any part of it is possibly being altered by another thread.
- Codes alter any part of a data structure while it is possibly in use by another thread.

Mutual Exclusion

A way of making sure that if one process is using a shared modifiable data, the other processes will be excluded from doing the same thing.

Formally, while one process executes the shared variable, all other processes desiring to do so at the same time moment should be kept waiting; when that process has finished executing the shared variable, one of the processes waiting; while that process has finished executing the shared variable, one of the processes waiting to do so should be allowed to proceed. In this fashion, each process executing the shared data (variables) excludes all others from doing so simultaneously. This is called Mutual Exclusion.

The mutual exclusion needs to be enforced only when processes access shared modifiable data - when processes are performing operations that do not conflict with one another they should be allowed to proceed concurrently.

Mutual Exclusion Conditions

If we could arrange matters such that no two processes were ever in their critical sections simultaneously, we could avoid race conditions. We need four conditions to hold to have a good solution for the critical section problem (mutual exclusion).

- No two processes may at the same moment inside their critical sections.
- No assumptions are made about relative speeds of processes or number of CPUs.
- No process should outside its critical section should block other processes.
- No process should wait arbitrary long to enter its critical section.

Semaphores

A semaphore is a protected variable whose value can be accessed and altered only by the operations P and V and initialization operation called 'Semaphoiinitislize'.

Binary Semaphores can assume only the value 0 or the value 1 counting semaphores also called general semaphores can assume only nonnegative values.

Synchronization

In computer science, synchronization refers to one of two distinct but related concepts: synchronization of processes, and synchronization of data. Process synchronization refers to the idea that multiple processes are to join up or handshake at a certain point, in order to reach an agreement or commit to a certain sequence of action. Data Synchronization refers to the idea of keeping multiple copies of a dataset in coherence with one another, or to maintain data integrity. Process synchronization primitives are commonly used to implement data synchronization.

Concurrency

Concurrency is the tendency for things to happen at the same time in a system. Concurrency is a natural phenomenon, of course. In the real world, at any given time, many things are happening simultaneously. When we design software to monitor and control real-world systems, we must deal with this natural concurrency.

When dealing with concurrency issues in software systems, there are generally two aspects that are important: being able to detect and respond to external events occurring in a random order, and ensuring that these events are responded to in some minimum required interval.

If each concurrent activity evolved independently, in a truly parallel fashion, this would be relatively simple: we could simply create separate programs to deal with each activity. The challenges of designing concurrent systems arise mostly because of the interactions which happen between concurrent activities. When concurrent activities interact, some sort of coordination is required.

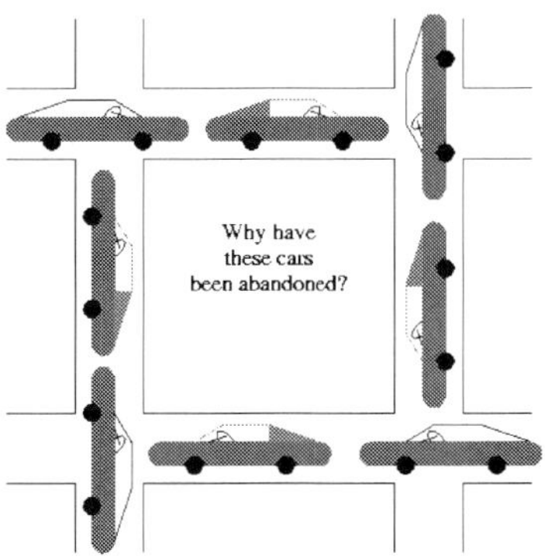

Why are we interested in Concurrency?

Some of the driving forces for concurrency are external. That is, they are imposed by the demands of the environment. In real-world systems many things are happening simultaneously and must be addressed "in real-time" by software. To do so, many real-time software systems must be "reactive." They must respond to externally generated events which may occur at somewhat random times, in some-what random order, or both.

Designing a conventional procedural program to deal with these situations is extremely complex. It can be much simpler to partition the system into concurrent software elements to deal with each of these events. The key phrase here is "can be", since complexity is also affected by the degree of interaction between the events.

There can also be internally inspired reasons for concurrency. Performing tasks in parallel can substantially speed up the computational work of a system if multiple CPUs are available. Even within a single processor, multitasking can dramatically speed things up by preventing one activity from blocking another while waiting for I/O, for example. A common situation where this occurs is during the start-up of a system. There are often many components, each of which requires time to be made ready for operation. Performing these operations sequentially can be painfully slow.

Controllability of the system can also be enhanced by concurrency. For example, one function can be started, stopped, or otherwise influenced in mid-stream by other concurrent functions—something extremely difficult to accomplish without concurrent components.

3 Deadlock

A set of process is in a deadlock state if each process in the set is waiting for an event that can be caused by only another process in the set. In other words, each member of the set of deadlock processes is waiting for a resource that can be released only by a deadlock process. None of the processes can run, none of them can release any resources, and none of them can be awakened. It is important to note that the number of processes and the number and kind of resources possessed and requested are unimportant.

The resources may be either physical or logical. Examples of physical resources are Printers, Tape Drivers, Memory Space, and CPU Cycles. Examples of logical resources are Files, Semaphores, and Monitors.

The simplest example of deadlock is where process 1 has been allocated non-shareable resources A, say, a tap drive, and process 2 has be allocated non-sharable resource B, say, a printer. Now, if it turns out that process 1 needs resource B (printer) to proceed and process 2 needs resource A (the tape drive) to proceed and these are the only two processes in the system, each is blocked the other and all useful work in the system stops. This situation its termed deadlock. The system is in deadlock state because each process holds a resource being requested by the other process neither process is willing to release the resource it holds.

Preemptable and Non-preemptable Resources

Resources come in two flavors: preemptable and nonpreemptable. A preemptable resource is one that can be taken away from the process with no ill effects. Memory is an example of a preemptable resource. On the other hand, a nonpreemptable resource is one that cannot be taken away from process (without causing ill effect). For example, CD resources are not preemptable at an arbitrary moment.

Reallocating resources can resolve deadlocks that involve preemptable resources. Deadlocks that involve nonpreemptable resources are difficult to deal with.

4 CPU Scheduling

The assignment of physical processors to processes allows processors to accomplish work. The problem of determining when processors should be assigned and to which processes is called processor scheduling or CPU scheduling.

When more than one process is runnable, the operating system must decide which one first. The part of the operating system concerned with this decision is called the scheduler, and algorithm it uses is called the scheduling algorithm.

Goals of scheduling (objectives)

Many objectives must be considered in the design of a scheduling discipline. In particular, a scheduler should consider fairness, efficiency, response time, turnaround time, throughput, etc., Some of these goals depends on the system one is using for example batch system, interactive system or real-time system, etc. but there are also some goals that are desirable in all systems.

General Goals

- Fairness: Fairness is important under all circumstances. A scheduler makes sure that each process gets its fair share of the CPU and no process can suffer indefinite postponement. Note that giving equivalent or equal time is not fair. Think of safety control and payroll at a nuclear plant.

- Policy Enforcement: The scheduler has to make sure that system's policy is enforced. For example, if the local policy is safety then the safety control processes must be able to run whenever they want to, even if it means delay in payroll processes.
- Efficiency: Scheduler should keep the system (or in particular CPU) busy cent percent of the time when possible. If the CPU and all the Input/output devices can be kept running all the time, more work gets done per second than if some components are idle.
- Response Time: A scheduler should minimize the response time for interactive user.
- Turnaround: A scheduler should minimize the time batch users must wait for an output.
- Throughput: A scheduler should maximize the number of jobs processed per unit time.

Preemptive vs. Non-preemptive Scheduling

The Scheduling algorithms can be divided into two categories with respect to how they deal with clock interrupts.

Non-preemptive Scheduling

A scheduling discipline is non-preemptive if, once a process has been given the CPU, the CPU cannot be taken away from that process.

Following are some characteristics of non-preemptive scheduling

- In non-preemptive system, short jobs are made to wait by longer jobs but the overall treatment of all processes is fair.
- In non-preemptive system, response times are more predictable because incoming high priority jobs cannot displace waiting jobs.
- In non-preemptive scheduling, a scheduler executes jobs in the following two situations.

  When a process switches from running state to the waiting state.

  When a process terminates.

Preemptive Scheduling

A scheduling discipline is preemptive if, once a process has been given the CPU can take away.

The strategy of allowing processes that are logically runnable to be temporarily suspended is called Preemptive Scheduling and it is contrast to the "run to completion" method.

We will discuss four major scheduling algorithms here which are following

First Come First Serve (FCFS)

- Jobs are executed on first come, first serve basis.
- Easy to understand and implement.
- Poor in performance as average wait time is high.

Shortest Job First (SJF)

- Best approach to minimize waiting time.
- Impossible to implement
- Processer should know in advance how much time process will take.

Priority Based Scheduling

- Each process is assigned a priority. Process with highest priority is to be executed first and so on.
- Processes with same priority are executed on first come first serve basis.
- Priority can be decided based on memory requirements, time requirements or any other resource requirement.

Round Robin Scheduling

- Each process is provided a fix time to execute called quantum.

- Once a process is executed for given time period. Process is preempted and other process executes for given time period.
- Context switching is used to save states of preempted processes.

Multi Queue Scheduling

- Multiple queues are maintained for processes.
- Each queue can have its own scheduling algorithms.
- Priorities are assigned to each queue.

5 Memory Management and Virtual Memory

Memory management is the functionality of an operating system which handles or manages primary memory. Memory management keeps track of each and every memory location either it is allocated to some process or it is free. It checks how much memory is to be allocated to processes. It decides which process will get memory at what time. It tracks whenever some memory gets freed or unallocated and correspondingly it updates the status.

Memory management provides protection by using two registers, a base register and a limit register. The base register holds the smallest legal physical memory address and the limit register specifies the size of the range. For example, if the base register holds 300000 and the limit register is 1209000, then the program can legally access all addresses from 300000 through 411999.

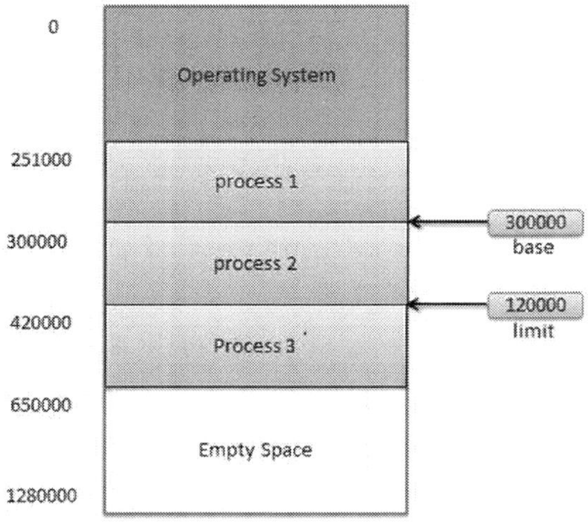

Instructions and data to memory addresses can be done in following ways

Compile time -- When it is known at compile time where the process will reside, compile time binding is used to generate the absolute code.

Load time -- When it is not known at compile time where the process will reside in memory, then the compiler generates re-locatable code.

Execution time -- If the process can be moved during its execution from one memory segment to another, then binding must be delayed to be done at run time

Dynamic Loading

In dynamic loading, a routine of a program is not loaded until it is called by the program. All routines are kept on disk in a re-locatable load format. The main program is loaded into memory and is executed. Other routines methods or modules are loaded on request. Dynamic loading makes better memory space utilization and unused routines are never loaded.

Dynamic Linking

Linking is the process of collecting and combining various modules of code and data into a executable file that can be loaded into memory and executed. Operating system can link system level libraries to a program. When it combines the libraries at load time, the linking is called static linking and when this linking is done at the time of execution, it is called as dynamic linking.

In static linking, libraries linked at compile time, so program code size becomes bigger whereas in dynamic linking libraries linked at execution time so program code size remains smaller.

Logical versus Physical Address Space

An address generated by the CPU is a logical address whereas address actually available on memory unit is a physical address. Logical address is also known a Virtual address.

Virtual and physical addresses are the same in compile-time and load-time address-binding schemes. Virtual and physical addresses differ in execution-time address-binding scheme.

The set of all logical addresses generated by a program is referred to as a logical address space. The set of all physical addresses corresponding to these logical addresses is referred to as a physical address space.

The run-time mapping from virtual to physical address is done by the memory management unit (MMU) which is a hardware device. MMU uses following mechanism to convert virtual address to physical address.

The value in the base register is added to every address generated by a user process which is treated as offset at the time it is sent to memory. For example, if the base register value is 10000, then an attempt by the user to use address location 100 will be dynamically reallocated to location 10100.

The user program deals with virtual addresses; it never sees the real physical addresses.

Swapping

Swapping is a mechanism in which a process can be swapped temporarily out of main memory to a backing store, and then brought back into memory for continued execution.

Backing store is a usually a hard disk drive or any other secondary storage which fast in access and large enough to accommodate copies of all memory images for all users. It must be capable of providing direct access to these memory images.

Major time consuming part of swapping is transfer time. Total transfer time is directly proportional to the amount of memory swapped. Let us assume that the user process is of size 100KB and the backing store is a standard hard disk with transfer rate of 1 MB per second. The actual transfer of the 100K process to or from memory will take

100KB / 1000KB per second

= 1/10 second

= 100 milliseconds

Fragmentation

As processes are loaded and removed from memory, the free memory space is broken into little pieces. It happens after sometimes that processes can not be allocated to memory blocks considering their small size and memory blocks remains unused. This problem is known as Fragmentation.

Paging

External fragmentation is avoided by using paging technique. Paging is a technique in which physical memory is broken into blocks of the same size called pages (size is power of 2, between 512 bytes and 8192 bytes). When a process is to be executed, it's corresponding pages are loaded into any available memory frames.

Logical address space of a process can be non-contiguous and a process is allocated physical memory whenever the free memory frame is available. Operating system keeps track of all free frames. Operating system needs n free frames to run a program of size n pages.

Segmentation

Segmentation is a technique to break memory into logical pieces where each piece represents a group of related information. For example, data segments or code segment for each process, data segment for operating system and so on. Segmentation can be implemented using or without using paging.

Unlike paging, segment is having varying sizes and thus eliminates internal fragmentation. External fragmentation still exists but to lesser extent.

Virtual Memory

Virtual memory is a technique that allows the execution of processes which are not completely available in memory. The main visible advantage of this scheme is that programs can be larger than physical memory. Virtual memory is the separation of user logical memory from physical memory.

This separation allows an extremely large virtual memory to be provided for programmers when only a smaller physical memory is available. Following are the situations, when entire program is not required to be loaded fully in main memory.

- User written error handling routines are used only when an error occured in the data or computation.
- Certain options and features of a program may be used rarely.
- Many tables are assigned a fixed amount of address space even though only a small amount of the table is actually used.
- The ability to execute a program that is only partially in memory would counter many benefits.
- Less number of I/O would be needed to load or swap each user program into memory.
- A program would no longer be constrained by the amount of physical memory that is available.
- Each user program could take less physical memory; more programs could be run the same time, with a corresponding increase in CPU utilization and throughput.

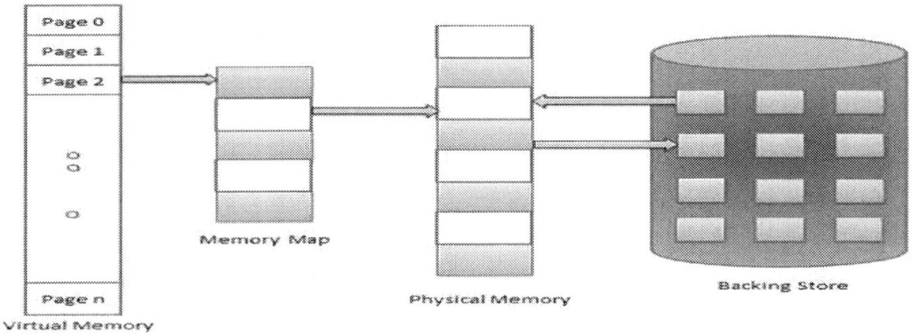

Virtual memory is commonly implemented by demand paging. It can also be implemented in a segmentation system. Demand segmentation can also be used to provide virtual memory.

Demand Paging

A demand paging system is quite similar to a paging system with swapping. When we want to execute a process, we swap it into memory. Rather than swapping the entire process into memory, however, we use a lazy swapper called pager.

When a process is to be swapped in, the pager guesses which pages will be used before the process is swapped out again. Instead of swapping in a whole process, the pager brings only those necessary pages into memory. Thus, it avoids reading into memory pages that will not be used in any way, decreasing the swap time and the amount of physical memory needed.

Hardware support is required to distinguish between those pages that are in memory and those pages that are on the disk using the valid-invalid bit scheme. Where valid and invalid pages can be checked by checking the bit. Marking a page will have no effect if the process never attempts to access the page. While the process executes and accesses pages that are memory resident, execution proceeds normally.

Advantages

Following are the advantages of Demand Paging

- Large virtual memory.
- More efficient use of memory.
- Unconstrained multiprogramming. There is no limit on degree of multiprogramming.

Disadvantages

Following are the disadvantages of Demand Paging

- Number of tables and amount of processor overhead for handling page interrupts are greater than in the case of the simple paged management techniques.

- Due to the lack of explicit constraints on jobs address space size.

Page Replacement Algorithm

Page replacement algorithms are the techniques using which Operating System decides which memory pages to swap out, write to disk when a page of memory needs to be allocated. Paging happens whenever a page fault occurs and a free page cannot be used for allocation purpose accounting to reason that pages are not available or the number of free pages is lower than required pages.

When the page that was selected for replacement and was paged out, is referenced again then it has to read in from disk, and this requires for I/O completion. This process determines the quality of the page replacement algorithm: the lesser the time waiting for page-ins, the better is the algorithm. A page replacement algorithm looks at the limited information about accessing the pages provided by hardware, and tries to select which pages should be replaced to minimize the total number of page misses, while balancing it with the costs of primary storage and processor time of the algorithm itself. There are many different page replacement algorithms. We evaluate an algorithm by running it on a particular string of memory reference and computing the number of page faults.

6 I/O and File System, Protection and Security

File systems

File type refers to the ability of the operating system to distinguish different types of file such as text files source files and binary files etc. Many operating systems support many types of files. Operating systems like MS-DOS and UNIX have the following types of files:

Ordinary Files

- These are the files that contain user information.
- These may have text, databases or executable program.
- The user can apply various operations on such files like add, modify, delete or even remove the entire file.

Directory Files

- These files contain list of file names and other information related to these files.

Special files

- These files are also known as device files.

- These files represent physical device like disks, terminals, printers, networks, tape drive etc.

These files are of two types

- Character special files - data is handled character by character as in case of terminals or printers.
- Block special files - data is handled in blocks as in the case of disks and tapes.

File Access Mechanisms

File access mechanism refers to the manner in which the records of a file may be accessed. There are several ways to access files

- Sequential access
- Direct/Random access
- Indexed sequential access

Sequential access

A sequential access is that in which the records are accessed in some sequence i.e the information in the file is processed in order, one record after the other. This access method is the most primitive one. Example: Compilers usually access files in this fashion.

Direct/Random Access

- Random access file organization provides, accessing the records directly.
- Each record has its own address on the file with by the help of which it can be directly accessed for reading or writing.
- The records need not be in any sequence within the file and they need not be in adjacent locations on the storage medium.

Indexed Sequential Access

- This mechanism is built up on base of sequential access.
- An index is created for each file which contains pointers to various blocks.
- Index is searched sequentially and its pointer is used to access the file directly.

Space Allocation

Files are allocated disk spaces by operating system. Operating systems deploy following three main ways to allocate disk space to files.

- Contiguous Allocation
- Linked Allocation
- Indexed Allocation

Contiguous Allocation

- Each file occupies a contiguous address space on disk.
- Assigned disk address is in linear order.
- Easy to implement.
- External fragmentation is a major issue with this type of allocation technique.

Linked Allocation

- Each file carries a list of links to disk blocks.
- Directory contains link / pointer to first block of a file.
- No external fragmentation
- Effectively used in sequential access file.
- Inefficient in case of direct access file.

Indexed Allocation

- Providessolutionstoproblemsofcontiguousandlinkedallocation.
- An index block is created having all pointers to files.
- Each file has its own index block which stores the addresses of disk space occupied by the file.
- Directory contains the addresses of index blocks of files.

I/O System

The CPU hardware uses an interrupt request line wire which helps CPU to sense after executing every instruction. When the CPU checks that a controller has put a signal on the interrupt request line, the CPU saves a state, such as the current value of the instruction pointer, and jumps to theinterrupthandlerroutineatafixedaddress.Theinterrupthandlerpart determines the cause of the interrupt performs the necessary processing and executes a interrupt instruction to return the CPU to its execution state.

The basic mechanism of interrupt enables the CPU to respond to an asynchronous event, such as when a device controller becomes ready for service. Most CPUs have two interrupt request lines.

- Non-mask able interrupt - Such kind of interrupts are reserved for events like unrecoverable memory errors.
- Mask-able interrupt - Such interrupts can be switched off by the CPU before the execution of critical instructions that must not be interrupted.

The interrupt mechanism accepts an address - a number that selects a specific interrupt handling routine/function from a small set. In most architecture, this address is an offset stored in a table called the interrupt vector table. This vector contains the memory addresses of specialized interrupt handlers.

Application I/O Interface

Application I/O Interface represents the structuring techniques and interfaces for the operating system to enable I/O devices to be treated in a standard, uniform way. The actual differences lies kernel level modules called device drivers which are custom tailored to corresponding devices but show one of the standard interfaces to applications. The purpose of the device-driver layer is to hide the differences among device controllers from the I/O subsystem of the kernel, such as the I/O system calls. Following are the characteristics of I/O interfaces with respected to devices.

- Character-stream / block - A character-stream device transfers bytes in one by one fashion, whereas a block device transfers a complete unit of bytes.
- Sequential / random-access - A sequential device transfers data in a fixed order determined by the device, random-access device can be instructed to seek position to any of the available data storage locations.
- Synchronous / asynchronous - A synchronous device performs data transfers with known response time whereas an asynchronous device shows irregular or unpredictable response time.
- Sharable / dedicated - A sharable device can be used concurrently by several processes or threads but a dedicated device cannot be used.
- Speed of operation - Device speeds may range from a few bytes per second to a few gigabytes per second.
- Read-write, read only, or writes only - Some devices perform both input and output, but others support only one data direction that is read only.

Kernel I/O Subsystem

Kernel I/O Subsystem is responsible to provide many services related to I/O. Following are some of the services provided.

- Scheduling - Kernel schedules a set of I/O requests to determine a good order in which to execute them. When an application issues a blocking I/O system call, the request is placed on the queue for that device. The Kernel I/O scheduler rearranges the order of the queue to improve the overall system efficiency and the average response time experienced by the applications.

- Buffering - Kernel I/O Subsystem maintains a memory area known as buffer that stores data while they are transferred between two devices or between a device with an application operation. Buffering is done to cope with a speed mismatch between the producer and consumer of a data stream or to adapt between devices that have different data transfer sizes.
- Caching - Kernel maintains cache memory which is region of fast memory that holds copies of data. Access to the cached copy is more efficient than access to the original.
- Spooling and Device Reservation A spool is a buffer that holds output for a device, such as a printer, that cannot accept interleaved data streams. The spooling system copies the queued spool files to the printer one at a time. In some operating systems, spooling is managed by a system daemon process. In other operating systems, it is handled by an in kernel thread.
- Error handling: An operating system that uses protected memory can guard against many kinds of hardware and application errors.

Operating System - Security

Security refers to providing a protection system to computer system resources such as CPU, memory, disk, software programs and most importantly data/information stored in the computer system. If a computer program is run by unauthorized user then he/she may cause severe damage to computer or data stored in it. So a computer system must be protected against unauthorized access, malicious access to system memory, viruses, worms etc. We're going to discuss following topics in this article.

- Authentication
- One Time passwords

- Program Threats
- System Threats
- Computer Security Classifications

Authentication

Authentication refers to identifying the each user of the system and associating the executing programs with those users. It is the responsibility of the Operating System to create a protection system which ensures that a user who is running a particular program is authentic. Operating Systems generally identifies/authenticates users using following three ways:

- *Username/Password* - User need to enter a registered username and password with Operating system to login into the system.
- *User card/key* - User need to punch card in card slot, or enter key generated by key generator in option provided by operating system to login into the system.
- *User attribute* - fingerprint/ eye retina pattern/ signature - User need to pass his/her attribute via designated input device used by operating system to login into the system.

One Time passwords

One time passwords provides additional security along with normal authentication. In One-Time Password system, a unique password is required every time user tries to login into the system. Once a one-time password is used then it cannot be used again. One time password are implemented in various ways.

- *Random numbers* - Users are provided cards having numbers printed along with corresponding alphabets. System asks for numbers corresponding to few alphabets randomly chosen.
- *Secret key* - User are provided a hardware device which can create a secret id mapped with user id. System asks for such secret id which is to be generated every time prior to login.
- *Network password* - Some commercial applications send one time

password to user on registered mobile/ email which is required to be entered prior to login.

Program Threats

Operating system's processes and kernel do the designated task as instructed. If a user program made these process do malicious tasks then it is known as Program Threats. One of the common examples of program threat is a program installed in a computer which can store and send user credentials via network to some hacker. Following is the list of some well-known program threats.

Trojan Horse - Such program traps user login credentials and stores them to send to malicious user who can later on login to computer and can access system resources.

Trap Door - If a program which is designed to work as required, have a security hole in its code and perform illegal action without knowledge of user then it is called to have a trap door.

Logic Bomb - Logic bomb is a situation when a program misbehaves only when certain conditions met otherwise it works as a genuine program. It is harder to detect.

Virus - Virus as name suggests can replicate them on computer system .They are highly dangerous and can modify/delete user files, crash systems. A virus is generally a small code embedded in a program. As user accesses the program, the virus starts getting embedded in other files/ programs and can make system unusable for user.

System Threats

System threats refer to misuse of system services and network connections to put user in trouble. System threats can be used to launch program threats on a complete network called as program attack. System threats create such an environment that operating system resources/ user files are miss-used. Following is the list of some well-known system threats.

Worm - Worm is a process which can choke down a system performance by using system resources to extreme levels. A Worm process generates its multiple copies where each copy uses system resources, prevents all other processes to get required resources. Worms processes can even shut down an entire network.

Port Scanning - Port scanning is a mechanism or means by which a hacker can detects system vulnerabilities to make an attack on the system.

Denial of Service - Denial of service attacks normally prevents user to make legitimate use of the system. For example user may not be able to use internet if denial of service attacks browser's content settings.

Computer Security Classifications

As per the U.S. Department of Defense Trusted Computer System's Evaluation Criteria there are four security classifications in computer systems: A, B, C, and D. this is widely used specifications to determine and model the security of systems and of security solutions.

A Handbook on Computer Science

9

Databases

CONTENTS

1 ER-Model and Relational Model

ER-MODEL

The ER model defines the conceptual view of a database. It works around real-world entities and the associations among them. At view level, the ER model is considered a good option for designing databases.

- *Entity*: Entities ar e represented by means of rectangles. Rectangles are named with the entity set they represent.
- *Entity Set*: It is not a data modeling construct; it does not describe the structure of data. Instead, an entity set provides a construct for a hosting or storage environment to group entity type instances so that they can be mapped to a data store.
- *Attributes*: Attributes are the properties of entities. Attributes are represented by means of ellipses. Every ellipse represents one attribute and is directly connected to its entity.
- *Relationship*: A Relationship describes relations between entities. Relationship is represented using diamonds.
- *Relationship Sets*: Entity-relationship diagrams do not show single entities or single instances of relations.
- *Super Key*: A superkey is a combination of attributes that can be uniquely used to identify a database record.
- *Candidate Key*: A minimal super key is called a candidate key. An

entity set may have more than one candidate key.

- *Primary Key*: A primary key is one of the candidate keys chosen by the database designer to uniquely identify the entity set.
- *Weak Entity*: Weak entity is an entity that depends on another entity. Weak entity doen't have key attribute of their own. Double rectangle represents weak entity.
- *Strong Entity*: If an entity type has a key attribute specified then it is a strong entity type.

Structural Constraints

- *D*egree: number of participating entity sets.
- *Cardinality constraints*: one to one, one to many, many to many.
- *Participation* canstraints: partial or total.

ER Diagram Symbols

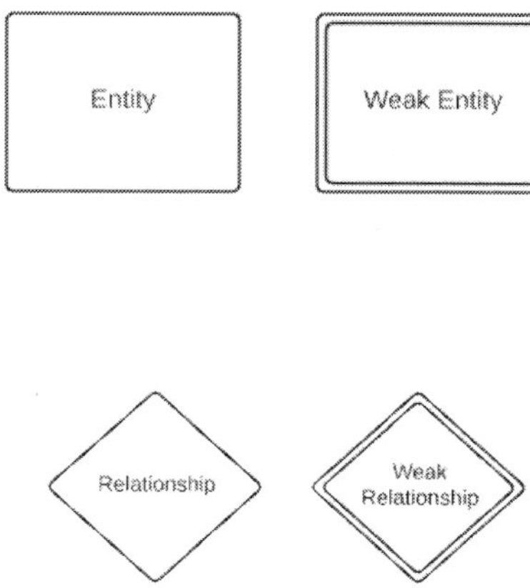

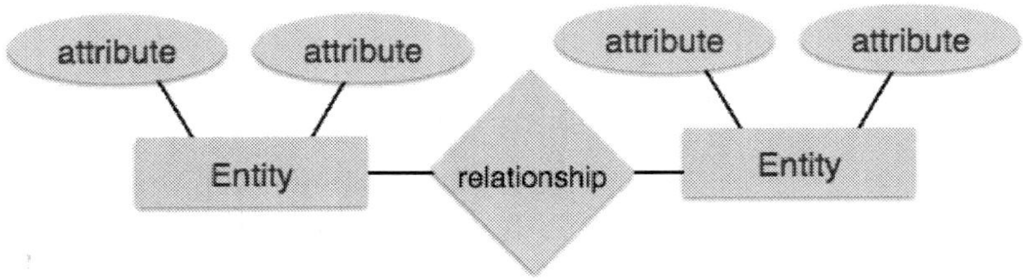

One to One: One entity from entity set A can be associated with at most one entity of entity set B and vice versa.

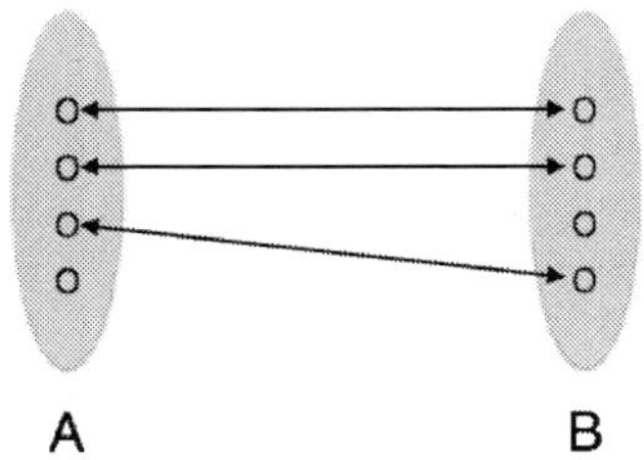

One to Many: One entity from entity set A can be associated with more than one entities of entity set B however an entity from entity set B, can be associated with at most one entity.

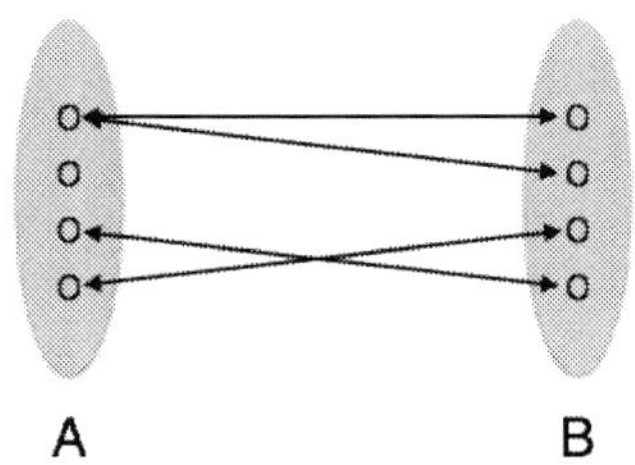

Many to One: More than one entities from entity set A can be associated with at most one entity of entity set B.

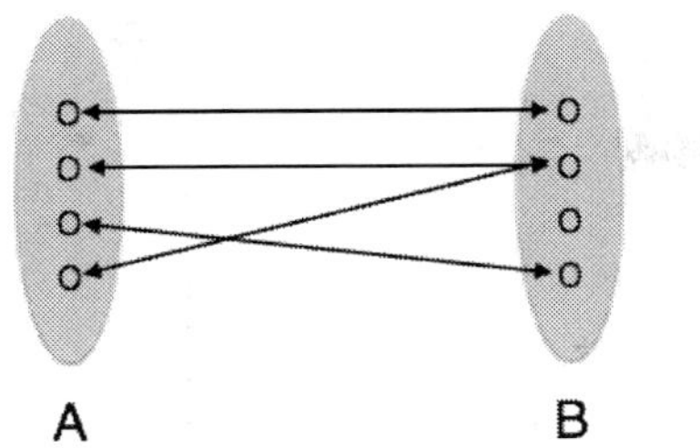

ManytoMany: One entity from A can be associated with more than one entity from B and vice versa.

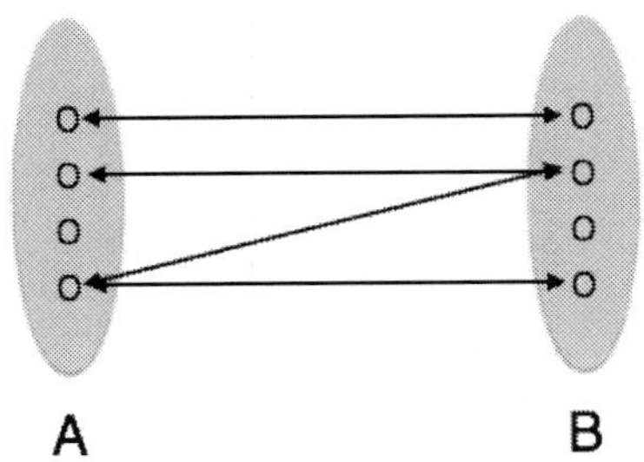

Command

DDL: Create, Drop and Alter

- Create:

  create table table-name (column-name1 datatype1, column-name2 datatype2, column-name3 datatype3, column-name4 datatype4)
- Drop

  DROP TABLE (table_name)
- Alter:

  ALTER TABLE <table_name>

  ADD(<NewColumnName> <Data_Type>(<size>),......n)

DML: Insert, Update, Delete

- INSERT:

  INSERT into table-name values (data1,data2,..)

- UPDATE:
  UPDATE table-name set column-name = value where condition;
- DELETE:
  DELETE from Student
  Where Condition;

DCL: Data Control Language (DCL) is used to control privilege in Database. DCL defines two commands,

Grant: Gives user access privileges to database.

GRANT [privilege]
ON [object]
TO [user]
[WITH GRANT OPTION]

Revoke: Take back permissions from user.

REVOKE [GRANT OPTION FOR] [permission]
ON [object]
FROM [user]
[CASCADE]

Relational Command

Cartesian product (×)

- $\text{Deg}(R \times S) = \text{deg}(R) + \text{deg}(s)$

$|(R \times S)| = |R| \times |S|$

Natural Join (⋈)

$$R \bowtie S = \{t \cup s \mid t \in R \ \wedge \ s \in S \ \wedge \ Fun(t \cup s)\}$$

The result of the natural join is the set of all combinations of tuples in R and S that are equal on their common attribute names.

Order by

The SQL ORDER BY clause is used to sort the data in ascending or descending order, based on one or more columns.

Aggregation Operation

Aggregate Functions are functions that provide mathematical operations. If you need to add, count or perform basic statistics, these functions will be of great help.

The functions include:

- count() - counts a number of rows
- sum() - compute sum
- avg() - compute average
- min() - compute minimum
- max() - compute maximum

Selection Operation

It selects tuples that satisfy the given predicate from a relation.

select * from tbl_name

OR

<Selection condition>(R)

Projection operation (π)

It projects column(s) that satisfy a given predicate.

Notation--πA1, A2, An (r)

Where A1, A2 , An are attribute names of relation r.

Duplicate rows are automatically eliminated, as relation is a set.

$\Pi_{subject,\ author}$ (Books)

Selects and projects columns named as subject and author from the relation Books.

Rename

The RENAME operator is used to give a name to results or output of queries.

EXEC sp_rename 'Sales.SalesTerritory', 'SalesTerr';

OR

$\rho_{s(Birth\_Date,\ Employee\_Number)}(EMPLOYEE) \leftarrow \pi_{dob,\ empno}(EMPLOYEE)$

Union Operation

The UNION operator is used to combine the result-set of two or more SELECT statements.

SELECT column_name(s) FROM table1

UNION

SELECT column_name(s) FROM table2;

In algebraic function

$$r \cup s = \{ t \mid t \in r \text{ or } t \in s\}$$

Intersection Operation

SELECT expression1, expression2, ... expression_n

FROM tables

WHERE conditions

INTERSECT

SELECT expression1, expression2, ... expression_n

FROM tables

WHERE conditions;

OR, Two relation should be union compatible

$\deg(R \cap S) = \deg(R) = \deg(S)$

$0 \leq |(R \cap S)| \leq \min(|R|, |S|)$

Set Difference (-)

The result of set difference operation is tuples, which are present in one relation but are not in the second relation.

Two relations should be union compatible

- $\text{Deg}(R\text{-}S) = \deg(R) = \deg(S)$

$0 \leq |(R - S)| \leq |R|$

Tuple Relational Calculus The Tuple Relational Calculus is based on specifying a number of tuple variables which are variables that range over a relation (theirs values are tuples of the relation).

A formal query in TRC is expressed as {t | P (t)} where t is a tuple variable and P(t) is a expression involving variable t. The result of the query is considered as a set of tuple t so predicate P is true for t.

Example of basic queries in Tuple Relational Calculus

Consider the COMPANY relational database schema (From chapter 3)

EMPLOYEE (SSN, Name, Bdate, Address, Salary, DeptId)

DEPARTMENT (DeptId, Dname, Office, Mng-SSN)

PROJECT (Code, Name, Budget, DeptId)

JOIN (ESSN, PCode, StartDate)

EMP-DEPENDENT (ESSN, Dependent-Name, Bdate, Relationship)

2 Database Design

Database design is the process of producing a detailed data model of a database. This logical data model contains all the needed logical and physical design choices and physical storage parameters needed to generate a design in a data definition language, which can then be used to create a database.

Limitation of File System

File system has many advantages over manual record keeping system, but it has some limitations. The conventional file processing system suffers from the following shortcomings.

- Data Redundancy
- Data Inconsistency
- Data Isolation
- Data Atomicity
- Data Security
- Incompatible File Format
- Data Dependence

Database Design Goals

There are many goals for the design of a database. Here are some of them listed:

- The database is comprehensive: it includes all the needed data and connections.
- The database is understandable: there is a clear structure which leads to easy, flexible and fast reading and updating of the data.
- The database is expandable: it is possible to change the structure of the database with a minimum change to the existing software.
- The database can be used in many organizations: the database can be adapted to different kinds of environments and customers without the need to change the database structure.
- The integrity of the data: data must be correct, it must be consistent.

According to Codd

No two record of the table should be equal. A relational database management system must manage its stored data using only its relational capabilities.

There are 12 rule of Codd, that are must require for database operation, such as:

- The information rule
- The guaranteed access rule
- Systematic treatment of null values
- Active online catalog based on the relational model
- The comprehensive data sublanguage rule
- The view updating rule
- High-level insert, update, and delete
- Physical data independence
- Logical data independence
- Integrity independence
- Distribution independence
- The non-subversion rule

Difference between Primary and Alternet key

A primary key is a constraint on a table uniquely identifying each row. No two rows may have the same key attribute. In some designs, more than one column determine the unique descriptor for a row. Alternate keys contain one or more columns whose combined values uniquely identify every row in a table. An alternate key is a key associated with one or more columns whose values uniquely identify every row in the table, but which is not the primary key.

Primary Key: Unique + not null

Super Key: Set of attributes used to differentiate all the tuples of the relation or super set of condidate key.

Functional Dependency

Functional dependency is a relationship that exists when one attribute uniquely determines another attribute. Functional dependency in a database serves as a constraint between two sets of attributes. Defining functional dependency is an important part of relational database design and contributes to aspect normalization.

Trivial Functional Dependency

- *Trivial*: If a functional dependency (FD) X □ Y holds, where Y is a subset of X, then it is called a trivial FD. Trivial FDs always hold.
- *Non-trivial*: If an FD X □ Y holds, where Y is not a subset of X, then it is called a non-trivial FD.
- *Completely non-trivial*: If an FD X□ Y holds, where x intersect Y = □, it is said to be a completely non-trivial FD.

Non Trivial Functional Dependency

If x □ y = ϕ and if x□y setisfy functional dependecy definition.

For example,

Cid□Cname

Armstrong's Axioms

Armstrong's Axioms are a set of rules, that when applied repeatedly, generates a closure of functional dependencies.

- Reflexive rule: If alpha is a set of attributes and beta is_subset_of alpha, then alpha holds beta.
- Augmentation rule: If a □ b holds and y is attribute set, then ay □ by also holds. That is adding attributes in dependencies, does not change the basic dependencies.
- Transitivity rule: Same as transitive rule in algebra, if a□b holds and b □ c holds, then a □ c also holds. a □ b is called as a functionally that determines b.

Closure of Attribute Sets

- Given a set of attributes □, the closure of □ under F (denoted by □+) is the set of attributes that are functionally determined by □ under F

  Application: whether □ is a super key?
- Algorithm to compute □+, the closure of □ under F

  result := □;

  while (changes to result) do

  for each □ □ □ in F do

  begin

  if □ ⊆ result then result := result ∪ □

  end

Example of Attribute Set Closure

- R = (A, B, C, G, H, I)
- F = {A → B
  A → C
  CG → H
  CG → I
  B → H}
- $(AG)^+$
  1. result = AG
  2. result = ABCG (A → C and A → B)
  3. result = ABCGH (CG → H and CG ⊆ AGBC)
  4. result = ABCGHI (CG → I and CG ⊆ AGBCH)

- Is AG a candidate key?
  - Is AG a super key?
    - Does AG → R?
    - Yes, $(AG)^+ \supseteq R$
  - Is any subset of AG a superkey?
    - Does A → R? Is $(A)^+ \supseteq R$?
    - Does G → R? Is $(G)^+ \supseteq R$?

Closure of a Set of Functional Dependencies

- Given a set F set of functional dependencies, there are certain other functional dependencies that are logically implied by F.
- The set of all functional dependencies logically implied by F is the closure of F.
- We denote the closure of F by F+.
- We can find all of F+ by applying Armstrong's Axioms:

– if □ ⊆ □, then □ □ □ (reflexivity)

– if □ □ □, then □□ □ □□ (augmentation)

– if □ □ □ and □ □ □, then □ □ □ (transitivity)

These rules are sound and complete.

Property of Decompotion

A rule that suggests if you have a table that appears to contain two entities that are determined by the same PK, consider breaking them up into two tables. Decomposition is the reverse of the Union rule. If you have a table that appears to contain two entities that are determined by the same PK, consider breaking them up into two tables.

Lossless-Join Decomposition

The lossless join property is a feature of decomposition supported by normalization. It is the ability to ensure that any instance of the original relation can be identified from corresponding instances in the smaller relations.

Let R be a relation schema and let F be a set of FDs over R. A decomposition of R into two schemas with attribute sets X and Y is said to be a lossless-join decomposition with respect to F if, for every instance r of R that satisfies the dependencies in F, $\prod_x$ (r), $\prod_y$ (r) = r. In other words, we can recover the original relation from the decomposed relations.

Dependency Preserving Decompotion

DependencypreservingDecompositionmeanthatdecompositionshould be such that every dependency of relation R must be implied in sub-relations or in combination of dependencies implied in sub relation.

LetRbeanyrelationwithFDsetF,decomposedintosub-relationsR1 and R2 with FD sets F1 and F2 respectively.

Then every dependency of R must be implied in F1 or F2 or in combination of these two.

F1∪F2 = F (dependency must be preserved in decomposition)

If F1∪F2 ⊂ F (not dependency preserving decomposition)

F1∪F2 ⊃ F (this is not possible)

Database Normalization

Database normalization is the process of efficiently organizing data in a database. There are two reasons of the normalization process:

- Eliminating redundant data, for example, storing the same data in more than one tables.
- Ensuring data dependencies make sense.

First normal form (1NF)

- Define the data items required, because they become the columns in a table. Place related data items in a table.

Second Normal Form (2NF)

Second normal form states that it should meet all the rules for 1NF and there must be no partial dependences of any of the columns on the primary key.

Third Normal Form (3NF)

- It is in second normal form.
- All nonprimary fields are dependent on the primary key.
- The dependency of nonprimary fields is between the data.

Boyce-Codd Normal Form

Boyce-Codd Normal Form (BCNF) is an extension of Third Normal Form on strict terms. BCNF states that for any non-trivial functional dependency, X □ A, X must be a super-key.

In the above example, Stu_ID is the super-key in the relation Student_Detail and Zip is the super-key in the relation ZipCodes. So,

Stu_ID □ Stu_Name, Zip

and

Zip □ City

Which confirms that both the relations are in BCNF.

Normalization Goal

The goal of database normalization is to ensure that every non-key column in every table is directly dependent on the key, the whole key and nothing but the key and with this goal come benefits in the form of reduced redundancies, fewer anomalies, and improved efficiencies.

Side Effect of Normalization

- More tables to join: By spreading out your data into more tables, you increase the need to join tables.

- Tables contain codes instead of real data: Repeated data is stored as codes rather than meaningful data. Therefore, there is always a need to go to the lookup table for the value.
- Data model is difficult to query against: The data model is optimized for applications, not for ad hoc querying.

Partial Dependency

In database management systems, partial dependency is a functional dependency that refers to the phenomenon where a primary key determines the outcome of another attribute or set of attributes. It occurs when a non-key attribute of a table in a database is dependent on the value of only a part of the table's primary key but not the entire primary key.

Multivalued Dependency (MVD)

Multivalued dependencies occur when the presence of one or more rows in a table implies the presence of one or more other rows in that same table.

- MVD requires other tuples of a certain form be present
- Consequence of 1NF that disallows a set of values for an attribute in a tuple
- If two or more multivalued independent attributes in the relation, every value of one attribute must be repeated with every value of other attribute to keep it consistent

Complement Rule

- Test relations to determine whether they are legal under a given set of FDs and MVDs
- Specify constraints on a set of relations

Equality of FD set

- A set of functional dependencies E is covered by a set of functional dependencies F if every FD in E is also in F+.
- Two sets of functional dependencies E and F are equivalent if E + = F+.
- If two sets of functional dependencies E and F are equivalent, then E covers F and F covers E.

Minimal Cover or Conical Cover

Sets of functional dependencies may have redundant dependencies that can be inferred from the others

- E.g.: A → C is redundant in: {A → B, B → C, A → C}
- Parts of a functional dependency may be redundant

  E.g. on RHS: {A → B, B → C, A → CD} can be simplified to
  {A → B, B → C, A → D}

  E.g. on LHS: {A → B, B → C, AC → D} can be simplified to
  {A → B, B → C, A → D}

Intuitively, a canonical cover of F is a "minimal" set of functional dependencies equivalent to F, having no redundant dependencies or redundant parts of dependencies.

Referential Integrity Constraint

Referential integrity is a relational database concept in which multiple tables share a relationship based on the data stored in the tables, and that relationship must remain consistent.

Foreign Key

It is a set of attributes that references primary key of the same relation or other relation.

Figure:

Referenced Relation

- *Insertion*: no validation
- *Deletion*:

  On deletion no action: Means if it causes problem on delete then not allowed to delete.

  On delete cascade: if we want to delete primary key value from referenced table then it will delete that value from referencing table also.

  On delete set null: if we want to delete primary key from referenced table then it will try to set the null values in place of that values in referencing table
- Updation:

  On update no action

  On update cascade

  On update set null

Referencing Relation

- *Insertion*: may cause violation
- *Deletion*: no violation
- *Updation*: May Cause Violation

3 SQL (Structure Query Language)

SQL is a database computer language designed for the retrieval and management of data in relational database. SQL stands for Structured Query Language.

Why SQL?

- Allows users to access data in relational database management systems.
- Allows users to describe the data.
- Allows users to define the data in database and manipulate that data.
- Allows users to create and drop databases and tables.
- Allows users to create view, stored procedure, functions in a database.
- Allows users to set permissions on tables, procedures, and views

SQL Process

When you are executing an SQL command for any RDBMS, the system determines the best way to carry out your request and SQL engine figures out how to interpret the task.

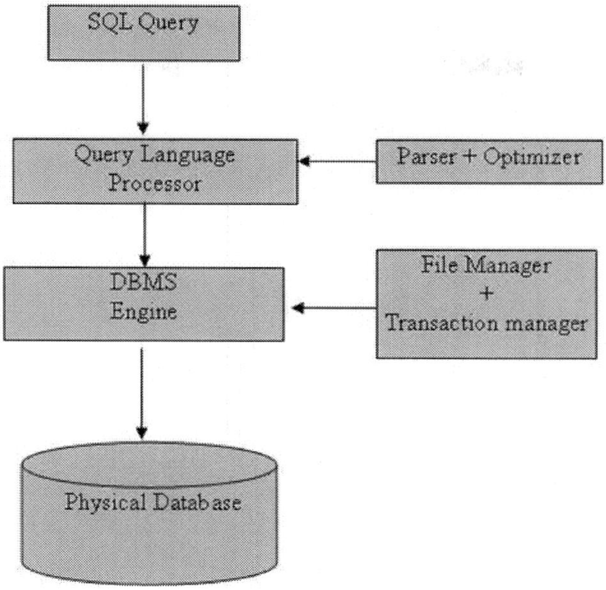

RDBMS

A Relational database management system (RDBMS) is a database management system (DBMS) that is based on the relational model as introduced by E. F. Codd.

The data in RDBMS is stored in database objects called tables. The table is a collection of related data entries and it consists of columns and rows. Following is the example of a CUSTOMERS table:

ID	NAME	AGE	ADDRESS
1	John	26	New york
2	Finch	24	Sydney
3	Joseph	30	Florida
4	Mitchel	32	Miami

Field

A field is a column in a table that is designed to maintain specific information about every record in the table. The fields in the CUSTOMERS table consist of ID, NAME, AGE, and ADDRESS.

Record or Row

A record, also called a row of data, is each individual entry that exists in a table. There are 4 records in the above CUSTOMERS table.

Column

A column is a vertical entity in a table that contains all information associated with a specific field in a table.

NULL Value

A NULL value in a table is a value in a field that appears to be blank, which means a field with a NULL value is a field with no value.

SQL Data Type

SQL data type is an attribute that specifies type of data of any object. Each column, variable and expression has related data type in SQL.

Exact Numeric Data Types:

DATA TYPE	FROM	TO
bigint	-9,223,372,036,854,775,808	9,223,372,036,854,775,807
int	-2,147,483,648	2,147,483,647
smallint	-32,768	32,767
tinyint	0	255
bit	0	1
decimal	-10^38 +1	10^38 -1

numeric	-10^38 +1	10^38 -1
money	-922,337,203,685,477.5808	+922,337,203,685,477.5807
smallmoney	-214,748.3648	+214,748.3647

SQL Constraints

Constraints are the rules enforced on data columns on table. These are used to limit the type of data that can go into a table. This ensures the accuracy and reliability of the data in the database.

NOTNULL Constraint: Ensures that a column cannot have NULL value. *For example*;

DEFAULT Constraint: The DEFAULT constraint provides a default value to a column when the INSERT INTO statement does not provide a specific value.

UNIQUE Constraint: The UNIQUE Constraint prevents two records from having identical values in a particular column.

Primary Key: A primary key is a field in a table which uniquely identifies each row/record in a database table.

Foreign key: A foreign key is a key used to link two tables together. This is sometimes called a referencing key.

CHECK Constraint: The CHECK Constraint enables a condition to check the value being entered into a record.

INDEX Constraint

The INDEX is used to create and retrieve data from the database very quickly. Index can be created by using single or group of columns in a table.

SQL Joins

The SQL Joins clause is used to combine records from two or more tables in a database. A JOIN is a means for combining fields from two tables by using values common to each.

There are different types of joins available in SQL:

- INNER JOIN: returns rows when there is a match in both tables.
- LEFT JOIN: returns all rows from the left table, even if there are no matches in the right table.
- RIGHT JOIN: returns all rows from the right table, even if there are no matches in the left table.
- FULL JOIN: returns rows when there is a match in one of the tables.
- SELF JOIN: is used to join a table to itself as if the table were two tables, temporarily renaming at least one table in the SQL statement.
- CARTESIAN JOIN: returns the Cartesian product of the sets of records from the two or more joined tables.

Alias Syntax

You can rename a table or a column temporarily by giving another name known as alias.

```
SELECT column1, column2....
FROM table_name AS alias_name
WHERE [condition];
```

SQL Transactions

A transaction is a unit of work that is performed against a database. A transaction is the propagation of one or more changes to the database.

Properties of Transactions:

- *Atomicity*: ensures that all operations within the work unit are completed successfully; otherwise, the transaction is aborted at the point of failure, and previous operations are rolled back to their former state.

- *Consistency*: ensures that the database properly changes states upon a successfully committed transaction.
- *Isolation*: enables transactions to operate independently of and transparent to each other.
- *Durability*: ensures that the result or effect of a committed transaction persists in case of a system failure.

Transaction Control

There are following commands used to control transactions:

- COMMIT: to save the changes.
- ROLLBACK: to rollback the changes.
- SAVEPOINT: creates points within groups of transactions in which to ROLLBACK
- SET TRANSACTION: Places a name on a transaction.

SQL Injection

Injection usually occurs when you ask a user for input, like their name, and instead of a name they give you a SQL statement that you will unknowingly run on your database.

In the example below, the name is restricted to alphanumerical chars plus underscore and to a length between 8 and 20 chars (modify these rules as needed).

```
if (preg_match("/^\w{8,20}$/", $_GET['username'], $matches))
{
  $result = mysql_query ("SELECT * FROM CUSTOMERS
                WHERE name=$matches[0]");
}
else
{
  echo "user name not accepted";
```

```
}
```

To demonstrate the problem, consider this excerpt:

```
// supposed input
$name = "Qadir'; DELETE FROM CUSTOMERS;";
mysql_query("SELECT * FROM CUSTOMSRS WHERE name='{$name}'");
```

SQL Using Views

A view is nothing more than a SQL statement that is stored in the database with an associated name. A view is actually a composition of a table in the form of a predefined SQL query.

Views, which are kind of virtual tables, allow users to do the following:

- Structure data in a way that users or classes of users find natural or intuitive.
- Restrict access to the data such that a user can see and (sometimes) modify exactly what they need and no more.
- Summarize data from various tables which can be used to generate reports.

4 File Structure (B and B+ Trees)

Relative data and information is stored collectively in file formats. A file is a sequence of records stored in binary format. A disk drive is formatted into several blocks that can store records. File records are mapped onto those disk blocks.

File Organization

File Organization defines how file records are mapped onto disk blocks. We have four types of File Organization to organize file records –

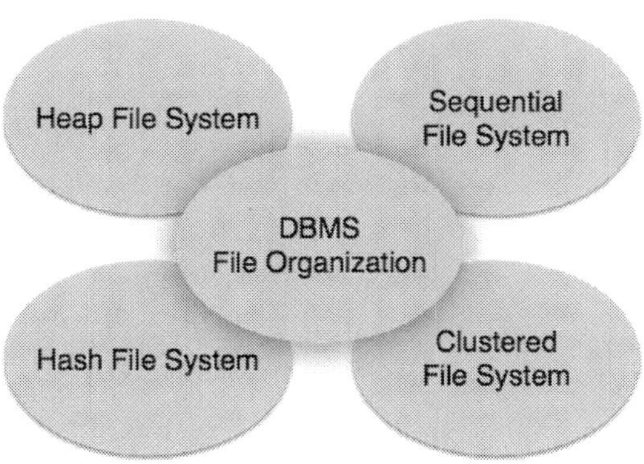

Heap File Organization

When a file is created using Heap File Organization, the Operating System allocates memory area to that file without any further accounting details. File records can be placed anywhere in that memory area. It is the responsibility of the software to manage the records. Heap File does not support any ordering, sequencing, or indexing on its own.

Sequential File Organization

Every file record contains a data field (attribute) to uniquely identify that record. In sequential file organization, records are placed in the file in some sequential order based on the unique key field or search key. Practically, it is not possible to store all the records sequentially in physical form.

$$\text{Blocking Factor} : \left\lfloor \frac{\text{Block size}}{\text{Record size}} \right\rfloor$$

$$\text{Number of Record Block} = \left\lceil \frac{\text{Total no. of record}}{\text{Blocking factor}} \right\rceil$$

$$\text{Average number of block accessed by linear search} : \left\lceil \frac{\#\text{ of Record block}}{2} \right\rceil$$

$$\text{Average number of block aceessed by search} : \left\lceil \log_2 \#\text{ of record block} \right\rceil$$

Hash File Organization

Hash File Organization uses Hash function computation on some fields of the records. The output of the hash function determines the location of disk block where the records are to be placed.

Clustered File Organization

Clustered file organization is not considered good for large databases. In this mechanism, related records from one or more relations are kept in the same disk block, that is, the ordering of records is not based on primary key or search key.

Indexed File

An indexed file is a computer file with an index that allows easy random access to any record given its file key. The key must be such that it uniquely identifies a record. If more than one index is present the other ones are called alternate indexes.

$$\text{Index file factor} = \left\lceil \frac{\#\text{ of record block} + 1}{2} \right\rceil$$

- First (single) level index blocks: $\left\lceil \dfrac{\#\text{ of record blocks}}{\text{index blocking factor}} \right\rceil$
- Number of block accesses $= \lceil \log_2(\text{first level index block}) \rceil + 1$
-

Indexing Types

1. Single level Index
   Primary index (sparse): Ordered with key field
   Clustered index (sparse): Ordered with non-key field
   Secondary index (dense): Ordered with either key or non-key field
2. Multilevel Index
   Indexed sequential access method
   B-tree index
   B^+ tree index

Single Level Index

Dense Index

- For every data base record there exists entry in the index file.
- Number of data base records = Number of entries of the index file.

Sparse Index

- For set of database records there exists single entry in the index files.
- Number of index file entries < Number of database records
- Number of index file entries = Number of database blocks.

Clustered Index

- Search key should be used to physically order the DB.
- Search key is non-key.
- Almost one clustering index is possible.
- Single level index blocks: (No. of distinct values over non key field/ Index blocking factor) +1
- Number of block accesses: [$\log_2$ (single level index blocks) + 1

Secondary Index

- Search key is used to non-ordered the DB file.
- Search key is primary or alternative key.
- Dense indexing is used.
- Number of block accesses ($\log_2$ (single level index block) +1
- Index blocking factors same for all indexes.

Multilevel Index (Static Level Index)

Second level index is always sparse.

Level 1 = "first level index blocks' computed by index.

Level 2 - # of blocks in level (1)/ [index blocking factor]

Level In = [-#of blocks in level (n-1)/ index blocking factor = 1

Number of levels: n

$$\text{Number of blocks} = = \sum_{i=1}^{n} \left(\textit{Number of blocks in level } i \right)$$

Tree (Bayes's/Balan CED Search Tree)

Root node: 2 to n children (pointers)

Internal node: [n/2] to n children

leaf nodes are all at same level.

Block Size = p x (Size of block pointer) + (p - 1) x (Size of key field + size of record pointer)

Minimum number of nodes = $=1+\left(\frac{2[(p/2)^h-1]}{(p/2)-2}\right)$

Maximum number of nodes = $=\frac{p^{h+1}-1}{p-1}$

Maximum possible height $=[1+\log_{p/2}| \quad /2]$

B⁺ Tree

It is same as B-tree.

AU the records are available at leaf (last) level.

Itallowsbothrandomandsequentialaccess,butinB-treeonlyrandom access allowed.

AU the leaf nodes are connected to next leaf node by block pointers [every leaf node has one block pointer]

Order of non-leaf Node: [p x size of block pointer] + [(p - 1) x size of key field] < Block size.

Order of Leaf Node: [(peat - 1) x (size of key field + size of record pointer) + p x (size of block pointer) < Block size.]

5 Transactions and Concurrency Control

A transaction can be defined as a group of tasks. A single task is the minimum processing unit which cannot be divided further.

Whereas the concurrency control ensures that correct results for concurrent operations are generated, while getting those results as quickly as possible.

Transaction Property (ACDI)

A transaction is a very small unit of a program and it may contain several lowlevel tasks.

- *Atomicity*: This property states that a transaction must be treated as an atomic unit, that is, either all of its operations are executed or none.
- *Consistency*: The database must remain in a consistent state after any transaction. No transaction should have any adverse effect on the data residing in the database.
- *Durability*: The database should be durable enough to hold all its latest updates even if the system fails or restarts.
- *Isolation*: In a database system where more than one transaction are being executed simultaneously and in parallel, the property of isolation states that all the transactions will be carried out and executed as if it is the only transaction in the system.

Schedules

A transaction schedule is a tabular representation of how a set of transactions were executed over time. The sequence of the read/write operations of several transactions as they are executed in the Database.

Serial Schedule: A Schedule that does not interleave the actions of different transactions.

- Transaction execute full
- One at a time
- No interleaving

Concurrent schedule: In concurrent schedule, CPU time is shared among two or more transactions in order to run them concurrently. However, this creates the possibility that more than one transaction may need to access a single data item for read/write purpose and the database could contain inconsistent value if such accesses are not handled properly.

Conflict in Concurrent Execution

The DBMS interleaves the actions of different transactions to improve performance, in terms of increased throughput or improved response times for short transactions, but not all interleaving should be allowed.

Ensuring transaction isolation while permitting such concurrent execution is difficult but is necessary for performance reasons. First, while one transaction is waiting for a page to be read in from disk, the CPU can process another transaction. This is because I/O activity can be done in parallel with CPU activity in a computer.

Classification of Schedule Based Serializability

Serializability: When multiple transactions are being executed by the operating system in a multiprogramming environment, there are possibilities that instructions of one transactions are interleaved with some other transaction.

Conflict Serializibilty: Conflict Serializability deals with detecting whether the instructions are conflicting in any way, and specifying the order in which these two instructions will be executed in case there is any conflict. A conflict arises if at least one (or both) of the instructions is a write operation.

Conflict Equivalent: Two schedules having multiple transactions with conflicting operations are said to be conflict equivalent if and only if:

- Both the schedules contain the same set of Transactions.
- The order of conflicting pairs of operation is maintained in both the schedules.

Conflict Serializable: A schedule is said to be conflict-serializable when the schedule is conflict-equivalent to one or more serial schedules.

View Serialisibility: This is another type of serializability that can be derived by creating another schedule out of an existing schedule, involving the same set of transactions.

Irrecoverable Schedule: It's not possible to roll back after the commitment of a transaction as the initial data is no where

Recoverable schedule: A recoverable schedule is a schedule which can recover form the failures.

Recoverale and Cascadeless Schedule

A recoverable schedule is one where, for each pair of Transaction Ti and Tj such that Tj reads data item previously written by Ti the commit operation of Ti appears before the commit operation Tj .

T8	T9	
read(A)		T9 is dependent on T8
write(A)		Non recoverable schedule if T9 commits before T8
	read(A)	
read(B)		

Cascadeless Schedule

T10	T11	T12
read(A)		
read(B)		
write(A)		
	read(A)	
	write(A)	
		read(A)

Strict Recoverable Schedule

If transaction T_i updates the data item A, any other transaction T_j not allowed to R (A) or W (A) untill commit or roll back of T*i*

T_i	T_j
W (A) Commit or rollback	
	R (A) or W (A)

- S: $r_3(x)\ r_1(x)\ w_3\ (x)\ r_2\ (x)\ w_1\ (x)\ r_2\ (y)\ w_2\ (x)\ c_3\ c_1\ c_2$ is recoverable schedule but not cascadless schedule.
- S: $r_1(x)\ r_2\ (z)\ r_3\ (x)\ r_3\ (y)\ w_1\ (x)\ w_3\ (y)\ r_2\ (y)\ w_2\ (z)\ w_2\ (y)\ c_1\ c_2\ c_3$ is recoverable schedule but not cascadless schedule.

Serializibility Checking

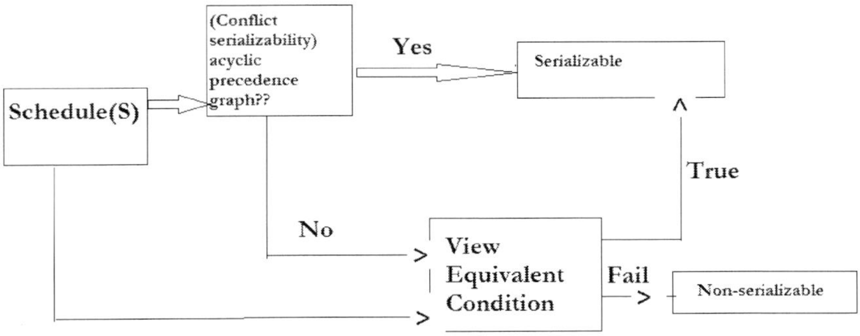

Concurrency Control with lock

A DBMS must be able to ensure that only serializable, recoverable schedules are allowed, and that no actions of committed transactions are lost while undoing aborted transactions. A DBMS typically uses a locking protocol to achieve this. A locking protocol is a set of rules to be followed by each transaction (and enforced by the DBMS), in order to ensure that even though actions of several transactions might be interleaved, the net effect is identical to executing all transactions in some serial order.

Lock Granularity

It deals with the cost of implementing locks depending upon the space and time. Here, space refers to data structure in DBMS for each lock and time refers to handling of lock request and release.

There are two types of lock granularity:

- Fine granularity
- Coarse granularity

Fine granularity refers for small item sizes and coarse granularity refers for large item Sizes.

Database Level

There are two types of database-level in SQL: fixed database that are predefined in the database and flexible database that you can create.

Fixed database are defined at the database level and exist in each database. Members of the db_owner and db_securityadmin database can manage fixed database membership. However, only members of the db_owner database can add members to the db_owner fixed database. There are also some special-purpose fixed database roles in the msdb database.

Table-level

Table-level or referential integrity is managed by the database Jet engine, which establishes rules to maintain table relationships. Understanding table components, and their relationships, is fundamental to complying with the rules of integrity.

Page level

If two customers have accounts on the same page, then only one may be serviced at a time. This is analogous to a page level lock in a database.

Row level

A technique used in database management systems, where a row is locked for writing to prevent other users from accessing data being while it is being updated.

Field level

- It allow concurrent transaction to access the same row, as long as they require the use of different field.
- The most flexible multi user data access, but cost extremely high level of computer overhead.

Lock Type

Database systems equipped with lock-based protocols use a mechanism by which any transaction cannot read or write data until it acquires an appropriate lock on it. Locks are of two kinds:

Binary Locks: A lock on a data item can be in two states; it is either locked or unlocked.

Shared/exclusive: This type of locking mechanism differentiates the locks based on their uses. If a lock is acquired on a data item to perform a write operation, it is an exclusive lock. Allowing more than one transaction to write on the same data item would lead the database into an inconsistent state. Read locks are shared because no data value is being changed.

Basically this lock work on two mode; these are

- Shared(S mode)
- Exclusive(X mode)

Two Phase Locking

The use of locks has helped us to create neat and clean concurrent schedule. The Two Phase Locking Protocol defines the rules of how to acquire the locks on a data item and how to release the locks.

The Two Phase Locking Protocol assumes that a transaction can only be in one of two phases.

Growing Phase

In this phase the transaction can only acquire locks, but cannot release any lock. The transaction enters the growing phase as soon as it acquires the first lock it wants. It cannot release any lock at this phase even if it has finished working with a locked data item. Ultimately the transaction reaches a point where all the lock it may need has been acquired. This point is called Lock Point.

Shrinking Phase

After Lock Point has been reached, the transaction enters the shrinking phase. In this phase the transaction can only release locks, but cannot acquire any new lock. The transaction enters the shrinking phase as soon as it releases the first lock after crossing the Lock Point. From now on it has no option but to keep releasing all the acquired locks.

Basic 2PL Protocol

- Equal serial schedule based on lock point.
- Problemswithbasic2PL;irrecoverableity,Deadlockandstarvation.

Strict 2PL protocol

- Basic 2Pl with all exclusive lock should be hold until commit/roll back.
- It ensure sreializability strict recoverable.
- Problems with strict 2PL; starvation and irrecoverably.

Rigorous 2PL protocol

- Basic 1PL with all locks (S/X) should be hold until commit.
- Equivalent serial schedule based on order of commit.

Class Diagram of Schedules with Serializability

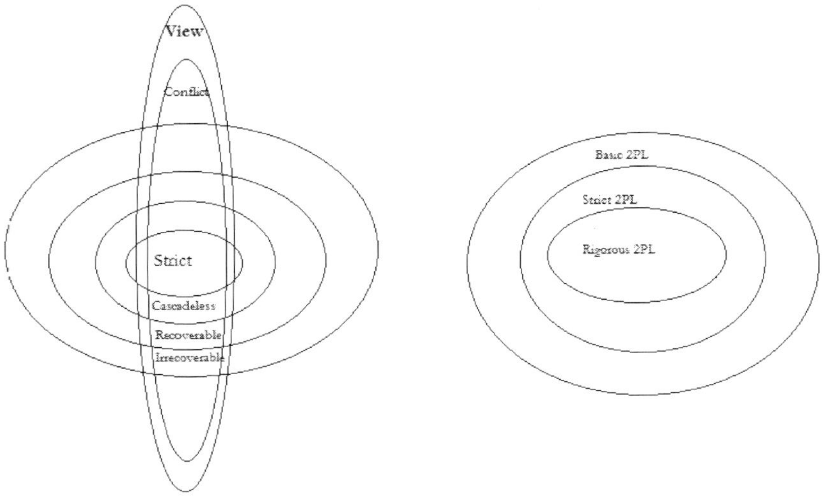

Timestamp Ordering Protocol

The timestamp-ordering protocol ensures serializability among transactions in their conflicting read and write operations. This is the responsibility of the protocol system that the conflicting pair of tasks should be executed according to the timestamp values of the transactions.

- The timestamp of transaction T_i is denoted as TS (T_i).
- Read time-stamp of data-item X is denoted by R-timestamp(X).
- Write time-stamp of data-item X is denoted by W-timestamp(X).

Basic Time stamp ordering Protocol

1. Transaction T issues R (A) option:
   If WTS (A) > TS (T) then roll back T
   Otherwise allow to execute R (A) successfully
   Set RTS (A) = max {(TS (T), RTS (A)}

2. *Transaction T issues W (A) Operation:*
   If RTS (A) > TS (T) then roll back.
   If WTS (A) > TS (T) then roll back.
   Otherwise execute W (A) option set WTS (A) = {TS (T)}

Thomas Write Rule Stamp ordering Protocol

1. Transaction T issues R (A) option:
   If WTS (A) > TS (T) then roll back T
   Otherwise execute successfully
   Set RTS (A) = max {TS (T), RTS (A)}
2. *Transaction T issues W (A) Operation:*
   If RTS (A) > TS (T) then roll back T.
   If WTS (A) > TS (T) then ignore W (A) and continue execution of Trans T.

Strict Time Stamp Ordering Protocol

A transaction T_2 that issues a R (A) or W (A) such that TS (T_2) > WTS (X) has its read write option delayed until the transaction T_1 that write the value X has committed or roll back.

Wait Die Protocol

- Write the transaction in ascending order of time stamp values.
- If T_1 required resources that is hold by T_2 T_1 wait for T_2 to unlock.
- If T_2 required resources that is hold by T_1 then roll back T_2 and restart with same time stamp value.

Wound Wait Protocol

- Write the transaction in ascending order of TS values.
- If T_1 required resources that is hold by T_2 then roll back T_2 restart with same time stamp value.

- If T_2 required resources that is hold by T_1 than T_2 wait for T_1 to unlock.
- Both wait die and wound wait protocols may have starvation.

A Handbook on Computer Science

10

Information Systems and Software Engineering

CONTENTS

1 Information Gathering, Requirement & Feasibility Analysis

Software engineering is an engineering branch associated with development of software product using well-defined scientific principles, methods and procedures. The outcome of software engineering is an efficient and reliable software product.

Software project management has wider scope than software engineering process as it involves communication, pre and post-delivery support etc.

Typical formal definitions of software engineering are:

- "The application of a systematic, disciplined, quantifiable approach to the development, operation, and maintenance of software";
- "An engineering discipline that is concerned with all aspects of software production";
- "The establishment and use of sound engineering principles in order to economically obtain software that is reliable and works efficiently on real machines."

Software Engineering Phases

The following are different phases in software development.

- Analysis
- Design
- Implementation
- Testing
- Deployment and Maintenance

Analysis

This phase is to collect all the required information for developing the software. Here the analyst makes use of various information gathering tools and technique. After a careful analysis of the system the analyst come up with an analysis report.

Design

In the design phase we convert the requirements in the analysis report into a form that can be used to design the software. The design involves the software Architecture, the data structure and the procedures in detail.

Implementation

In this phase the design is translated into a machine readable form. We can use the appropriate programming language for this purpose.

Testing

Once coding is completed we have to test our software to find out if any error exists. The testing focus on the logical internals of the software assuring that all statements have been tested. And on the functional externals the testing is to assure that the sample input will produce the expected output.

Deployment and Maintenance

After a successful testing Deployment starts. Software may definitely undergo changes after it is delivered to the customer. This is because of the following.

- Any new error has been encountered.
- The customer may have new additional requirements.

Requirement Engineering

The process to gather the software requirements from client, analyze and document them is known as requirement engineering.

The goal of requirement engineering is to develop and maintain sophisticated and descriptive 'System Requirements Specification' document.

Requirement Engineering Process

It is a four step process, which includes –

- Feasibility Study
- Requirement Gathering
- Software Requirement Specification
- Software Requirement Validation

Feasibility Study

When the client approaches the organization for getting the desired product developed, it comes up with rough idea about what all functions the software must perform and which all features are expected from the software.

Referencing to this information, the analysts does a detailed study about whether the desired system and its functionality are feasible to develop.

This feasibility study is focused towards goal of the organization. This study analyses whether the software product can be practically materialized in terms of implementation, contribution of project to organization, cost constraints and as per values and objectives of the organization. It explores technical aspects of the project and product such as usability, maintainability, productivity and integration ability. The output of this phase should be a feasibility study report that should contain adequate comments and recommendations for management about whether or not the project should be undertaken.

Requirement Gathering

If the feasibility report is positive towards undertaking the project, next phase starts with gathering requirements from the user. Analysts and engineers communicate with the client and end-users to know their ideas on what the software should provide and which features they want the software to include.

Software Requirement Specification

SRS is a document created by system analyst after the requirements are collected from various stakeholders.

SRS defines how the intended software will interact with hardware, external interfaces, speed of operation, response time of system, portability of software across various platforms, maintainability, speed of recovery after crashing, Security, Quality, Limitations etc.

The requirements received from client are written in natural language. It is the responsibility of system analyst to document the requirements in technical language so that they can be comprehended and useful by the software development team.

SRS should come up with following features:

- User Requirements are expressed in natural language.
- Technical requirements are expressed in structured language, which is used inside the organization.
- Design description should be written in Pseudo code.
- Format of Forms and GUI screen prints.
- Conditional and mathematical notations for DFDs etc.

Software Requirement Validation

After requirement specifications are developed, the requirements mentioned in this document are validated. User might ask for illegal, impractical solution or experts may interpret the requirements incorrectly. This results in huge increase in cost if not nipped in the bud. Requirements can be checked against following conditions -

- If they can be practically implemented
- If they are valid and as per functionality and domain of software
- If there are any ambiguities
- If they are complete
- If they can be demonstrated

Requirement Elicitation Process

Requirement elicitation process can be depicted using the following diagram:

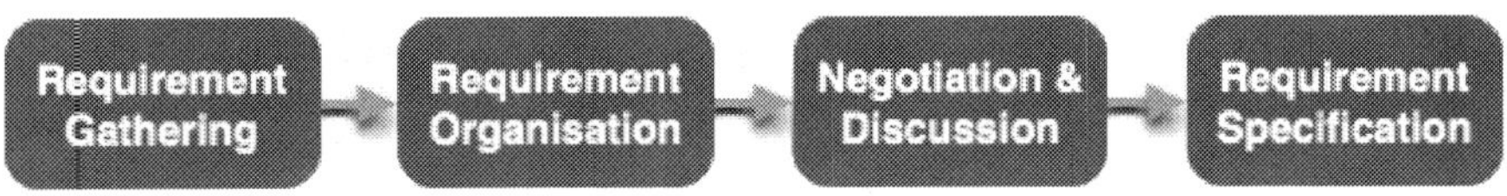

Requirements gathering - The developers discuss with the client and end users and know their expectations from the software.

Organizing Requirements - The developers prioritize and arrange the requirements in order of importance, urgency and convenience.

Negotiation & discussion - If requirements are ambiguous or there are some conflicts in requirements of various stakeholders, if they are, it is then negotiated and discussed with stakeholders. Requirements may then be prioritized and reasonably compromised.

The requirements come from various stakeholders. To remove the ambiguity and conflicts, they are discussed for clarity and correctness. Unrealistic requirements are compromised reasonably.

Documentation- All formal & informal, functional and non-functional requirements are documented and made available for next phase processing.

Requirement Elicitation Techniques

Requirements Elicitation is the process to find out the requirements for an intended software system by communicating with client, end users, system users and others who have a stake in the software system development.

There are various ways to discover requirements

Interviews: Interviews are strong medium to collect requirements. Organization may conduct several types of interviews such as:

- Structured (closed) interviews, where every single information to gather is decided in advance, they follow pattern and matter of discussion firmly.
- Non-structured (open) interviews, where information to gather is not decided in advance, more flexible and less biased.
- Oral interviews
- Written interviews
- One-to-one interviews which are held between two persons across the table.
- Group interviews which are held between groups of participants. They help to uncover any missing requirement as numerous people are involved.

Surveys

Organization may conduct surveys among various stakeholders by querying about their expectation and requirements from the upcoming system.

Questionnaires

A document with pre-defined set of objective questions and respective options is handed over to all stakeholders to answer, which are collected and compiled.

A shortcoming of this technique is, if an option for some issue is not mentioned in the questionnaire, the issue might be left unattended.

Task analysis

Team of engineers and developers may analyse the operation for which the new system is required. If the client already has some software to perform certain operation, it is studied and requirements of proposed system are collected.

Domain Analysis

Every software falls into some domain category. The expert people in the domain can be a great help to analyse general and specific requirements.

Brainstorming

An informal debate is held among various stakeholders and all their inputs are recorded for further requirements analysis.

Prototyping

Prototyping is building user interface without adding detail functionality for user to interpret the features of intended software product. It helps giving better idea of requirements. If there is no software installed at client's end for developer's reference and the client is not aware of its own requirements, the developer creates a prototype based on initially mentioned requirements. The prototype is shown to the client and the feedback is noted. The client feedback serves as an input for requirement gathering.

Observation

Team of experts visit the client's organization or workplace. They observe the actual working of the existing installed systems. They observe the workflow at client's end and how execution problems are dealt. The team itself draws some conclusions which aid to form requirements expected from the software.

Software Requirements Characteristics

Gathering software requirements is the foundation of the entire software development project. Hence they must be clear, correct and well-defined.

A complete Software Requirement Specifications must be:

- Clear
- Correct
- Consistent
- Coherent
- Comprehensible
- Modifiable
- Verifiable
- Prioritized
- Unambiguous
- Traceable
- Credible source

Software Requirements

We should try to understand what sort of requirements may arise in the requirement elicitation phase and what kinds of requirements are expected from the software system.

Broadly software requirements should be categorized in two categories:

Functional Requirements

Requirements, which are related to functional aspect of software fall into this category.

They define functions and functionality within and from the software system.

Examples -

- Search option given to user to search from various invoices.
- User should be able to mail any report to management.
- Users can be divided into groups and groups can be given separate rights.
- Should comply business rules and administrative functions.
- Software is developed keeping downward compatibility intact.

Non-Functional Requirements

Requirements, which are not related to functional aspect of software, fall into this category. They are implicit or expected characteristics of software, which users make assumption of.

Non-functional requirements include -

- Security
- Logging
- Storage
- Configuration
- Performance
- Cost
- Interoperability
- Flexibility
- Disaster recovery
- Accessibility

Requirements are categorized logically as

- Must Have: Software cannot be said operational without them.
- Should have: Enhancing the functionality of software.
- Could have: Software can still properly function with these requirements.

- Wish list: These requirements do not map to any objectives of software.

While developing software, 'Must have' must be implemented, 'Should have' is a matter of debate with stakeholders and negation, whereas 'could have' and 'wish list' can be kept for software updates.

User Interface Requirements

UI is an important part of any software or hardware or hybrid system. A software is widely accepted if it is -

- easy to operate
- quick in response
- effectively handling operational errors
- providing simple yet consistent user interface

User acceptance majorly depends upon how user can use the software. UI is the only way for users to perceive the system. A well performing software system must also be equipped with attractive, clear, consistent and responsive user interface. Otherwise the functionalities of software system cannot be used in convenient way. A system is said be good if it provides means to use it efficiently. User interface requirements are as: -

- Content presentation
- Easy Navigation
- Simple interface
- Responsive
- Consistent UI elements
- Feedback mechanism
- Default settings
- Purposeful layout
- Strategically use of colour and texture.
- Provide help information
- User centric approach
- Group based view settings.

Software System Analyst

System analyst in an IT organization is a person, who analyses the requirement of proposed system and ensures that requirements are conceived and documented properly & correctly. Role of an analyst starts during Software Analysis Phase of SDLC. It is the responsibility of analyst to make sure that the developed software meets the requirements of the client.

System Analysts have the following responsibilities:

- Analysing and understanding requirements of intended software
- Understanding how the project will contribute in the organization objectives
- Identify sources of requirement
- Validation of requirement
- Develop and implement requirement management plan
- Documentation of business, technical, process and product requirements
- Coordination with clients to prioritize requirements and remove and ambiguity
- Finalizing acceptance criteria with client and other stakeholders

Software Metrics and Measures

Software Measures can be understood as a process of quantifying and symbolizing various attributes and aspects of software.

Software Metrics provide measures for various aspects of software process and software product.

Software measures are fundamental requirement of software engineering. They not only help to control the software development process but also aid to keep quality of ultimate product excellent.

According to Tom DeMarco, a (Software Engineer), "You cannot control what you cannot measure." By his saying, it is very clear how important software measures are.

Let us see some software metrics:

- Size Metrics - LOC (Lines of Code), mostly calculated in thousands of delivered source code lines, denoted as KLOC.
- Function Point Count is measure of the functionality provided by the software. Function Point count defines the size of functional aspect of software.
- Complexity Metrics - McCabe's Cyclamate complexity quantifies the upper bound of the number of independent paths in a program, which is perceived as complexity of the program or its modules. It is represented in terms of graph theory concepts by using control flow graph.
- Quality Metrics - Defects, their types and causes, consequence, intensity of severity and their implications define the quality of product.
- The number of defects found in development process and number of defects reported by the client after the product is installed or delivered at client-end, define quality of product.
- Process Metrics - In various phases of SDLC, the methods and tools used, the company standards and the performance of development are software process metrics.
- Resource Metrics - Effort, time and various resources used, represents metrics for resource measurement.

2 DFD and Process Specification

Data flow diagram (DFD) represents the flows of data between different processesinabusiness.Itisagraphicaltechniquethatdepictsinformation flowandthetransformsthatareappliedasdatamoveforminputtooutput. It provides a simple, intuitive method for describing business processes withoutfocusingonthedetailsofcomputersystems.DFDsareattractive techniquebecausetheyprovidewhatusersdoratherthanwhatcomputers do.

DFDs only involve four symbols. They are:

- Process
- Data Object
- Data Store
- External entity

Process

Transform of incoming data flow(s) to outgoing flow(s).

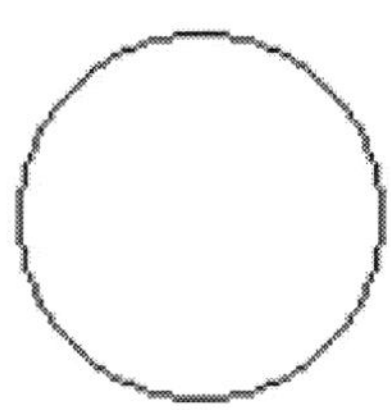

Data Flow

Movement of data in the system.

Data Store

Data repositories for data that is not moving. It may be as simple as a buffer or a queue or a s sophisticated as a relational database.

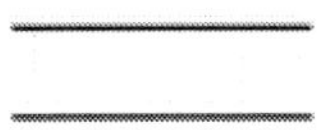

External Entity

Sources of destinations outside the specified system boundary.

Process Specification

A process specification is a method used to document, analyse and explain the decision-making logic and formulas used to create output data from process input data. Its objective is to flow down and specify regulatory/engineering requirements and procedures. High-quality, consistent data requires clear and complete process specifications.

A process specification reduces ambiguity, allowing an individual or organization to obtain a precise description of executed tasks and accomplishments and validate system design, including the data dictionary and data flow diagrams.

Process specifications are created for primitive processes and data flow diagram processes of a higher level (minispecs). Process logic is best represented through structured English, decision tables, decision trees or specified formulas or algorithms and is used to communicate engineering requirements and procedures to businesses involved in the creation of a process. Process descriptions may exist on a form or in a computer aided software engineering (CASE) tool repository.

Process specifications are not created for processes requiring physical input or output, processes representing simple data validation or processes with pre-existing and prewritten code.

3 I/O Design, Process Life Cycle

Software Life Cycle Model

A systems development life cycle is the method of organizing the creation, use and disposal of new hardware and software in the computer industry. A systems development life cycle follows the same pattern as most new inventions: find a problem, design the solution and then implement the solution. The term is a catchall for a large number of different methodologies and processes, all of which follow this same basic pattern.

There isn't a single process called a systems development life cycle--rather, there are many different methodologies and models that all fall under the term. The most basic model, often called the Waterfall Method, consists of seven steps. These steps are taken in a specified order, each building on the last. While this makes the Waterfall one of the most complete models, it also makes it the slowest and most expensive.

Other developmental methods work on similar, but different, principles. Other systems development life cycle methods skip, combine or reorder the basic steps. Generally, this is done to speed up the creative process or lower developmental costs. In addition, models exist to take advantage of alternate computing styles and business structures.

The basic steps of a systems development life cycle are broken into four areas. The first three, design, construction and implementation, are common parts of many new systems and inventions. The forth, disposal, is relatively uncommon. Most of these four areas have 'sub steps' that make up the full cycle.

Design is the first step in nearly every model, because without an idea there isn't anything to build. The design step has the largest number of sub steps of any of the areas. Initiation requires that a project be brought to the design team to begin the process. The systems concept and planning steps centre on internal accounting and feasibility studies for the designing company. Requirements analysis centres on focusing on user needs, and design is the initial creation of the software or hardware model.

The construction phase in a software development life cycle is often one of the longest. During these sub stages, the hardware or software is actually built and tested. The first step, development, is the actual creation of the system, and depending on the project, this can take anywhere from days to years to complete. The second step, testing, involves non-developers using the product in order to generate feedback. Based on that feedback, the project will return to development or go onto the next phase.

Implementation is when users are actually using the software or hardware. During the first sub step, also called implementation, the project is integrated into existing systems, and user training takes place. Operations and maintenance comprise the second step. During this time, its target audience uses the project normally and performs regular maintenance on the system.

The last area, disposal, has no sub steps. During this phase, the project is pulled out of the users' systems. If it is hardware, it is disposed of normally. Software is migrated out, and existing data is converted to a newer system that is entering its implementation phase.

Waterfall Model

The waterfall Model is a linear sequential flow. In which progress is seen as flowing steadily downwards (like a waterfall) through the phases of software implementation. This means that any phase in the development process begins only if the previous phase is complete. The waterfall approach does not define the process to go back to the previous phase to handle changes in requirement. The waterfall approach is the earliest approach that was used for software development.

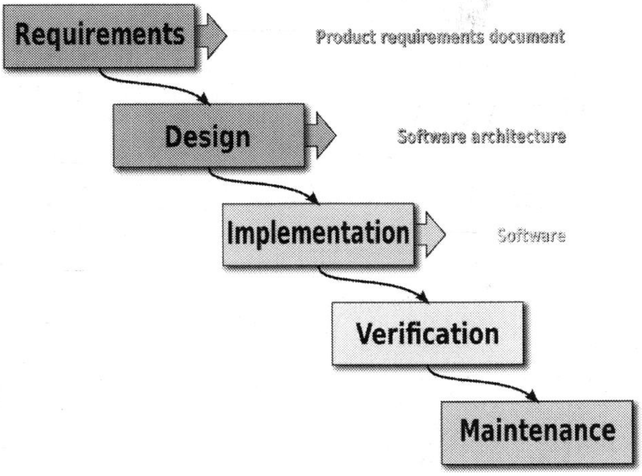

Spiral Method (SDM)

It is combining elements of both design and prototyping-in-stages, in an effort to combine advantages of top-down and bottom-up concepts. This model of development combines the features of the prototyping model and the waterfall model. The spiral model is favored for large, expensive, and complicated projects. This model uses many of the same phases as the waterfall model, in essentially the same order, separated by planning, risk assessment, and the building of prototypes and simulations.

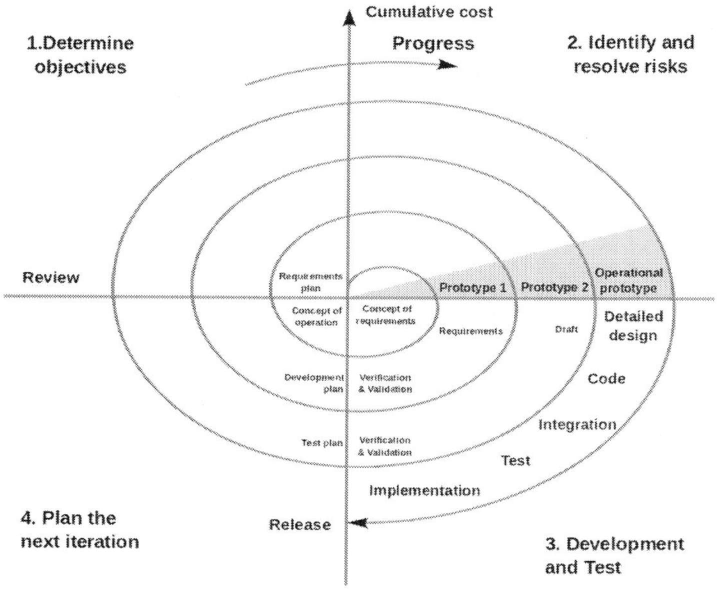

Iterative and Incremental Method

It is developed to overcome the weaknesses of the waterfall model. It starts with an initial planning and ends with deployment with the cyclic interactions in between. The basic idea behind this method is to develop a system through repeated cycles (iterative) and in smaller portions at a time (incremental), allowing software developers to take advantage of what was learned during development of earlier parts or versions of the system.

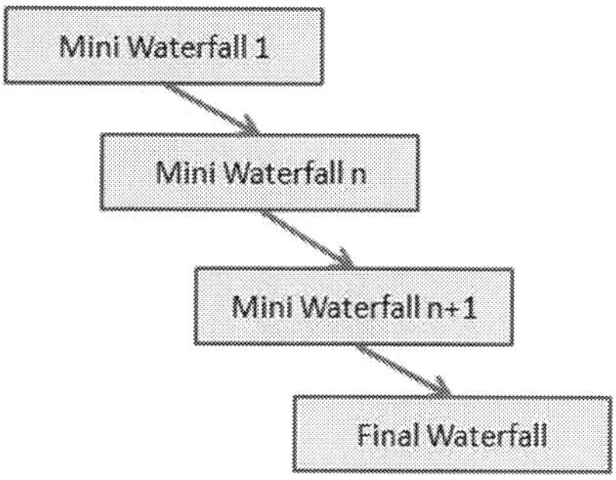

Prototyping Model

The Prototyping Model is a systems development method (SDM) in which a prototype (an early approximation of a final system or product) is built, tested, and then reworked as necessary until an acceptable prototype is finally achieved from which the complete system or product can now be developed. This model works best in scenarios where not all of the project requirements are known in detail ahead of time. It is an iterative, trial-and-error process that takes place between the developers and the users.

There are several steps in the Prototyping Model:

The new system requirements are defined in as much detail as possible. This usually involves interviewing a number of users representing all the departments or aspects of the existing system.

A preliminary design is created for the new system.

A first prototype of the new system is constructed from the preliminary design. This is usually a scaled-down system, and represents an approximation of the characteristics of the final product.

The users thoroughly evaluate the first prototype, noting its strengths and weaknesses, what needs to be added, and what should to be removed. The developer collects and analyzes the remarks from the users.

The first prototype is modified, based on the comments supplied by the users, and a second prototype of the new system is constructed.

The second prototype is evaluated in the same manner as was the first prototype.

The preceding steps are iterated as many times as necessary, until the users are satisfied that the prototype represents the final product desired.

The final system is constructed, based on the final prototype.

The final system is thoroughly evaluated and tested. Routine maintenance is carried out on a continuing basis to prevent large-scale failures and to minimize downtime.

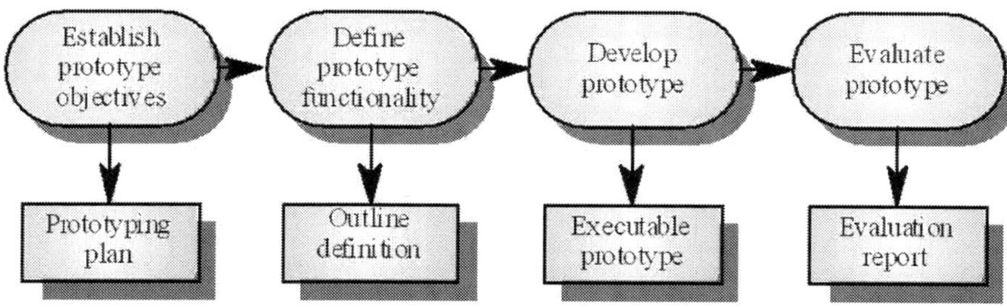

Evolutionary Prototyping Model

Evaluation prototyping requirements are gathered in this phase. This evolutionary prototyping model is the main focus of the project managers and stakeholders. Meetings with managers, stakeholders and users are held in order to determine the requirements. Who is going to use the system? How will they use the system? What data should be input into the system?

What data should be output by the system? These are general questions that get answered during a requirements gathering phase. This produces a nice big list of functionality that the system should provide, which describes functions the system should perform, business logic that processes data, what data is stored and used by the system, and how the user interface should work. The overall result is the system as a whole and how it performs, not how it is actually going to do it.

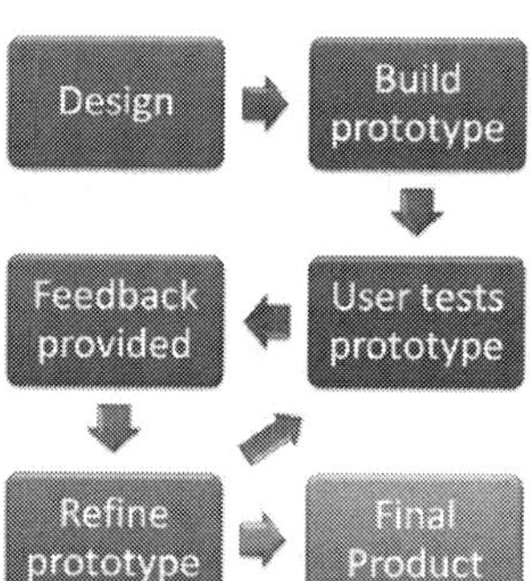

Rapid Application Development Model

RAD model is Rapid Application Development model. It is a type of incremental model. In RAD model the components or functions are developed in parallel as if they were mini projects. The developments are time boxed, delivered and then assembled into a working prototype. This can quickly give the customer something to see and use and to provide feedback regarding the delivery and their requirements.

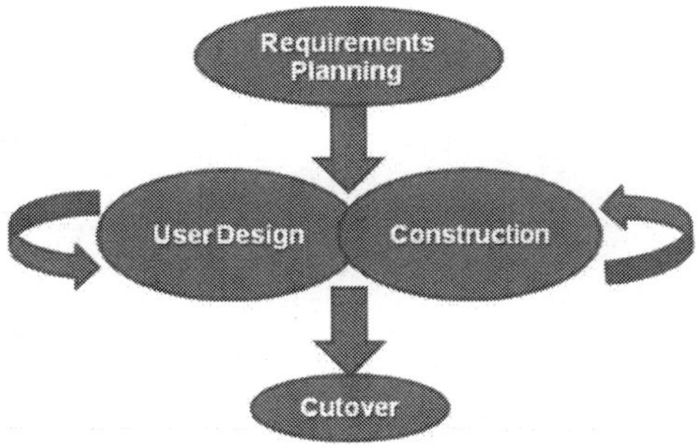

Agile Methodology

- Development team focuses on construction than design and documentation
- Intended to deliver software quickly

4 Planning and Management the Project

Software Project Planning

Planning provides a road map for the software development process.

Objective of Software Project Planning

The objective of software project planning is to provide a frame work that enables the manager to make reasonable estimates of resources, cost and schedule.

Software Scope

The first activity in software project planning is the determination of software scope. A software project scope must be unambiguous and understandable at the management and technical levels. The software scope means the actual operation that is going to carried out by the software and its plus points and limitations.

Resources

The second task of software planning is the estimation of resources required. Each resource is specified with the following characteristic. Resource descriptions, details of availability, when it is required, how long it is required.

- Human Resource
- Hardware Resource
- Software Resource

People are the primary software development resource. The planner evaluate the scope and select the appropriate people for appropriate positions.

COCOMO

The Constructive Cost Model is an algorithmic software cost estimation model developed by Barry W. Boehm. The model uses a basic regression formula with parameters that are derived from historical project data and current as well as future project characteristics. COCOMO was first published in Boehm's 1981 book Software Engineering Economics as a model for estimating effort, cost, and schedule for software projects. It drew on a study of 63 projects at TRW Aerospace where Boehm was Director of Software Research and Technology. The study examined projects ranging in size from 2,000 to 100,000 lines of code, and programming languages ranging from assembly to PL/me. These projects were based on the waterfall model of software development which was the prevalent software development process in 1981. References to this model typically call it COCOMO 81. In 1995 COCOMO II was developed and finally published in 2000 in the book Software Cost Estimation with COCOMO II. COCOMO II is the successor of COCOMO 81 and is better suited for estimating modern software development projects. It provides more support for modern software development processes and an updated project database. The need for the new model came as software development technology moved from mainframe and overnight batch processing to desktop development, code reusability and the use of off-the-shelf software components.

Basic COCOMO

Basic COCOMO: computes software development effort and cost as a function of program size expressed in estimated DSIs. There are three modes within Basic COCOMO:

- Organic Mode: Development projects typically are uncomplicated and involve small experienced teams. The planned software is not considered innovative and requires a relatively small amount of DSIs (typically under 50,000).
- Semidetached Mode: Development projects typically are more complicated than in Organic Mode and involve teams of people with mixed levels of experience. The software requires no more than 300,000 DSIs. The project has characteristics of both projects for Organic Mode and projects for Embedded Mode.
- Embedded Mode: Development projects must fit into a rigid set of requirements because the software is to be embedded in a strongly joined complex of hardware, software, regulations and operating procedures.
- Intermediate COCOMO: an extension of the Basic model that computes software development effort by adding a set of "cost drivers," that will determine the effort and duration of the project, such as assessments of personnel and hardware.
- Detailed COCOMO: an extension of the Intermediate model that adds effort multipliers for each phase of the project to determine the cost drivers impact on each step.

The Basic COCOMO equations take the form:

$$E = a_b \, KLOC^{b_b}$$

$$D = c_b \, E^{d_b}$$

Where E is the effort applied in person-months, D is the development time in chronological months and KLOC is the estimated number of delivered lines of code for the project (express in thousands). The coefficients a_b and c_b and the exponent's b_b and d_b are given in Table 1.

Table 1. Basic COCOMO Model

Software Project	a_b	b_b	c_b	d_b
organic	2.4	1.05	2.5	0.38
Semi-detached	3.0	1.12	2.5	0.35

embedded	3.6	1.20	2.5	0.32

Software Configuration Management (SCM)

SCM tool helps in maintaining different version of the configurable item.

Maintenance

Mean time between failure (MTBF) = MTTF + MTTR

$$\text{Availability} = \frac{\text{MTTF}}{\text{MTBF}} = \frac{\text{MTTF}}{\text{MTTF} + \text{MTTR}}$$

$$\text{Software Maturity Index} = \frac{\left[M_T - (f_a + f_d + f_c)\right]}{M_T}$$

M_T = Number of modules released

f_a = Number of modules added

f_d = Number of modules deleted

f_c = Number of modules changed

5 Design, Coding, Testing, Implementation & Maintenance

Design

Software design is a process to transform user requirements into some suitable form, which helps the programmer in software coding and implementation.

For assessing user requirements, an SRS (Software Requirement Specification) document is created whereas for coding and implementation, there is a need of more specific and detailed requirements in software terms. The output of this process can directly be used into implementation in programming languages.

Software design is the first step in SDLC (Software Design Life Cycle), which moves the concentration from problem domain to solution domain. It tries to specify how to fulfill the requirements mentioned in SRS.

Cohesion Coupling

Cohesion is a measure that defines the degree of intra-dependability within elements of a module. The greater the cohesion, the better is the program design.

There are seven types of cohesion, namely –

- **Co-incidental cohesion** - It is unplanned and random cohesion, which might be the result of breaking the program into smaller modules for the sake of modularization. Because it is unplanned, it may serve confusion to the programmers and is generally not-accepted.
- **Logical cohesion** - When logically categorized elements are put together into a module, it is called logical cohesion.
- **Temporal Cohesion** - When elements of module are organized such that they are processed at a similar point in time, it is called temporal cohesion.
- **Procedural cohesion** - When elements of module are grouped together, which are executed sequentially in order to perform a task, it is called procedural cohesion.
- **Communicational cohesion** - When elements of module are grouped together, which are executed sequentially and work on same data (information), it is called communicational cohesion.
- **Sequential cohesion** - When elements of module are grouped because the output of one element serves as input to another and so on, it is called sequential cohesion.
- **Functional cohesion** - It is considered to be the highest degree of cohesion, and it is highly expected. Elements of module in functional cohesion are grouped because they all contribute to a single well-defined function. It can also be reused.

Module Coupling

Coupling is a measure that defines the level of inter-dependability among modules of a program. It tells at what level the modules interfere and interact with each other. The lower coupling is the better for the program.

There are five levels of coupling, namely -

- **Content Coupling** - When a module can directly access or modify or refer to the content of another module, it is called content level coupling.

- **Common Coupling-** When multiple modules have read and write access to some global data, it is called common or global coupling.
- **Control Coupling-** Two modules are called control-coupled if one of them decides the function of the other module or changes its flow of execution.
- **Stamp Coupling-** When multiple modules share common data structure and work on different part of it, it is called stamp coupling.
- **Data Coupling-** Data coupling is when two modules interact with each other by means of passing data (as parameter). If a module passes data structure as parameter, then the receiving module should use all its components.

Software Testing

- Testing is the process of executing a program with the intent of finding errors.
- All tests should be traceable to customer requirements.
- Tests should be planned long before testing begins.
- The Pareto principle (80% of all errors will likely be found in 20% of the code) applies to software testing.
- Testing should begin in the small and progress to the large.
- Exhaustive testing is not possible.
- To be most effective, testing should be conducted by an independent third party.

Verification

Verification is a process of evaluating the intermediary work products of a software development lifecycle to check if we are in the right track of creating the final product.

Validation

Validation is the process of evaluating the final product to check whether the software meets the business needs.

Acceptance Testing

Testing is conducted to determine if the requirements of a specification or contract are met. It may involve chemical tests, physical tests, or performance tests.

Alpha and Beta Testing

- Used when the software is developed as a product for anonymous customers.
- The alpha tests are conducted at the developer's site by a customer.
- The beta tests are conducted by the customers/end users at their sites.

Testing and debugging are two different processes which occur at same time which identify bug and other removes the bug (respectively).

Unit Tests

Tests the smallest unit of functionality, typically a method/function (e.g. given a class with a particular state, calling x method on the class should cause y to happen).

Integration Tests

Integration tests build on unit tests by combining the units of code and testing that the resulting combination functions correctly.

Functional Tests

Functional tests check a particular feature for correctness by comparing the results for a given input against the specification. It is also known as "Black Box testing".

- Boundary value analysis

  Boundary value analysis and equivalence partitioning both are test case design strategies in black box testing.

- Equivalence Class Testing

  In this method the input domain data is divided into different equivalence data classes. This method is typically used to reduce the total number of test cases to a finite set of testable test cases, still covering maximum requirements. In short it is the process of taking all possible test cases and placing them into classes. One test value is picked from each class while testing.

For example: If you are testing for an input box accepting numbers from 1 to 1000 then there is no use in writing thousand test cases for all 1000 valid input numbers plus other test cases for invalid data.

Using equivalence partitioning method test cases can be divided into three sets of input data called as classes. Each test case is a representative of respective class.

Decision Table Based Testing

A decision table is most widely adopted graphical tool for representing process specification.

Decision table are useful for describing situation in which a number of combinations of action are taken under varying set of conditions. These are used to represent and analyse complex logical relationship.

The four quadrants

Conditions	Condition alternatives
Actions	Action entries

Structural Testing

- The structural testing is the testing of the structure of the system or component.
- Structural testing is often referred to as 'white box' or 'glass box' or

'clear-box testing' because in structural testing we are interested in what is happening 'inside the system/application'.

- In structural testing the testers are required to have the knowledge of the internal implementations of the code. Here the testers require knowledge of how the software is implemented, how it works.

Static White Box Testing: It is a type of testing in which the program source code is tested without running it.

Dynamic White Box Testing: This involves testing a running program. So, now binaries and executable are desired.

Loop Testing

Loop testing a white box testing technique performed to validate the loops. There are four kinds of loops as:

- Simple Loops
- Nested Loops
- Concatenated Loops
- Unstructured Loops

Stress Testing

- It is a type of non-functional testing.
- It involves testing beyond normal operational capacity, often to a breaking point, in order to observe the results.

It is better to prevent the injection of defects rather than finding them and fixing them.

Testing Performed?

Integration testing is performed after unit testing and before system testing.

Big Bang: It is an approach to Integration Testing where all or most of the units are combined together and tested at one go. Top Down: It is an approach to Integration Testing where top level units are tested first and lower level units are tested step by step after that.

Bottom Up: It is an approach to Integration Testing where bottom level units are tested first and upper level units step by step after that.

Sandwich/Hybrid: It is an approach to Integration Testing which is a combination of Top Down and Bottom Up approaches.

Testing phase requires largest manpower.

Maintenance

Software maintenance is widely accepted part of SDLC now a days. It stands for all the modifications and updations done after the delivery of software product.

Types of Maintenance

Following are some types of maintenance based on their characteristics:

- **Corrective Maintenance** - This includes modifications and updations done in order to correct or fix problems, which are either discovered by user or concluded by user error reports.
- **Adaptive Maintenance** - This includes modifications and updations applied to keep the software product up-to date and tuned to the ever changing world of technology and business environment.
- **Perfective Maintenance** - This includes modifications and updates done in order to keep the software usable over long period of time. It includes new features, new user requirements for refining the software and improve its reliability and performance.
- **Preventive Maintenance** - This includes modifications and updations to prevent future problems of the software. It aims to attend problems, which are not significant at this moment but may cause serious issues in future.

Implementation

In the implementation phase, the team builds the components either from scratch or by composition. Given the architecture document from the design phase and the requirement document from the analysis phase, the team should build exactly what has been requested, though there is still room for innovation and flexibility. For example, a component may be narrowly designed for this particular system, or the component may be made more general to satisfy a reusability guideline.

The implementation phase deals with issues of quality, performance, baselines, libraries, and debugging. The end deliverable is the product itself.

Software Implementation Challenges

There are some challenges faced by the development team while implementing the software. Some of them are mentioned as:

- Code-Reuse - Programming interfaces of present-day languages are very sophisticated and are equipped huge library functions. Still, to bring the cost down of end product, the organization management prefers to re-use the code, which was created earlier for some other software. There are huge issues faced by programmers for compatibility checks and deciding how much code to re-use.
- Version Management - Every time new software is issued to the customer, developers have to maintain version and configuration related documentation. This documentation needs to be highly accurate and available on time.
- Target-Host - The software program, which is being developed in the organization, needs to be designed for host machines at the customers end. But at times, it is impossible to design software that works on the target machines.

A Handbook on Computer Science

11

Computer Networks

CONTENTS

1 ISO/OSI Stack, LAN Technology (Ethernet, Topology)

A computer network or data network is a telecommunications network which allows computers to exchange data. In computer networks, networked computing devices pass data to each other along data connections (network links). Data is transferred in the form of packets. The connections between nodes are established using either cable media or wireless media. The best-known computer network is the Internet.

Characteristics of a computer network

- Share Resources from one computer to another
- Create files and store them in one computer, access those files from the other computer(s) connected over the network
- Connect a printer, scanner, or a fax machine to one computer within the network and let other computers of the network use the machines available over network.

Following is the list of hardware's required to setup a computer network.

- Network Cables
- Distributors
- Routers
- Internal Network Cards
- External Network Cards

OSI Model

There are n numbers of users who use computer network and are located over the world. So to ensure national and worldwide data communication systems can be developed and are compatible to each other. ISO has developed this. ISO stands for International organization of Standardization. This is called a model for open system interconnection (OSI) and is normally called as OSI model.

The ISO-OSI model consists of seven layer architecture. It defines seven layers or levels in a complete communication system.

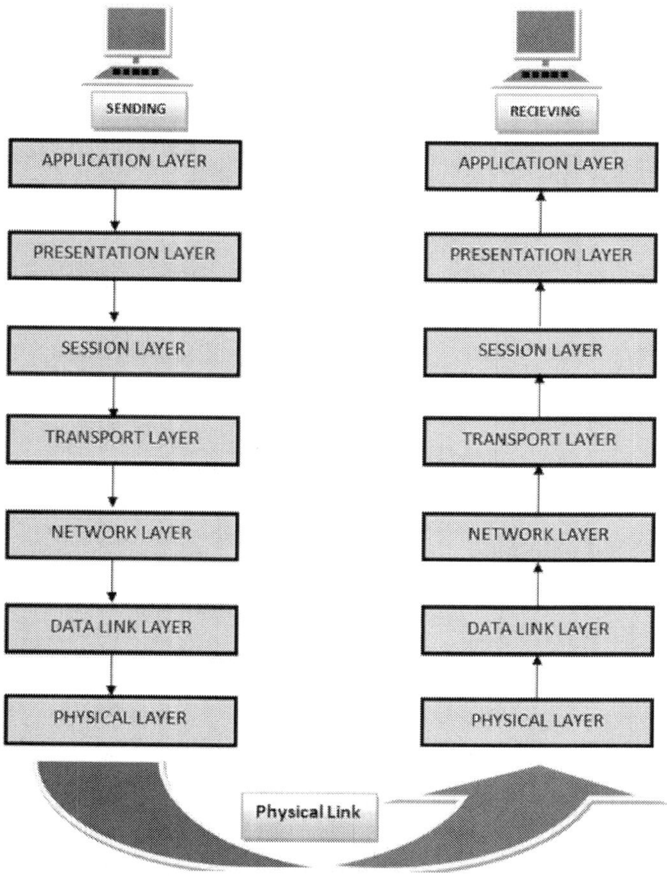

Feature of OSI Model

- Big picture of network is understandable through this OSI model.
- We see how hardware and software work together.
- We can understand new technologies as they are developed.
- Troubleshooting is easier by separate networks.
- Can be used to compare basic functional relationships on different networks.

Functions of Different Layers

Layer 1: The Physical Layer

It activates, maintain and deactivate the physical connection. Voltages and data rates needed for transmission is defined in the physical layer. It converts the digital bits into electrical signal.

Layer 2: Data Link Layer

Data link layer synchronizes the information which is to be transmitted over the data. Error controlling is easily done. The encoded data are then passed to physical. Error detection bits are used by the data link on layer. It also corrects the errors. Outgoing messages are assembled into frames. Then the system waits for the acknowledgements to be received after the transmission. It is reliable to send message.

Layer 3: The Network Layer

It routes the signal through different channels to the other end. It acts as a network controller. It decides by which route data should take. It divides the outgoing messages into packets and to assemble incoming packets into messages for higher levels.

Layer 4: Transport Layer

It decides if data transmission should be on parallel path or single path. Functions such as multiplexing, segmenting or splitting on the data done by layer four that is transport layer. Transport layer breaks the message (data) into small units so that they are handled more efficiently by the network layer.

Layer 5: The Session Layer

Session layer manages and synchronize the conversation between two different applications. Transfer of data from one destination to another session layer streams of data are marked and are resynchronized properly, so that the ends of the messages are not cut prematurely and data loss is avoided.

Layer 6: The presentation Layer

Presentation layer takes care that the data is sent in such a way that the receiver will understand the information (data) and will be able to use the data. Languages (syntax) can be different of the two communicating systems. Under this condition presentation layer plays a role translator.

Layer 7: Application Layer

It is the top layer. Manipulation of data (information) in various ways is done in this layer. Transferring of files disturbing the results to the user is also done in this layer. Mail services, directory services, network resource etc. are services provided by application layer.

Merits of OSI Reference Model

- OSI model distinguish between the services, interfaces and protocols.
- Protocols of OSI model are very well hidden.
- They can be replaced by new protocols as technology changes.
- Supports connection oriented as well as connectionless service.

Demerits of OSI reference Model

- Model was devised before the invention of protocols.
- Fitting of protocols is tedious task.

LAN Technologies

A local area network (LAN) is a group of computers and associated devices connected to a server using a shared common communications line or wireless link.

Ethernet

A local-area network (LAN) architecture developed by Xerox Corporation in cooperation with DEC and Intel in 1976. Ethernet uses a bus or star topology and supports data transfer rates of 10 Mbps. The Ethernet specification served as the basis for the IEEE 802.3 standard, which specifies the physical and lower software layers. Ethernet uses the CSMA/CD access method to handle simultaneous demands. It is one of the most widely implemented LAN standards.

A newer version of Ethernet, called 100Base-T (or Fast Ethernet), supports data transfer rates of 100 Mbps. And the newest version, Gigabit Ethernet supports data rates of 1 gigabit (1,000 megabits) per second.

Network Topology

Network topology is the arrangement of the various elements (links, nodes, etc.) of a computer network. Essentially, it is the topological structure of a network and may be depicted physically or logically.

- *BUS Topology:* Bus topology is a network type in where every computer and network device is connected to single cable.
- *RING Topology:* It is called ring topology because it forms a ring as each computer is connected to another computer, with the last one connected to the first. Exactly two neighbours for each device.
- *STAR Topology:* In this type of topology all the computers are connected to a single hub through a cable. This hub is the central node and all others nodes are connected to the central node.
- *MESH Topology:* It is a point-to-point connection to other nodes or devices. Traffic is carried only between two devices or nodes to which it is connected. Mesh has n (n-2)/2 physical channels to link h_n devices.
- *TREE Topology:* It has a root node and all other nodes are connected to it forming a hierarchy. It is also called hierarchical topology. It should at least have three levels to the hierarchy.
- *HYBRID Topology:* It is two different types of topologies which is a mixture of two or more topologies. For example if in an office in one department ring topology is used and in another star topology is used, connecting these topologies will result in Hybrid Topology (ring topology and star topology).

2 Flow and Error Control, Congestion Control

Flow Control

When a data frame (Layer-2 data) is sent from one host to another over a single medium, it is required that the sender and receiver should work at the same speed. That is, sender sends at a speed on which the receiver can process and accept the data. What if the speed (hardware/software) of the sender or receiver differs? If sender is sending too fast the receiver may be overloaded, (swamped) and data may be lost.

Two types of mechanisms can be deployed to control the flow:

- *Stop and Wait:* This flow control mechanism forces the sender after transmitting a data frame to stop and wait until the acknowledgement of the data-frame sent is received.
- *Sliding Window:* In this flow control mechanism, both sender and receiver agree on the number of data-frames after which the acknowledgement should be sent. As we learnt, stop and wait flow control mechanism wastes resources, this protocol tries to make use of underlying resources as much as possible.

Error Control

When data-frame is transmitted, there is a probability that data-frame may be lost in the transit or it is received corrupted. In both cases, the receiver does not receive the correct data-frame and sender does not know anything about any loss. In such case, both sender and receiver are equipped with some protocols which help them to detect transit errors such as loss of data-frame. Hence, either the sender retransmits the data-frame or the receiver may request to resend the previous data-frame.

Requirements for error control mechanism:

- *Error detection* - The sender and receiver, either both or any, must ascertain that there is some error in the transit.
- *Positive ACK* - When the receiver receives a correct frame, it should acknowledge it.
- *Negative ACK* - When the receiver receives a damaged frame or a duplicate frame, it sends a NACK back to the sender and the sender must retransmit the correct frame.
- *Retransmission:* - The sender maintains a clock and sets a timeout period. If an acknowledgement of a data-frame previously transmitted does not arrive before the timeout the sender retransmits the frame, thinking that the frame or it is acknowledgement is lost in transit.
- *Cyclic Redundancy Checksum (CRC):* We have an n-bit message. The sender adds a k-bit Frame Check Sequence (FCS) to this message before sending. The resulting (n + k) bit message is divisible by some (k + 1) bit number. The receiver divides the message ((n + k)-bit) by the same (k + 1)-bit number and if there is no remainder, assumes that there was no error.

Congestion Control

Congestion is an important issue that can arise in packet switched network. Congestion is a situation in Communication Networks in which too many packets are present in a part of the subnet, performance degrades. Congestion in a network may occur when the load on the network (i.e. the number of packets sent to the network) is greater than the capacity of the network (i.e. the number of packets a network can handle.)

How to correct the Congestion Problem

Congestion Control refers to techniques and mechanisms that can either prevent congestion, before it happens, or remove congestion, after it has happened. Congestion control mechanisms are divided into two categories, one category prevents the congestion from happening and the other category removes congestion after it has taken place.

These two categories are:

- Open loop
- Closed loop

Open Loop Congestion Control

- In this method, policies are used to prevent the congestion before it happens.
- Congestion control is handled either by the source or by the destination.
- The various methods used for open loop congestion control are:
- Retransmission Policy: The sender retransmits a packet, if it feels that the packet it has sent is lost or corrupted.
- Window Policy: To implement window policy, selective reject window method is used for congestion control. Selective reject method sends only the specific lost or damaged packets.
- Acknowledgement Policy: The acknowledgement policy imposed by the receiver may also affect congestion. If the receiver does not acknowledge every packet it receives it may slow down the sender and help prevent congestion.
- Discarding Policy: A router may discard less sensitive packets when congestion is likely to happen.
- Admission Policy: An admission policy, which is a quality-of-service mechanism, can also prevent congestion in virtual circuit networks.

Closed Loop Congestion Control

- Backpressure: Backpressure is a node-to-node congestion control that starts with a node and propagates, in the opposite direction of data flow.
- Choke Packet: In this method of congestion control, congested router or node sends a special type of packet called choke packet to the source to inform it about the congestion.
- Implicit Signalling: In implicit signalling, there is no communication between the congested node or nodes and the source.
- Explicit Signalling: In this method, the congested nodes explicitly send a signal to the source or destination to inform about the congestion.

Congestion Control Algorithms

- Leaky Bucket Algorithm: leaky bucket algorithm shapes burst traffic into fixed rate traffic by averaging the data rate.
- Token bucket Algorithm: A token bucket algorithm is a modification of leaky bucket in which leaky bucket contains tokens.

3 TCP/UDP and Socket

TCP/UDP Socket and Port

To manage the connection between application layer network protocols, TCP and UDP use ports and sockets. TCP and UDP operate at the host-to-host layer in the IP communication model and provide host-to-host communication services for the application layer protocol. This means an application layer protocol is on one IP host connecting to an application layer protocol on another IP host.

TCP is one of the main protocols in TCP/IP networks. Whereas the IP protocol deals only with packets, TCP enables two hosts to establish a connection and exchange streams of data. TCP guarantees delivery of data and also guarantees that packets will be delivered in the same order in which they were sent.

UDP (User Datagram Protocol) is a communications protocol that offers a limited amount of service when messages are exchanged between computers in a network that uses the Internet Protocol (IP). UDP is an alternative to the Transmission Control Protocol (TCP) and, together with IP, is sometimes referred to as UDP/IP.

A network socket is an endpoint of an inter-process communication across a computer network. Today, most communication between computers is based on the Internet Protocol; therefore most network sockets are Internet sockets.

4 IP(v4), Application Layer Protocol

IPv4

Internet Protocol version 4 (IPv4) is the fourth version in the development of the Internet Protocol (IP) and the first version of the protocol to be widely deployed. IPv4 is described in IETF publication RFC 791 (September 1981), replacing an earlier definition (RFC 760, January 1980).

IPv4 is a connectionless protocol for use on packet-switched networks. It operates on a best effort delivery model; in that it does not guarantee delivery, nor does it assure proper sequencing or avoidance of duplicate delivery. These aspects, including data integrity, are addressed by an upper layer transport protocol, such as the Transmission Control Protocol (TCP).

Application Layer

An application layer is an abstraction layer that specifies the shared protocols and interface methods used by hosts in a communications network. The application layer abstraction is used in both of the standard models of computer networking; the Internet Protocol Suite (TCP/IP) and the Open Systems Interconnection model (OSI model).

There are several protocols which work for users in Application Layer. Application layer protocols can be broadly divided into two categories:

- Protocols which are used by users. For email for example, eMail.

- Protocols which help and support protocols used by users. For example DNS.

ICMP: ICMP (Internet Control Message Protocol) is an error-reporting and message-control protocol that network devices use to report problems in IP packet delivery.

Domain Name System: The Domain Name System (DNS) is a hierarchical distributed naming system for computers, services, or any resource connected to the Internet or a private network. It associates various information with domain names assigned to each of the participating entities.

SMTP: Simple Mail Transfer Protocol (SMTP) is an Internet standard for electronic mail (e-mail) transmission. First defined by RFC 821 in 1982, it was last updated in 2008 with the Extended SMTP additions by RFC 5321 - which is the protocol in widespread use today. SMTP by default uses TCP port 25.

POP: Post Office Protocol (POP) is an application-layer Internet standard protocol used by local e-mail clients to retrieve e-mail from a remote server over a TCP/IP connection. POP has been developed through several versions, with version 3 (POP3) being the current standard.

FTP: The File Transfer Protocol (FTP) is a standard network protocol used to transfer computer files from one host to another host over a TCP-based network, such as the Internet. FTP is built on client-server architecture and uses separate control and data connections between the client and the server.

HTTP: The Hypertext Transfer Protocol (HTTP) is an application protocol for distributed, collaborative, hypermedia information systems. HTTP is the foundation of data communication for the World Wide Web.

5 Routing Algorithm

Routing is the process of selecting best paths in a network. In the past, the term routing was also used to mean forwarding network traffic among networks.

How do we get packets from one end point to another? Here's what would be nice for a routing algorithm: correctness, simplicity, robustness, stability, fairness, optimality.

- Robustness: The world changes, software changes, use changes, topology and hardware change, things go wrong in lots of different ways. How well does the routing algorithm handle all this?
- Stability: Does the algorithm find a routing table quickly (convergence)? How does it adapt to abrupt changes in topology or state of the routers? Is it possible to have oscillations?
- Fairness & Optimality: May be at odds with one another. What might be fair for a single link may hurt throughput. Must decide on what is meant by optimality before thinking about algorithms. For example, optimal could be for an individual packet (least amount of time in transit) or could be for the system as a whole (greatest throughput). Often times number of hops is chosen as the metric to minimize as this represents both in some sense.

Shortest Path

Links between routers have a cost associated with them. In general it could be a function of distance, bandwidth, average traffic, communication cost, mean queue length, measured delay, router processing speed, etc. The shortest path algorithm just finds the least expensive path through the network, based on the cost function.

Flooding

Every incoming packet is sent out on every other link by every router. Super simple to implement, but generates lots of redundant packets. Interesting to note that all routes are discovered, including the optimal one, so this is robust and high performance (best path is found without being known ahead of time).

Flow-based

Similar in spirit to minimum distance, but takes traffic flow into consideration.

Distance Vector

Also known as Bellman-Ford or Ford-Fulkerson. Used in the original ARPANET, and in the Internet as RIP.

6 Hub, Switches, Gateways and Routers

Hub

A common connection point for devices in a network. Hubs are commonly used to connect segments of a LAN. A hub contains multiple ports. When a packet arrives at one port, it is copied to the other ports so that all segments of the LAN can see all packets.

Hubs and switches serve as a central connection for all of your network equipment and handles a data type known as frames. Frames carry your data. When a frame is received, it is amplified and then transmitted on to the port of the destination PC.

Switch

In a telecommunications network, a switch is a device that channels incoming data from any of multiple input ports to the specific output port that will take the data toward its intended destination.

Gateway

A gateway is a node (a router) on a TCP/IP network that serves as an access point to another network. A default gateway is the node on the computer network that the network software uses when an IP address does not match any other routes in the routing table.

A gateway is a network point that acts as an entrance to another network.

Router

In packet-switched networks such as the Internet, a router is a device or, in some cases, software in a computer, that determines the next network point to which a packet should be forwarded toward its destination.

7 Network Security Basic Concept

Network security

Network security consists of the provisions and policies adopted by a network administrator to prevent and monitor unauthorized access, misuse, modification, or denial of a computer network and network-accessible resources.

Public Key

In cryptography, a public key is a value provided by some designated authority as an encryption key that, combined with a private key derived from the public key, can be used to effectively encrypt messages and digital signatures.

Private Key

A private key in the context of Bit coin is a secret number that allows bit coins to be spent. Every Bit coin wallet contains one or more private keys, which are saved in the wallet file. The private keys are mathematically related to all Bit coin addresses generated for the wallet.

Because the private key is the "ticket" that allows someone to spend bitcoins, it is important that these are kept secure. Private keys can be kept on computer files, but in some cases are also short enough that they can be printed on paper.

Digital Signature

A digital signature is a mathematical scheme for demonstrating the authenticity of a digital message or document. A valid digital signature gives a recipient reason to believe that the message was created by a known sender, such that the sender cannot deny having sent the message (authentication and non-repudiation) and that the message was not altered in transit (integrity). Digital signatures are commonly used for software distribution, financial transactions, and in other cases where it is important to detect forgery or tampering.

Firewall

A firewall is a system designed to prevent unauthorized access to or from a private network. Firewalls can be implemented in both hardware and software, or a combination of both. Firewalls are frequently used to prevent unauthorized Internet users from accessing private networks connected to the Internet, especially intranets. All messages entering or leaving the intranet pass through the firewall, which examines each message and blocks those that do not meet the specified security criteria.

Hardware and Software Firewalls

Firewalls can be either hardware or software but the ideal firewall configuration will consist of both. In addition to limiting access to your computer and network, a firewall is also useful for allowing remote access to a private network through secure authentication certificates and logins.

Hardware firewalls can be purchased as a stand-alone product but are also typically found in broadband routers, and should be considered an important part of your system and network set-up. Most hardware firewalls will have a minimum of four network ports to connect other computers, but for larger networks, business networking firewall solutions are available. Software firewalls are installed on your computer (like any software) and you can customize it; allowing you some control over its function and protection features. A software firewall will protect your computer from outside attempts to control or gain access your computer.

Index

D

E

F

G

H

I

K

L

T

U

V

W